KU-204-294

N 0091255 7

CREATIVE CRAFTS IN EDUCATION

SEONAID M. ROBERTSON

Diploma in Design and Crafts, Edinburgh College of Art
Art Teachers Diploma, Moray House Training College
Diploma in Psychology, University College, London
Senior Lecturer in Art and Crafts at Bretton Hall

CREATIVE CRAFTS IN EDUCATION

by

SEONAID M. ROBERTSON

Foreword by

HERBERT READ

ROUTLEDGE & KEGAN PAUL LIMITED
Broadway House, Carter Lane
London

First published in 1952

by Routledge & Kegan Paul Limited
Broadway House, 68–74 Carter Lane
London E.C.4

Second Impression 1955
Third Impression 1957
Fourth Impression 1961
Fifth Impression (with some corrections) 1964

Reprinted by lithography in Great Britain
by William Clowes and Sons, Limited
London and Beccles

DEDICATED

TO THOSE FRIENDS

WHOSE HOSPITALITY AND LONG-SUFFERING

MADE THE WRITING OF THIS BOOK POSSIBLE

CONTENTS

ILLUSTRATIONS

PLATES

NOTES ON SCHOOLS IN WHICH THE WORK ILLUSTRATED WAS DONE

In most cases the teacher supplied the information in writing. In some they are my own notes after a visit. But in any case, the information given was that received at the time the photograph was taken, in a few cases as long as three years ago. An apology is therefore made to any school about which the information is now out of date.

The photographic illustrations, nos. I, III*b*, VIII, IX, X, XIV, XVII, XVIII, XX, XXII, are by Margaret Harker, through the kind permission of the Society for Education in Art. The others are by the author.

ILLUSTRATIONS

TEXT FIGURES

FOREWORD

One of the most unhappy effects of the economic developments of the past century and a half has been the divorce of the crafts, not merely from industrial production, but also from the arts. By 'the arts' we mean certain crafts, such as painting and carving, which acquired a special prestige from their association, first with religious instruction, and then with bourgeois ostentation; and which even without the encouragement of the industrial revolution, tended to separate themselves as an upper class of craftsmanship. There are, of course, hierarchies of skill, and it takes more skill to paint a portrait of a successful soldier or merchant than to paint a door. But it is a vulgar error to assume that the quality of the skill engaged in painting a portrait is necessarily higher than the quality of skill engaged in throwing a pot or making a chair. More *ideas* are conveyed by pictorial images, or by poetry; and ideas have great importance for civilized communities. But the only element in art which can be taught is skill, and in the school all the arts should have equal status in order that the child can find its proper aptitudes. What is important is not that the child should be taught painting in preference to woodwork, but that all practical activities should be taught as arts; in one or more of which the child, according to its disposition, will discover creative potentialities.

Miss Robertson insists on that unity of the arts and crafts, and because her book is the product of wide and successful experience in teaching, we may hope that what she has to say on this subject will influence those who plot the structure of national education. She also uses the word 'creative', even in her title—a question-begging word, but necessary as an emphasis in a world where values have become blurred. We need a word to indicate whatever is not uniform, ready-made, mass-produced: to indicate whatever is individual, freshly-conceived, expressive of feeling. We need a word to indicate the relationship which should exist between a human being and the things shaped by his will: to describe the effect which our ideals can have on the actual: a word to describe the work we love. Creative is the only such word, and in education we may use it freely and without sentimentality, conscious of its practical connotation.

The crafts could, more than any other form of education, transform our social environment. As an instinctive revolt against the shoddy products of our factories, they could immediately bring into the home an undercurrent of good taste, in furnishings, in clothing, in utensils. In the long run they could transform the factories themselves, by creating a taste to which, if only for economic reasons, the producers would have to conform. This is placing a heavy burden of social responsibility on the schools, and on the art teacher in particular. But the necessary revolution can begin nowhere else: in tender human shoots, not yet distorted in mind and body by a world grown ugly. Miss Robertson has a brave belief in such a possibility, and this gives her book its wider social appeal.

HERBERT READ

INTRODUCTION

FIFTY years ago education in this country was a desert so far as crafts were concerned. To-day it is a jungle where every sort of indiscriminate growth flourishes, where the educationalists' recent recognition of the value of handwork results equally in sound satisfying pieces of craftsmanship and in monstrosities fit for the white elephant bazaar. If one asks in a school to see the craft work one may be shown models of arctic villages; plastic napkin rings; carpentry; white cotton stitched underwear; spun, dyed and woven tweeds; match-box chests of drawers; printed and illustrated books; cardboard comb cases; painted lampshades; thrown, glazed and fired pottery; embroidered pictures; paper flowers.

Are such activities all equally crafts? Is it desirable that our children should be making one rather than another? Is match-box furniture acceptable at one age but not at another? Or does it not matter very much what children are doing in the handwork period—as one would be likely to conclude from this list—if they are using their hands?

Does the fact that a child has done one craft rather than another make any difference to him as a person when he grows up?

In search of an answer to my questions I returned to the northern industrial town where I had taught five years before. I wanted to see again the community of which I had been a part, and reconsider my teaching in the light of the achievements, the needs, the hopes of these people. So now, after some months back in Milltown, I am writing of the people, their homes and their ways.

It is a small town of woollen mills and machinery. It has an orderly centre, a Victorian Gothic town hall, and a parish church now tucked behind pubs and shops. There is a library, but no picture gallery, and travelling exhibitions seldom find their way here. Beyond these, little streets of bleak houses slope up the sides of the valley and crowd round the railway and the factories. These have few gardens, but the town is blessed with some trees, and on the outskirts the spaces between the big houses of the millowners and directors are patchworked with suburban dwellings of cream wash and red roof-tiles. The sight of the roofs thinning at the town fringes reminds me of the term or two we used to devote to the question of houses, and how the cherished hope of every girl—almost without exception—was for a house of her own with a garden all round. I pleaded for the compact city and the claims of agricultural land; I took excursions to see monumental housing schemes of workers' flats in a neighbouring town, to see Georgian streets and cloistered squares; I introduced them to the work of Le Corbusier and Gropius, but in vain. All the pressure of drab streets and crowded houses produced a healthy revolt, but one which could see no further than the suburban box. The great majority, I see, are still living in their little streets, but the architectural wilderness of prefabricated henhouses along the highway to the next city is a gigantic monument to this desire. But the little streets of Milltown are still saved from complete drabness on one day of the week. On Mondays the ropes are rigged diagonally across the 'setts' from house to house, and the streets prink themselves with clean clothes, white, spotted and striped. For one day while the wind blows, the moral fervour of the housewife flowers into a saving grace.

The girls I knew as juniors in white socks or striplings in gym tunics are now the young women of the town and I see them in the evenings with strange hairstyles and rather drab clothes, clustered at corners or strolling in the streets with their boy friends. Sometimes I am cheered by a bright coat or a gay dress which seems a protest tossed at the dingy tone which the buildings adopt as protective colouring in this smoky atmosphere. But how seldom is there any subtle combination of colours or any outfit which delights by its originality or imaginative thought. Except for the knitted jumpers, these clothes are almost all ready made. While we can feel thankful for the economic easement of cheap and fashionable clothes, it is depressing to observe that they are seldom appropriately chosen or combined with taste. There is a great preponderance of grey-fawn, 'which is so useful because it does not show the dirt'. Few of those young people sit or move with any natural grace, but then they mostly shuffled through childhood or were pushed around by overworked mothers. Their natural exuberance had to be curbed in a crowded home and, because at school they were taught jerky gymnastics, it was curbed into an awkward rigid gait, lacking spring or rhythm. I am cheered to see that on Saturday nights they flock to dance at the town hall, but there appear to be few for whom dancing is an end in itself, a satisfying means of expression. They go to the pictures, of course, but they queue in the rain as unthinkingly for a trivial and sentimental show as for one of the important films of our time.

The regional accent is pleasing, but lack of confidence prevents an easy flowing speech. If one works all day within the clatter of looms it is not easy to avoid a harsh intonation, and a raucous mother affects all her children.

Some of those I left as schoolgirls are married now and invite me to their homes. They are rightly proud of their cooking and cleaning—but what a desolate wilderness of neutral-coloured rooms, varied only by the recurring fawn and green sitting-room and the pink and cream bedroom. Remembering their lively colourful paintings, their collage embroideries, I look eagerly for an imaginative use of colour and texture, for a protest against the dull uniformity of the furniture and rugs offered by the shops within reach. (Those few who have obviously delighted in creating their surroundings—and there are several—still talk of the 'homes and clothes' course we initiated for one year in the school. I see now that this was of even more importance than I realized at the time.)

Where is the eager courage, the questioning spirit, the gay imagination of my schoolgirls? Why have most of them so soon acquiesced, so soon accepted the dullness of their surroundings, and given their life the outward stamp of mediocrity?

There is a sturdy robust strength about those people, a capacity to 'put up with things'. This is their attitude to their town and their life, to *put up with* the ugly buildings, the dirty atmosphere, the lack of pleasing and satisfying order. They accept it as the natural order of things. The most astounding thing to me is that *men* built this town and hundreds of others like it—and hundreds worse. Did they not believe that men could build beautifully, could arrange their lives in pleasing surroundings? Or, much more likely, were they just not concerned? Yet, in almost all its elements, our environment is man-made. Given our terrain and our weather we have made the rest, buildings, factories, soot, goods yards, streets of houses without gardens. Men need an environment in which they feel at home. They need open space for wide activities and vision, and enclosed space for comfort and intimacy. They need furniture adapted to the human body, and acceptable to the senses, colours and texture which give positive pleasure and minister to varying moods, and they need works of art inspiring to the spirit. How then do we come to live in such a town, in such a district, in houses which jar on every one of these sensibilities, barren of any expression of the spirit, till sensibility is stunted and finally dies off in the harsh atmosphere. Those children who came to school and set down their conception of a 'lovely pattern' in rich and glowing colours with every part related to the other parts and the whole, who wanted nothing less than a picture which was perfectly 'right', have grown up to accept the limitations of ugliness, harshness, the inappropriate and unsatisfying, and to take it for granted. They have lost that belief in themselves to create a harmony with the things which are around them, and have accepted the axiom that external conditions must dictate their lives. Their education has somehow failed to relate their creativeness to their material world.[1]

[1] The environment which surrounds growing men and women reflects the form of society which has been evolved. The physical differences in the landscape of Saxon strip-fields and the unfenced acres of a mechanized farm are directly related to the kind of life lived there. The plan and disposition of the conical huts of the Celtic monks, the blocked cells opening on an enclosed court of a Carthusian monastery, the students' rooms opening from a communal staircase, the hall and buttery of an Oxford college, reflect as clearly as a block of bachelors' flatlets the life of that section of the community in that age.

That the disposition of the material things around reflects our activities can be seen on a more intimate scale by looking at a room on the morning after a party. The position of the chairs, the rugs, the cushions, the glasses, will reveal a great deal about the sort of party it was—dancing, discussion, formal intercourse, intimate groups or couples, or a riotous binge!

But the environment not only reflects, it actually moulds to some extent the activities which take part in it. This is true, not only on the large scale of slums or countryside, but again on the scale of a room. The same group of adults or children will be considerably affected by whether the room they meet in is arranged with upright chairs facing the front, or an informal circle of arm-chairs.

All this will be easily acceptable, but we have all the time to be aware that we are inducing certain modes of thought and feeling in those whom we

Going among the homes and the people of Milltown I ask myself what their education has given them that must not be endangered; what I would have hoped that it would have given them which is obviously lacking; why the unfolding personalities of schooldays have so often failed to ripen into the rich, warm, varied individuals one envisaged? Firstly, we must reckon with the spheres over which education has no control. Each individual person probably has limits, physical, mental, intellectual and emotional, which must be accepted, but between those limits lie the possibilities which we have hardly begun to explore fully. Within these—rather than pressing for the unattainable—lies the educator's job. Next, his parents will be the greatest and most lasting influence in a child's life and his attitude to everything else will be in some measure a reflection of his attitude to them. Thirdly, the environment, the economic pressures, the ugly machine-dominated life of Milltown is not a field for the educationalist to tackle alone. Politicians, economic planners, architects, industrialists are all involved. But it is certain that it will only be tackled and remade in human terms by an informed, intelligent, determined and sensitive public. And if the foundations of knowledge, character and sensibility are not laid in the schools before sixteen, they never will be.

Of knowledge we have more than we can assimilate. The problem for the world to-day is not the gaining but the using of knowledge, so the handing on of knowledge can no longer be the school's paramount task. Of character these northern folk have more than most. Along with their sturdy common sense they are capable of an endurance which tends to despise and distrust anything gracious as 'soft'. They have a stubborn concentration on immediate realities which has atrophied their vision for further horizons. What the children of Milltown, who are to walk these streets and work in these factories, most need to derive from their education are confidence, sensitivity and imagination. They need imagination to reach beyond their conventional thought, their limited surroundings; imagination to envisage new uses of material in a new and comely town. They need

---

bring up to use certain furniture, tools, utensils, etc. And while children are necessarily presented with this ready-made environment, perhaps most important of all are the materials and opportunities we give them to make, in part, their own environment.

sensitivity to see their town as the material expression of a way of life, catering adequately for their work, their family activities, their leisure time, their spiritual aspirations, as they need vision to reach out to appreciate different ways of life and different faiths. They need confidence to believe that men, that *they*, can build an environment which does embody all this, and which satisfies senses, intellect, emotions and what (for want of a better word) we call spirit. And they need courage to set about it. In fact, what they need is faith in their own ability to create. They need a belief that to feel deeply, and find forms of expression for such feeling, is no shame, but the richest human experience. And they need their own firm core of values about what is ultimately good in life, to prevent confidence or courage or imagination or feeling from sweeping them off their balance. This core will serve not only as a measure to select or reject experiences, but as the very pattern of the personality which, interacting with experience, directs its growth.

Faith in the ability to create and values by which to create well —no small programme for an educationalist!

I, being a craftsman, have left to the last those qualities usually put first, a critical intelligence and well-developed social conscience. An education which neglected them would indeed be dangerously one-sided. But for hundreds of years the stress has been laid on intellect in education and during the last twenty years the conception of education for society or education for democracy has tended to loom increasingly larger. But education for society is a barren doctrine unless it is held in mind that the society is more rich and varied in proportion as those composing it are varied and richly developed individuals.

I know that here I am stating no revolutionary doctrine nor contributing to original thought. But the contribution which the practice of a craft can make to this has usually been missed.

Much of what must be said has been said with the authority of a poet and a critic by Dr. Herbert Read. His vision of the æsthetic education is something we can only hope to understand fully as we are fit to take part in it. But it would be the greatest tragedy if that day of which he speaks comes, when all education is education through art if that day comes of which Eric Gill speaks, when every man is seen as a particular kind of artist, and we find we have lost the essential thing, the power to recognize the values of art.

Looking to this revolution in education, which must come if we are to advance as human beings, I am concerned to protect those things I value within the present educational system so that when the artist in man is called for, art will not have been crushed out of existence between the millstones of our machine civilization and our so-called 'education for democracy'. And especially I am concerned to preserve and develop the creative crafts in education, because I believe they offer the most fundamental and most universally valid experience of creation which young human beings need.

I.—BEAR AND YOUNG

Clay is the ideal material for capturing and holding the impress of feeling. This quickly shaped bear and young, by an older boy used to working at more exacting crafts, shows not only the sturdiness and tenderness he sensed in the subject, but his gentle humour which comes only with a degree of detachment. The identification with his subject, which is the characteristic emotion of a younger child, has yielded, even in this playful piece, to a more mature appreciation.

Boy of 16.

Teacher: Donald Potter,
Bryanston,
Blandford.

I

1*a*

1*b*

1*a*.—CHILD'S HANDS

'Clay takes immediately the impress of the forming fingers.'

A child's hands pressing and prodding a lump of clay, feeling towards a shape. This exploratory period is a long stage in the introduction of any new material, and to some extent a preliminary to every single piece of craftsmanship.

1*b*.—MOTHER DUCK AND YOUNG

'The sincere effort to explain and convey some feeling, induces the child to search himself for its precise shade and mood, and to reconsider his expression, whether in words or paint or in some other form, to see whether it does in fact say what he wants to say.'

This simple little group shows clearly that it was not so much the *appearance* but his feeling for and with the mother duck that he wished to convey. The upward-thrusting bill of the youngster, the earth-pressed tail and nuzzling head of the mother, all bear the direct finger impressions which formed them. This child, left undisturbed, had immersed himself in the tenderness of his subject, and his feeling directed the pressure of his finger-tips. To insist at this age on more finish or greater detail, after his feeling about this had been exhausted, would be to cultivate insincerity.

Boy of 8.

Cort Crescent Junior School,
Leicester.

At this time this crowded school was working in temporary huts in extremely difficult conditions. There was no special accommodation for art and craft and the clay-bin stood outside the door, in a courtyard.

CHAPTER ONE

THE CHILDREN WE TEACH

It is the concern of this book to discuss which crafts are most valuable in schools and which approach can lead to the most rewarding study of those crafts. But before this can be considered, it is essential to discuss why we teach crafts in schools at all.

This book is particularly concerned with crafts, not because they ought to be separated off from what is called 'art' in schools, but because there are several good books which have played their part in helping forward the revolution in art teaching which has done an incalculable amount to make the life of children happier. Starting from the revolutionary contention of Professor Cizec that children's drawings have their own artistic validity, a change of thought has been brought about by many wise and thoughtful educationalists,[1] with the result that now the colourful expressionism of children's painting is generally accepted. This state has its own dangers of an indiscriminate enthusiasm or *laissez-faire* on the teacher's part, and a superficial decorativeness and failure to search deeply on the child's. But at least the main battle for freedom is won, the essential *condition* of progress is present, and all kinds of interesting experimental work are going on.

But the arguments which have raged about the purpose of art teaching have left the question of crafts bogged in a strange confusion and apathy. Even where more rigid methods and techniques have been dropped, the teaching of crafts usually lacks the clarity of purpose and inspiration to use this new freedom. A few craftsmen of the traditional type, believing in the value of their own experience, are working quietly away in the schools, initiating boys and girls into a love of good materials and sound workmanship. But craftsmen are inarticulate folk, and apt to feel that there

[1] Of whom, in our own country, Marion Richardson was, of course, outstanding.

is no place for their outlook and their values in the world to-day. Some painters, on the other hand, have seized on the materials of the craftsmen and played delightfully and frivolously with them, but have not given the time and thought necessary to understand and enter into the tradition of the craft. That tradition is the main stem through which all sound individual work draws its strength and in which it is rooted.

Each of us concerned with craft education needs a clear policy if we are to avoid the dull, safe repetition of traditional work and the stimulating but directionless frivolities of the constant experimenter. But a policy depends ultimately on a philosophy—a philosophy of education.

What we believe education is and does must depend on what we believe a child to be and what we know of his potentialities in the world in which he grows up. All the time we are brought up against the fact that so often *we do not know*. The old beliefs are sometimes confirmed by careful experiment, sometimes contradicted. 'It seems obvious,' said many intelligent well-intentioned people, 'that the sooner you teach *every* child to read, and the sooner you teach him to work carefully and accurately with his hands the better it will be for him and society.' These are just two of the beliefs accepted for many years which have been largely disproved by actual experiment. While the main questions have hardly been formulated, far less systematically answered, the psychologists have yet drawn our attention to many things which have some bearing on the teaching of crafts. This book originated as an attempt to relate some of those discoveries to the experience of years of practical teaching, and to reconsider why and what to teach.

It is impossible, if what is said is to have any general significance at all, to avoid using such expressions as 'the child' and 'the adolescent' which one would prefer to do without. No one knows with more certainty than the teacher how every child, every one of the hundreds who work in the studio or workshop each week, every one of the thousands she has taught through the years, is an *individual*, unique and fascinatingly himself. All we can say about the general development of children is only a framework to which we can relate the needs of that child who claims all our attention at the moment. But obviously the studies of how other children have behaved and other teachers responded cannot destroy, and may sharpen, the innate wisdom on which we must ultimately rely.

Out of the countless activities which might be practised, the teacher has the responsibility of making some choice for the child. She [1] takes on this responsibility when she orders and provides certain materials and certain conditions, when she suggests and encourages certain forms of activity and when she praises and approves certain kinds of work. Even the freest sort of 'free activity' is not completely free. Since we teachers cannot escape this very great responsibility it is incumbent on us to think very carefully about how we are to encourage a child to spend his precious time and energy—for childhood is not nearly long enough for all the delightful things there are to do! Now, so long as we are passing on or encouraging the child to find out practical information about the world in which we live or about the history of our civilization, we know that we are fairly safe in teaching something which will be necessary and useful if he is to take his place in the culture to which he was born. Again, so long as men and women were dependent on the work of their own hands for furniture, for utensils, for clothes, in giving them the useful skills which were necessary for their making, a teacher, a mother or a master craftsman could be sure that he was justified in demanding time and patience, and that his pupil would continue all his life to be thankful for such teaching. But when we encourage a child to paint a picture or to model an animal, to copy a galleon on to a lampshade or make a cast from a Woolworth rabbit, have we the same certainty? Are we really justified? Now that it is hardly ever *quite necessary* to sew a frock, to construct a shelf or make a tool, the range of useful skills which *must* be taught is reduced to a fraction. In fact, we have to confess that very many things we use in daily living can be mass-produced by a machine much better than we can make them. Before considering those things which cannot be mass-produced by machines, it is worth asking—is even the best of mass-produced frocks *always* right for an individual face and figure? Is there never a corner of the living-room or the kitchen which demands a fitment made just for that position?

However, craftsmanship must obviously have more and more

[1] Purely for convenience, the pronoun 'she' will be used for the teacher, and 'he' for the child, except where the craft discussed is associated particularly with one sex.

some justification other than the utilitarian if it is to make a claim as a necessary part of education. But this reduction of its range, this freedom from the necessity of making steadily for the urgent needs of to-morrow, opens up all sorts of possibilities of making *for other reasons*. But have these any educational value? It depends on what we conceive an educated human being to be. I suppose we would all give lip service to the idea that we are educating the *whole* man. Every piece of factual information comes to us through the senses, every feat of intellectual activity operates on matter presented in the first place through the senses, every æsthetic pleasure depends on the acuity of the senses. Yet how much of our education is devoted to the development of the senses? We know that every creative act is an act of the imagination; we set up the explorers, the great scientists, the far-seeing administrators and the imaginative writers as heroes for the child. But how are we actually helping him to develop imagination? Until we are prepared to encourage the development of the senses *as much as* we now do the intellect, the mental activity of imagination *as much as* we now do that of memory, and to find ways of expressing emotion as much as repressing it, until then, our talk of educating the whole man is eye-wash. Such a conception of education is not in the least to reduce it to an undisciplined self-expression. That would be almost as narrow a conception as that of factual learning. It means that we must be aware of and sensitive to the needs of the child, that we must search deeply for ways of meeting his needs and directing his activities, and that we must be prepared to wait years for results and honestly try to assess the value of our teaching. To 'assess the value' means that we have certain standards by which to judge, that we believe certain experiences are good in themselves, not just because they produce useful results. For me, one of the most important of these is that experience of entering afresh, through the senses, some part of life, focused and transformed for me by the expression of another human spirit, which is what we call art. And the experience of so selecting, focusing and transforming his own crowded and chaotic experience to present it to himself and others is one I wish all children to have continually. These assumptions will lie behind all I say in this book. So when we are free from the tyrant necessity of making—whether we enjoy it or not—*solely* because we urgently need something, we are left with the domain, so to speak, of craftsmanship, overlapping, but not co-extensive with the area of art. With this general approach to the question of crafts in education, we can consider the development of the child.

The baby develops into a young child and the child into an adolescent as a coherent whole which we recognize as a personality and call by his name. While it is impossible to separate completely one facet of his development from another, we ought here, since they are the aspects of his personality chiefly neglected in our education and those most strongly involved in the arts, to consider especially *the senses, the emotions and the imagination.* The next few pages are a very brief and necessarily extremely over-simplified attempt to do this. The approach taken and the work suggested in the practical chapters which make up the bulk of this book depend entirely on a view of the needs which these practical activities are designed to meet. The teacher who has a different view of the needs of the growing child will necessarily arrive at different forms of craftwork. So the serious reader is earnestly invited to read more fully in the appendix about some of the experimental work and experiences on which these conclusions are based.

All his knowledge of the outer world comes to the child through his senses, seeing, hearing, tasting, smelling, touching, and the kinæsthetic sense which gives him knowledge of the movement of his own muscles and of the extension of space. A great part of his 'education', before this begins formally in school, is devoted to learning discrimination—of colours, of shapes by touch and sight, of hardness and softness by handling and biting, of tastes by sucking everything within reach. Such knowledge and discrimination are absolutely necessary if the child is to grow up safely in this world, but they are also the prerequisite of almost all the pleasures of life. And the basis of all the arts lies in refined and discriminating senses.

The baby's appetite for exploring would bring him simply an endless succession of sense impressions were it not guided by his preferences; one texture or one taste is preferred to another, leading him to return to it and gain a greater discrimination within a narrower range. So, from very early days, sense impressions are linked to feelings and thereby given coherence. 'Sense training apparatus' such as the Montessori blocks and colour cards demand a more detached and intellectual approach than many children are ready for. Much apparently purposeless learning in unreal situations remains undigested. If we encourage children to feel and to express their pleasure or dislike or fear in the face of certain colours, sounds, textures, we are giving them a chance to savour, to become aware of, their own feelings, and we are also giving them the raw material with which to express or describe these feelings in the future. So we have to provide, as part of their normal environment in the early days, a wide variety of materials to develop this discrimination. We would pity an older child who grew up without many books from which to choose and through which to gain from other people's experience of life. More to be pitied is the little child whose physical environment may be hygienic to the point of sterility, but is poor in materials for *direct* experience, in colours, in textures, in things which make sounds and provide an interesting variety of smells.

And children must be *encouraged* in their simple sensuous enjoyment, and given positive approval in their pleasure, in their boundless curiosity about the things around them, and in their growing discrimination of colours, smell and sounds. It is absolutely essential that such exploration of their own senses and the world should be associated with feelings of pleasure and approval in the adults around if they are to grow up with courage and confidence to explore the world and confidence in the pleasures to be derived from their own senses. Probably the sense most ignored among us is that of touch, and yet it is the sense through which the baby has his first groping contact with his strange world, and that which will be of paramount importance in all his sexual life. The kinæsthetic sense is developed much more sensitively through the movement study now practised in an increasing number of schools than through gymnastics. That sensuous pleasure which children rightly have in the commonest of all human activities, just moving, is made the basis of future delight in dance and sports. It seems astonishing, when one considers it, that children have been allowed to lose, and we ourselves to lose, so much innocent pleasure in enjoying the things which we must in any case do every day.

One sense may be predominant in an individual's experience of the world, and in his comments on it. Some children will be most vividly aware of sound and seek a comparable form of expression. In art and craft the 'visual type' and the 'haptic type' [1] (who experi-

[1] These terms are explained more fully in Appendix A.

ence most vividly through their touch and muscle sensations) have been clearly differentiated, and the type of work they adopt when given a choice of crafts is quite different. But it seems probable that others will emerge more clearly as we teachers are more alive to individual forms of expression. While the intention is to develop every one of the senses more fully, and to widen the scope of its use and enjoyment, there still remain innate differences in the make-up of individuals. Those who tend to experience the world in visual terms will probably be happiest with two-dimensional work, painting and flat pattern making, while those whose kinæsthetic sense is dominant will find their fullest experience and expression in working with solid materials, modelling, pottery or perhaps carving. Again, there are physical differences in the rhythms which come more naturally to different individuals.[1] For some, the intermittent tapping and hammering of beaten metal will accord with their bodily rhythms, for some, the continuous side-to-side rhythm of weaving. Then again, some children dislike the tactile sensation of clay, some of plasticine; to some, fingering wool gives the utmost pleasure, to others wet wool is abhorrent. But many of the tactual dislikes of older children are not simple physical sensations but are built up by association, especially by parental warnings against getting dirty, and the child's life can be immeasurably enriched by encouraging him to explore and enjoy with all his senses as well as using them in the more humdrum aspects of living.

Many prominent educationalists have spoken of the need for educating not only the intellectual but the emotional capacities of the human being. This has come to be recognized by some as the particular responsibility of the arts side of the curriculum, and the inclusion of music, art and craft has often been justified on the grounds that they 'educate the emotions'. But the phrase needs to be defined more precisely if we are to regard this as more than a vague hope, and actually shape an art and craft course with this end in view. Faced with conflicting theories about the emotions and how they function, it is impossible to condense such a subject into a few paragraphs without dangerous oversimplification. Yet we cannot advocate the education of the whole man and refuse to commit ourselves on the education of the emotions.

It appears to me that between babyhood and adulthood the

[1] For a note on Rudolf Laban's study of movement, see Appendix B.

emotions develop along three main lines. They increase in number through progressive refinement, in strength, and in complexity through their interaction with one another.

From one general response to all emotional situations shown by the very young baby, two kinds of emotion, of satisfaction and dissatisfaction (called by others delight and distress), are very soon distinguished. Then the kind of satisfaction expressed is progressively shown as a more exact response to a *particular* situation, and satisfaction takes the form of delight or joy or affection, and soon the affection differs as it is directed towards parents or sisters or friends. So gradually, over many years, there becomes apparent the whole range of slightly different responses to varying objects and situations displayed by a sensitive adult.

No one has seriously questioned that this increase in the *number* of the emotions or emotional responses is desirable. But when we come to consider the *strength* of the emotions, the case is different. It has occasionally been said outright, but more often tacitly agreed, that one of the tasks of education is to stifle the strong emotions of the growing child. It is questionable whether anything school can do will alter their inherent strength—this is more probably an inborn characteristic—but education can certainly vary enormously the power to express and direct the emotions, and as teachers I believe it is our responsibility deliberately to do this. Fear of the undisciplined life at the mercy of feeling has produced —but only during the last hundred years—a strong tradition in our education of the suppression of the emotions in favour of the intellect. But the intellect alone does not serve as a driving force for the personality at any age, and least of all in childhood, and where basic emotions are not developed and directed fully enough, the emotions of competition, or patriotism, or social or family duty have to be artificially fostered instead to hold the group together. The instincts and the emotions are the most powerful forces we possess and 'the education of the emotions', if we can use the phrase at all, must mean preserving their initial force while finding better objects for their satisfaction. Affection, given by the baby first totally to his mother who satisfies his desires, will extend to the rest of his family, to friends, and townsfolk, till he cares about the welfare of people he has never seen. The same emotional drive is in the process growing not less strong, but more precisely directed towards one action or another which is appropriate. So there is no need to sacrifice emotion to the development of the intellect but rather to experience more deeply and fully any emotion which is recognized (and recognition implies intellectual appreciation too) as being a desirable and integral part of the personality. But integral to what? An increase in the number and in the strength of the emotions is not enough. The education of the emotions implies a growth in relation to something, with reference to a pattern of some kind.

The emotional life of any person is given coherence by the building up of certain 'clusters' of feelings called 'Sentiments'[1] which may centre round a person, or a subject, or an abstract idea. By constant reinforcement through the same emotions felt repeatedly for this object, there results a dominating pattern which influences all the field of the emotions rather as a magnet does a magnetic field. The 'centre patterns' discussed in Chapter XII might serve as an analogy here. The many shades of feeling experienced each day, instead of forming separate units in a chaotic mass, are organized into groups by the pull of these dominant groups of emotions. So the parts are brought into relationship with the whole and so with one another. The personality is unified and coherent to the extent that these complex centres are developed.

So it is possible to think of the development of the emotions as an increase in range, in strength, and in grouping or patterning. And as we come to consider specific forms of craft we shall have to ask how far each is capable of providing a harmless channel for expression or a form of activity pleasurable in itself. But however valuable 'self-expression' is to the one who expresses, as a release and a necessary safety valve, it does not make much positive contribution towards *educating* the emotions.

Any expression, any sound or mark, from the baby's first cry to a footprint in the snow, might be interpreted by someone. But it is only when there is *a desire to express to or for other people* that another strange effect becomes apparent on the producer himself. The sincere effort to explain and convey some feeling (whether in the face of distress or delight) induces him to search himself for its precise shade and mood and to reconsider his expression (whether in words or paint or other form) to see whether it does in fact say

[1] A precise term given by William MacDougall, and distinguished from the usual use of the word by a capital S.

what he wishes to say. And the knowledge he gains thus of his own feelings leads to a further refining of feeling in that the subtler shades are distinguished in the honest attempt to convey them. This communication of feeling—as distinct from fact—leads us straight to art in its widest sense. Both expression and communication are elements in art, but I would rather reserve the word for those instances in which there is at least the attempt to sift, to plumb experience before presenting its impact to others.

In tracing the development of the emotions we have considered only those ways in which the emotions respond to situations in 'real life'. I cannot accept the theory that art is a substitute for life when that offers too many frustrations, nor do I believe that art is intrinsically a higher form of activity than the working out of relationships in daily living. But art as an experience of creation or of contemplation embodies a peculiar concentration of life. A relationship of such intricacy as that between art and life can best perhaps be explained in terms of metaphor. I picture the experience of creating, as a lens focusing in the work of art the many elements of experience. Yet although this figure conveys the *concentration* at one point or at one moment, it will not suffice because it does not imply the *selection* of what is significant for the artist. It is as though his personality were a coloured filter which suppresses some elements and throws up others sharply. It is obvious that refined and discriminating emotions play a significant part in such selection.

Or shall I borrow the metaphor of a modern poetic painter, Paul Klee, and say that the artist is the trunk of a tree whose roots go down into the world and draw from our common environment. Stirred by his experience, the artist passes on what comes to him from the depths, but when it unfolds in the foliage, the crown of the tree, it is transformed. Many trees grow on and feed on the same ground, but the crowns produced by each may be different. So the productions of many men looking at the same object or undergoing the same experience may be different through this peculiar chemistry of art.

Thus emotions are clarified and defined in the act of their expression, and when the whole self is applied to making a satisfying work of art, in that act the feelings are related to one another within the pattern of the whole personality. The creation of a work of art implies, for a child as for an adult, some organization of the emotions felt, and therefore a step towards the organization of the whole personality. If contemplation of the product shows it to be incomplete or inco-ordinate the artist is sent back to search more deeply in his own consciousness.

Permitted to the intimacy of seeing such a self-revelation of another human being, we, his teachers, can only regard it with respect if not reverence. The one thing we can do with certainty is to cultivate sincerity in ourselves and the children in our care, and value it openly and consistently, above any subject, or method, or interpretation which *we* might consider more desirable.

While each individual can only be encouraged to develop within his own range, this emphasis on the individual vision is not the whole. Education is the induction of a child into his culture as well as being the development of faculties inherent in him. Thus there are two processes simultaneously at work: the unfolding of the self, and the adaptation of that unfolding of the self to outward conditions by its assimilation of the traditions and customs of society.

The teacher must provide the atmosphere and the materials within which this unfolding can take place. But her rôle is not a passive one. The small child has to be made aware of the great tradition to which he is heir, through the fairy tales, the myths and the religious stories in which the wisdom of the people is embodied. In the visual arts we now lack the corresponding traditional forms and are the poorer for it. The Dutch tiles, the slipware plates and embroidered aprons which were once the visual background to childhood are now rarities, and our picture books and toys are vitiated by being too self-consciously made for children, and are not sufficiently linked to the vital sources of adult culture to serve as substitutes. But at the later primary and secondary ages we can introduce him to his heritage of building and craftsmanship, of carving and painting, which is quite as fundamental a part of his tradition as is the literature.

Having glanced at the development of the senses and the emotions, we must turn to imagination, which draws on these and changes the quality of their experience to something new. This takes place constantly in childhood, and it takes place in that astonishing activity we call play. For young children, play is as absorbing, as demanding and as satisfying as will be the serious occupations of life. Even activities which seem prosaic and necessary to us adults, such as eating and washing, may be made opportunities for play. Why is there this extraordinary 'waste' of energy in childhood? There have been many theories of the nature of play which are too complex to summarize here. It is only necessary to remind ourselves that of all animals the human child has the longest period of childhood and that within that period he adopts the essential attitudes which will shape his manhood. It was Froebel who realized the educational value of play and set it at the heart of his teaching.

There are many different types of play and a full range of play is essential to the all-round development of the child.[1] It is helpful to make a distinction between the 'play attitude' and the 'work attitude'. The play attitude is shown towards an activity which is spontaneous, self-directed and the purpose of which ends with the play—that is, it is *the activity itself* which is enjoyed. But usually before five years children may adopt a 'work attitude' to their play. The initiation of the play may be spontaneous, the child saying perhaps, 'I shall build myself a bridge', but having set himself an aim he persists—even though he may find the intermediate activity hard—until he has finished his undertaking. This attitude is obviously the basis of all satisfactory work for the rest of his life, so it is vitally important that we should guard the element of pleasure and satisfaction in it and carry this over into school work. The chief reason that the pleasure persists through hard and even sometimes uncongenial work is that the child *wants* the finished product, so that he is willing to persevere for a comparatively distant end. If this attitude is not destroyed in the infant and early junior years, it is found intact at the stage of serious craft. It can be extended to embrace ends increasingly further away, as when an adolescent or adult applies himself to learning a skill, a trade or a new language which he knows he will not be able to use competently for years. For most people, unfortunately, the end is even further removed. We are willingly to do hard and uncongenial work not because we desire the end product (the coal we dig, or machinery we produce) but because other people want it and will pay us for it, so that with the money we

[1] The most illuminating study of play is Margaret Lowenfeld's *Play in Childhood*, mentioned in Appendix C, where the bearing of Ruth Griffiths' *Imagination in Early Childhood* is discussed. But parents and teachers would do well to go straight to these sources.

can buy the products which we want. But we cannot expect a young child to appreciate such remote ends, and the only way of developing the habit of persistence without constant external control is to develop it *in the making of something which is itself desired.*

Now, since craftsmanship is practised on and with the physical materials which surround us, the way in which the infant comes to know his environment through play has a special interest for us. At first, set down among sticks, blocks, sand, lumps of clay or bundles of straw, he will *explore* these materials without attempting to modify their shape or construct anything with them. The baby will pick up a pebble or a piece of wood and feel the shape and weight of it, smooth it in his fingers and look at it from all sides. This is an essential stage in getting to know any physical thing or substance, and this might equally be a description of a sculptor with a new block of stone before he begins to carve. It is a stage we too often tend to leave out of the craft lesson. Next he will pick up another piece and bang the two together. It is only at a later stage that he will attempt to make anything with them. So there are two stages in this play with the environment—getting to know the different materials of which it is made up, and secondly, making something out of them. Making of any sort is a valuable activity for the child since he needs the growing confidence, the *certainty* of achievement which the tangible result brings. Other types of socially desirable behaviour which we hope to encourage *may* bring the voiced approval of grown-ups and so give the child the sense of achievement, of having done well. But this is not invariable, it is dependent on the presence, the attention and understanding of others, and so it does not always follow automatically. But to have made a *thing*, which remains, to which he can return, a thing which exists assuringly in its own right—there is no question about that achievement. (The sense of confidence will of course be deepened if his product wins some praise as well.) This need recurs through the years and is perhaps most acute again in adolescence, when among the uncertainties and confusion of new demands and unexpected feelings, a tangible proof of one's achievement is a great comfort.

If the child is making something which he himself really wants, he has set his own goal and it will probably be within his scope with a little effort. In introducing a new material it is very important that the form of activity should allow for achievement *before* any technique is gained. This means that with clay, for instance, the first activity to be encouraged should be modelling, because there he can quickly shape a figure or an animal which will serve his purpose. If he started straight off with pottery it would be impossible for him to accomplish anything with a fair resemblance to a pot for a long time, and achievement would be delayed till enthusiasm wilted. The early stages of a craft should employ just so much technique as can be mastered with ease and satisfaction. On the impetus roused by this happy and successful performance, he can go on with the confidence gained to undertake more difficult jobs.

But how does the imagination develop through such activities? In order to explain more precisely the sense in which I am using the word 'imagination'—for it has to serve a wide number of uses in our language—I ought to point out that there are two types of thought. There is *controlled thought*, directed towards a specific end, keeping its aim always clearly before it, exemplified in that type of concentrated attention which attacks a problem directly. But there is another type of thinking, a mind-wandering, which cruises round the subject, drifts to apparently unrelated subjects and wild surmises, which includes phantasy, and is exemplified by day-dreaming. This type of thought is not un-controlled but is controlled *by inner necessity rather than outer demands*. Now, day-dreaming is usually frowned on and published in our schools as inattention. But ought it indeed to be eradicated? When we come to consider the facts we find that browsing is a necessary element in all creative thought. Not only the poets and composers, but the imaginative scientists and inventors need time and relief from the pressure of urgencies in which to brood. We can find the evidence for the necessity and the value of their day-dreaming in their letters and their biographies if we take the trouble to study them.

This then is the thought which is typical of childhood, and childhood is apparently the time biologically designed to free the human young from the pressure of practical cares. But how little do we foster the qualities which are then most untrammelled, hurrying instead our children towards rational, practical thought instead of developing and strengthening the attribute they have. This is not to suggest that phantasy and day-dreaming are enough, but it has been definitely proved that this is a *positive* and invaluable phase in the child's development, not just a negative stage marking time till he can think rationally. Children work out their problems in phantasy, problems of practical living, and try out in imagination adjustments and solutions which have the deepest significance for their social development. They also explore a much wider range of ideas and possibilities than the limitations of their actual environment permit. In their games of being cowboys, or playing families, they are gaining imaginative experience of projecting themselves into other situations, is which the forerunner of that understanding of other people's needs and problems, on which the relationships of our society are dependent.

In their day-dreaming and phantasy play, therefore, children need time and opportunity to wonder at and ponder on the nature of the physical world around them and of such facts as birth and death which have to be assimilated, time to work out solutions to their own problems in the family and group, to enter imaginatively into the situations of others.

For this they require time, quiet, freedom from external distractions and pressures, and suitable materials with which to play. But we think we have to distract children from day-dreaming and so we are always thinking up something 'interesting' for them to do. We are usually compelling the child's attention to something *other* than what is concerning him at the moment. We are destroying the conditions for phantasy. Even those teachers who accept the children's interests as their starting point often put too much stress on accomplishing something in actuality, and not enough on the solitary pausing, that quiet in which growth goes on.

For it is on the material of phantasy as much as the facts presented by the intellect and the senses that imagination operates. And in early childhood because he has little intellectual knowledge of the world and because of his physical limitations, it is very largely on the material of phantasy or on the 'play material' around, that a child's imagination can develop. The ability to pick out the significant from a mass of crowding ideas, to select the relevant fact, the beautifully appropriate action, depends on a certain freedom of the mind from the immediate and obvious. And this freedom, this strength of flight, this confidence in its power to leap, is developed by day-dreaming. Only the familiarity gained by brooding over, wandering round the situation, trying out fantastic combinations, gives that freedom. Not that phantasy alone is enough—by imagination it is *related* to the real situation—but it is the aspect usually neglected. In the act of imagination a new thing, a synthesis, is formed between the near and the far, the prosaic and the phantastic, the flesh and the word. But apparently, this is not possible until the far, the remote is encircled, entered into, pondered on, accepted as fully as the near. And I am convinced that if this faculty is not developed in early childhood it never will be. I believe that we are systematically destroying the possibility of the quality we most lack—imagination—through the conditions and organization of the homes and schools in which children spend the years up to nine or so.

In addition, since we have become aware of the part the school can play in social development through group activities, we have perhaps tended to let this obscure the solitary activity of which I am speaking. Human development is a rhythmical alternation between the individual subjective growth, and the responsive, socially adaptive growth. Some will develop full stature more through one, some more through the other, but both are necessary. We have hailed such activities as projects, games and choirs as an opportunity for that social development, but the 'arts' side of education must give time and opportunity for the secret development of the individual soul.

A great educationist [1] wrote something which sums up a great deal of what I have been trying to say: 'Culture (if it is not a superficial polish) is the growth of imagination in flexibility, in scope, in sympathy, till the life which the individual lives is informed with the life of nature and of society.' If we can do that we are indeed educating. And of course the process is not a one-sided affair. Anyone who is so 'informed with the life of nature and of society', selects some aspects of the one or the other and ponders on these, informs them with his own particular feeling, until he has made them in some sense his own. Such an individual provides the counterbalancing process, and by his perhaps quite small, but unique, contribution extends the imagination and understanding of others who come in contact with him. A child may do this for us through his wonder and admiration in the face of some new sight. An artist may do it by extending the range of experience of the whole community. A teacher must be doing it all the time in a hundred ways.

[1] John Dewey.

CHAPTER TWO

'COMBINED OPERATIONS' IN THE PRIMARY YEARS

IN the last chapter we traced certain needs of the growing child, to which the craft aspect of art teaching has its own contribution to make.

We now know that the child needs a wide variety of materials to stimulate his senses and through which to explore the nature of his physical environment; that these must be adaptable in countless ways to serve for the expression of feelings and ideas; that they should be capable of embodying such expression even before much technique has been acquired; that they should be such as will stimulate and not curb imaginative expression; and that they should be capable of being related to wider and more permanent interests in the world around.

We know that the forms of activity encouraged should be in themselves pleasurable to his senses and bodily rhythms.

We know that each child, in varying degrees, needs time and quietness for absorbtion in individual play without too much pressure to 'make something' or to participate too soon in the group. He needs opportunity and encouragement to work out his own emotional and social problems through becoming more aware of them in his concrete expression of them, and trying out in imagination ideas and solutions.

If these then are the needs of the growing child to which our aspect of education can minister, the practical problem is to select the materials and the activities most appropriate to each age. While the development of a human being is continuous, I am of the opinion that in early adolesence, there is a definite change of attitude towards work, and that craft, in the craftsman's sense of the word, is not to be expected before then. So I want to consider separately here the ways of playing and working suited chiefly to the years before that occurs.

'COMBINED OPERATIONS' IN THE PRIMARY YEARS

At this stage there is, less than ever, any distinction between art and craft, so I have adopted the term 'combined operations' for want of a better. But in what way does play with materials—other than drawing and painting—make a peculiar and necessary contribution in the Primary years? Indeed why teach 'handcrafts' at that age at all. Do not free painting and pattern work provide all the child needs with less material difficulties and less wear and tear on everyone's patience?

While all serious educationists now agree that painting is essential there are fundamental reasons why handcraft is also necessary. The child needs two things: contact with the physical world in which he will live, with the varied and individual nature of its substances, and a material in which to express his own feelings and ideas. For both reasons the small child must have around him an abundance of materials. The *exploration* of any new substance must always come first. Later he will begin to use it to *make* things. The change from aimless play to deliberate shaping marks, as was said, a new level. But the door is not closed on exploration. We all have to plunge back into it from time to time and 'play' with material. Moreover, the two processes interact constantly. In expressing himself, in constructing, the child is also learning more about the material he uses; and in using that material to express his feelings and ideas (as a sort of concrete language), he is defining those ideas by giving them shape in this particular form.

If that 'language' is to be comprehensive, teachers must provide other substances as well as paint. The child needs to handle actual things, to contrast, for example, the softness of fur with the smoothness of silk, the smoothness of metal with the roughness of stone, and to put these together as he would colours in a picture, for the sheer pleasure of combined textures. In the same way he will need as large a variety of materials as possible for his expressive play. Moreover, plastic cubes and ready-made constructional toys, well enough in their way, do not introduce the child to the natural materials in all their variety. For instance, there is no substitute for clay. Plasticine (while being more expensive) is less suggestive, less responsive, less permanent, and in addition, clay has thousands of years of tradition in its handling. So it is too with wood and cloth.

At the exploring stage orthodox teaching has little meaning.

The teacher provides the materials and encourages the children to enjoy themselves with them. And how delightful they find it to spend whole hours simply handling, smelling, gazing at different substances, knowing happily that it will not be considered a waste of time, if nothing seems to come of it all. So far from being a waste of time, to know materials, not just to know *about* them, is temporarily a sufficient end in itself. And this is the only basis for that subtle relationship between man and material which, later in life, is essential to craftsmanship. So, for everyone, this kind of experience of materials in childhood is desirable, and those who miss it find they have to go back and try to recapture this absorption hampered by the developing self-consciousness of adolescence. If only we could presume those opportunities in the home or nursery of pre-school years, there would be less need to stress them here, but if the Primary Schools do not afford them, many children will miss them altogether. In fact, I suspect this stage lasts much longer than is generally allowed for—perhaps it is never fully outgrown. And all through the Secondary School this need to explore aimlessly may be expected to recur from time to time.

If a number of these materials are provided in boxes and bins around the classroom, the child can be left to linger over them, getting to know them in his own way. He will take up pieces of wood perhaps, and stroke them first along the grain, then crosswise, or plunge his hands into a bin of soft clay and squeeze it through his fingers again and again. All this is good and a necessary part of his education. And inspiration arises *from* this handling of materials. In the first few years of the Primary School, at least, the children need not be hurried or urged to make something if they show a desire to linger over the handling and feeling stage. Maybe in the early years experience is so new that an action must be repeated constantly to be fully comprehended and enjoyed, as singing games and nursery rhymes are repeated. The ideal is to let the child remain at one thing as long as he will. A mis-timed enthusiasm about the riches around may lead us into hastening him from one experience to another. The results of these unhurried beginnings will be apparent at a later stage when growing control enables the older child to form something which is both satisfying in the making and permanent.

To go on to the second aspect of 'pre-craft' education, which

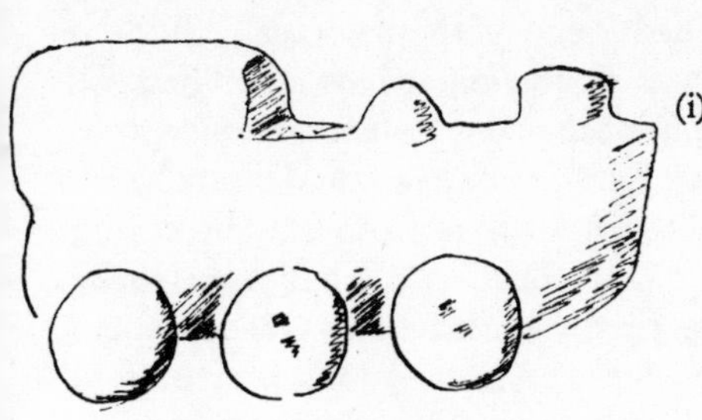

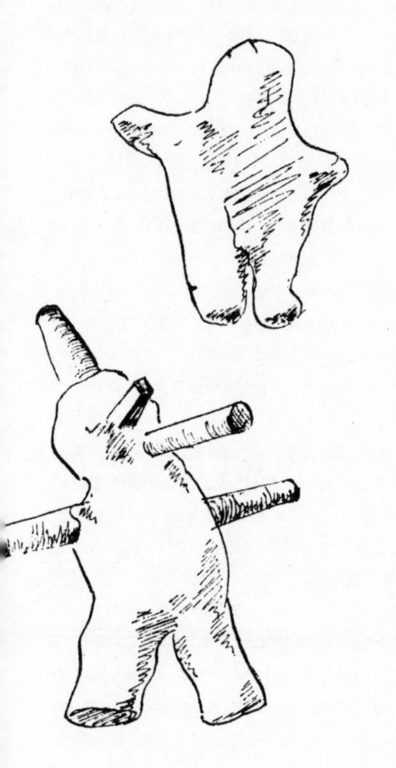

Fig. 1.

(i) Here a child of $4\frac{1}{2}$ has formed his conception of an engine in flour and salt paste. He has grasped that it has a long body with funnel and dome, a driver's cabin and wheels (these are buttons dipped in the paste and pressed on).

(ii) A first solid conception of a man by a child of 4. A roll of flour and salt paste has the arms pinched out and rudimentary legs rather like the leg buds of an embryo. The conception is limited by the possibilities of the material.

(iii) Another child of a few months older, given the same range of materials, has seized on the empty cardboard rolls which serve as packing round pencils and used them in his man. The legs are still pinched-out clay, but as well as using these rolls for arms this child with glee stuck one in his head for a hat and one in his mouth (for a cigar ?). The nose is a piece of wood stuck in. This little man is not merely a symbol but has already some character—a cocky confident appearance.

should more fittingly be called 'play with materials', children want to make things for many fundamental reasons. There is, very early, the need to give physical shape to mental concept, to tie down, as it were, the idea of an object in some definite form. There is the urge to realize his own feelings more fully by giving them material form. And there is the need to enter into the social environment by playing out past experiences to absorb them fully, or those which are to come in unconscious preparation. Such activities must be largely *self-directed*. We do not know his feelings or how he is situated, we can only help *him* to move towards knowing these things himself. Nevertheless, the teacher's rôle is far from passive. She it is who must see that there is an *adequate time* for such play. She it is, especially, who must evoke the *sympathetic atmosphere* in which the personality can best develop. And she must see that *appropriate materials* are to hand. She is responsible for these three conditions in which the child can grow.

The child's life is a whole, and there are no hard and fast divisions in his education, but there are differences of emphasis desirable at different phases of its development. And these phases correspond roughly with certain age levels. Approximately then, between two and five is especially the time when the child is becoming familiar with his feelings (getting control over his at one time ungovernable emotions) and gradually extending them through himself to his clothes and to his possessions as well as his family, his animals, and his friends. During this time his phantasies are as real and as valid to him as what we call his 'ordinary life'.

From four to six roughly he is turning a little more to external things, and has more energy to spend on them, but his play is still of a rather solitary type; he plays more in the presence of other children with an occasional exchange of comment, rather than in joint activity with them. On entering school about five he is suddenly thrust into a comparatively large community and forced all at once into many new social relationships. These are probably the first two years in which all children are in the teachers' care and they are vitally important years. The child has been living to a great extent in the world of his phantasy, especially if he is an only child or separated from brothers and sisters by difference of age or health or temperament. He is now suddenly presented with a complete new set of values. When he goes to school, not only is his physical and social world suddenly extended, but objects and experiences which were peculiarly his own have now to be brought into relation with a group of people. If his hidden imaginative life is not linked firmly to his overt social life, if his private emotional attitude to things is not related to their real qualities, the inner life may grow unreal and the outer life unimaginative. And if the imaginative life goes 'underground' not only does phantasy fail to fulfil its positive rôle, but the day-dreams will persist in later years at a childish level.

So it is the task of the Nursery, the Infant and Junior School actively to encourage the expression of phantasy, first as an essential step in the child's exploration of his own problems, secondly to bring his phantasy into a form where it can be seen and talked about with his playmates and teacher, and thirdly to encourage and strengthen his ability to transform phantasy by the power of imagination.

For this he must obviously be given time to himself and not have his whole life organized. So he must be allowed to go off and play by himself for long periods if he wants to. If we always encourage group activity and imitative social behaviour in the young and discourage the individual from pursuing his own interest, in later life he will be fitted only for regimented pursuits and mass entertainment. Nursery Schools and the best infant classes let the child play by himself, but this is often not true in the Junior School, where despite the natural tendency to work and play in groups there is still a need to 'stand and stare'.

Secondly the teacher must provide not only the time but the *atmosphere* in which the child feels at ease to explore both his environment and his phantasy world. This implies creating in the room an atmosphere of quiet confidence where there is no scorn to 'wither', no sense of pressure or hurry, but only of tranquillity and appreciation. The teacher is not expected to be an amateur psychiatrist, but rather to show sympathy and common sense, and be alert for signs of serious emotional trouble which do need expert handling.

The immediate environment of street or farm provides all sorts of interesting things which the child may want to shape in his material just because they have interested him. But usually it is experiences which have especially impressed him that he will choose to portray. We may expect him to recreate scenes either as a way of understanding more fully what has already happened to him or as wish fulfilment, wielding in them, perhaps, a power that compensates for his actual frailty. The very act of shaping or building with his fingers stimulates a flow of images, and releases feelings connected with them. In addition, he can let himself feel for these symbols of parents and others, emotions which he has had to suppress, and he can work off destructive impulses harmlessly on his little figures. Fear or triumph or hatred, instead of being stifled, can be recognized and acted out. Energy which would have been used unproductively in repressing such 'unacceptable' feelings and keeping them separate from the ordinary conscious life can now be released for more profitable ends. On the other hand potential situations can be explored, without embarrassing consequences, as the child pictures to himself 'what would happen if . . .' Moreover, in addition to exploring his own emotions he may, through this type of play, enter into the feelings of others by imaginatively entering into their situations.

In addition to the known he will want to express his ideas of the unknown, of giants, witches, dragons. To the child at this stage, as to our early forefathers and primitive peoples still, these fantastic creatures are more real than the dog in his kennel or the cat on the mat. He will want to clarify them in his own mind and to translate them from huge, vague and therefore terrifying beings to small tangible figures over which he has power. It is generally accepted that children have many irrational fears. But it needs to be more generally recognized that it is the smothering of such fears (and perhaps hopes) which does harm. If the child can talk about such things and find sympathetic help, he will more easily outgrow them. But paint or clay may be the language in which he can speak. If he can model the giant he fears, or draw the catastrophe he dreads, then he is in control of it, he has conquered it to some extent just by making it explicit. Now it is a thing existing on paper or in clay before him, and he can laugh at it or perhaps tear it up and so destroy it.

In this outpouring of a side of the nature not normally expressed, the value is largely therapeutic. There is no selection or arrangement, and so no art as we understand it. But I believe that no material or form of activity can be a satisfactory medium for artistic creation, until it has served any purpose it has for that individual as a therapeutic medium. Aggressive impulses may lead to the pounding up of several blocks of stone before carving proper can be begun. Clay may be used to work off anal or sexual impulses before modelling as a form of art can be attempted.

This means roughly that if we give children or adults any new material, paint or clay, or hard material to carve, they will not be able to achieve the detachment necessary to that selection and distilling of experience which goes to the making of a work of art, until they have worked off on it any impulses from which it can relieve them *at the moment.*

Such self-expression is certainly not art, and if we believe in the potency of the creative act itself to create a more formed and coherent personality, we cannot be content to let children stay at the stage of such outbursts of self-expression. Some pictures and craftwork exhibited as works of art are as far from being that as yells of laughter or cries of rage are from being song. They have served their function and should be quietly put away. True, they convey feeling, but feeling has to be transmuted by being brought into touch with the core of life. Self-expression which is not given form and orientated in this way, whose roots do not strike downward to the centre, cannot serve as a road for others to reach thither.

We can get only obscure hints and oblique illuminations on the process we have to study. From watching children and ourselves at the work of creation, and from reading what the artists have written about their own way of working, we can learn something (but certainly not the whole process) of the 'peculiar chemistry' which translates an experience into a work of art, and see something of the way in which the emotions are developed in this process.

The little boy who modelled the 'Duck and Young One' (Plate I*b*) or the girls who made the 'Two Old Men and Clown' (Plate III*a*) must have first *looked* at a duck, an old man, a clown. (These subjects were chosen by the children themselves.) Then something about this particular sight must have moved them to look more intently and to *allow themselves* to feel with, to identify themselves —for a moment at least—with this other life. This identification can be intensely real and it can be very painful, but it is one of the ways in which we all grow emotionally. It is constantly seen in play when a child 'is' an old man and hobbles round with drooping shoulders and bent knees, or laughing, tumbles around as a clown. It is seen in all the games of houses, Red Indians and battle-fields in which a whole gamut of emotions is constantly 'exercised'. But play is not art, although it is the activity from which it springs. In play the child or the adult can be completely absorbed, the whole of him gathered up in the experience of the moment. And that experience can be *expressed* in material, as when colours are poured on to paper, or clay thumped into shape. But it is only when there is a desire to *convey* the experience that a work of art is attempted. Then out of the whole (the total unity of the one lost in or identified with the other), the artist has to abstract or detach himself sufficiently to know which facets of this whole should be selected in what form. The result will depend on three things: the first, willingness to enter completely into the other thing (those who will not allow themselves to do this can portray the external form, but not the internal nature of the object or experience); then the power to detach himself and, having understood, to select what is to *him* the relevant and significant (this selection is necessarily individual, reflecting the artist's own nature); and then the ability to shape and form the work of art in a specific material to embody this for himself and for others. And it is only when a form is found which puts down feelers to these underlying universal forms inherent in ourselves and in the world, that a work of art, be it ever so slight, can be said to have been achieved.

A realization of what is involved in this process, the extension of the self, the concentration of the whole of past experience and association on this moment, this object, to grasp its significance, and the sincere search for that form which embodies the final work of art—a realization of the immensity of this experience brings understanding of the importance of the creative arts in education.

The teacher can help by encouraging, not just observation of but absorption in other things, and in the sincere search for those forms which do indeed convey his pupil's feeling and vision. His experience of the same object or scene is a different one; he cannot put the child right, or correct his work, he can only encourage him to search more deeply and describe more fully his own experience. The younger child has not enough language of words to discuss his work, but the atmosphere of the room will encourage this. An older child may find it clarifies his work to discuss it, and the critical appraisement of a sympathetic adult may send him back to it more thoughtful. Also, he will increasingly appreciate help with technique to convey what he has to say.

If handcraft is to serve this individual need or spring from this individual experience, the child must obviously choose his own subject, so far as is possible. Many small children will know quite certainly what they wish to make or model, and should be allowed to go ahead. Others will need to be stimulated by handling the material, and finding suggestive forms into which it falls naturally. The teacher can draw out suggestions in discussion and find in what directions the children's interests are running, so as to propose subjects they will enjoy. Any subject she proposes to a group should be rich enough for each child to find in it some figure or situation which will particularly appeal to him. Thus it is better not merely to ask the whole class to model or embroider say a 'tiger', but to get the children to talk about the different animals they might meet in a forest and to let them choose the one which excites them. But it is wise to let any child who is strongly moved to work on another subject to do so.

The third responsibility of the teacher is to provide the *material* most appropriate for the age and activity in question. I am concerned here not with finished toys (whose shape cannot be radically altered) or with material like bricks and meccano (which combine in many but in rigid and formulated ways) but with materials which can be *shaped* and *combined in personal ways*. Since we are concerned largely at this age with stimulating the senses and providing for emotional and imaginative expression, I shall suggest the materials most valuable for these ends, arranging them in related groups, as on page 36.

It will be seen that as well as clay, wood, carving materials, we have a group (cloth, net, beads and so on) which leads on to needlework, a group hinting at metal work, and a group leading directly to bookcraft. Although at this stage the child will use them in all kinds of fantastic combinations rather than work within strict limits as in a craft, yet he is gaining familiarity with their qualities. This prevents a break in continuity. Play with materials can pass imperceptibly into craft by a change in attitude and workmanship, as each child shows himself ready for it.

I said that when instead of *only* playing aimlessly with it, the infant begins to shape or construct something of the material around him, he has reached a new level of development. But for

THE INSPIRATION OF MATERIALS, AND THEIR POSSIBILITIES

Material	*Expressive in these ways*	*Stimulating to these senses*
Clay	Completely impressionable: capable of infinite forms	t.k.
Plasticine	Comparatively impressionable: capable of infinite forms	t. (to some unpleasant) k.
Dough, papier mâché	Able to be roughly moulded	t. (to some unpleasant) k.
Natural pieces of wood, lumps of chalk, soft stone	Original shapes suggestive / Can all be cut or shaped. Shape limited by hardness, and by original form	v.t.k.o.
Bricks, plaster, blocks	Original shapes less suggestive	v.t. (both slight) k.
Wooden boxes, Bottle tops, etc., Metal scraps, wire, tins	Can be combined with each other in constructions, limited by original shapes	v.t.o. v. (slight) v. & k. (slight)
Feathers, steelwool, pipe-cleaners, straw, miscellaneous objects	Can be shaped to a slight extent, can be combined with other groups	v.t.
Plain paper, cardboard	Can be cut and bent in a limited number of ways	v. (only if coloured)
Cellophane, silver paper, crinkly paper, doyleys, shelf-edging, corrugated card	Can be cut and bent in a number of ways, can be combined with cloth and thread	v.t.
Various cloths, sacking, net, lace, fur, leather	Can be cut and shaped in flat or the round	v.t.
Threads, string, wool, beads, sequins, buttons, rings	Can be combined with these or the following	v.t.
Shells, lichens, pebbles	Cannot be shaped, but can be combined together	v.t.k.

t = sense of touch. v = vision. o = olfactory (smell).
k = kinæsthetic (muscle and organ sense).

many years he will construct from what lies to hand, using paper for cups, clay for wheels, dressing a bundle of straw up as a doll. He imaginatively invests the materials he finds with qualities we cannot see. This is the chief difference between the attitude of the child to materials and the attitude of the adult, especially the craftsman, who searches around for the material most suited to his purpose, and shapes a form directly related to his material. But this serious craftsmanlike attitude must not be induced before its proper time, or qualities equally valuable, which can develop only during childhood, will be inhibited. Childhood is the precious period of exploration, in which the imagination is stimulated to try out strange combinations of materials in improvisation, without having to suffer serious consequences if they are not successful. As soon as the child despises his product because it does not serve a 'real' purpose, because it is not capable of fulfilling its utilitarian function, he will become dissatisfied and then he should be guided towards materials and tools with which he can construct on his new principles. Thus, so long as he is happy making a clay cart with clay wheels, he supplies the movement from his imagination. He may tell long stories about where this cart is going, and may lift it up and move its position among the other objects or may take it in his hand and slide it along. He is experiencing the movement in himself and it is real to him. To provide only carts with wheels which can run would be to deny him this experience, which he can get through identifying himself with his product. But the time will come when in his effort to understand the world about him he will want to understand the *mechanism* of movement and then he must have boxes, tin lids, wire, to construct revolving wheels. Since clay wheels will not turn, clay is no longer the material for a cart. Of course, his need will be for imaginative play one day or one hour, and for mental understanding the next. The two will continue together and sometimes one will grow out of the other in some project. For this reason all these materials should be available most of the time. Usually the child himself will find his way to what he needs by watching others using them, but sometimes he may have his attention drawn to the materials which will serve his present purpose. The greatest alertness and sensibility is demanded of the teacher to know with each child what he is aiming at and what materials will serve him best.

In what ways will children use these materials, clay, wood, chalk, cloth, tins for their play? Clay is quite indispensable in the Primary School. The activity of squeezing, thumping, patting clay is tremendously satisfying to small children, but clay also provides the best material for emotional expressions. Gesture, in mime and drama, is the most direct channel for such expression, but these have just one disadvantage. When they are past and over, nothing remains. Clay will take the imprint of a gesture and hold it in time It is the intimate pressure of the fingers, the push and thrust of the arm which forms it. Its inspiration is in feeling rather than in thought, and it can convey that with a peculiar intensity. Moreover, the young child's feelings are constantly changing, so he needs to make quickly an image to embody them. The child needs to learn no skill, needs to use no tool, his contact with the material is sensuous and direct, needing no interposing intellect to order the shaping. The discipline of the craft comes later. Meanwhile these priceless qualities it offers for childish expression can be used to the full.

In addition to serving as a material for predominantly emotional expression, clay, simply because it is so plastic, will be used either alone or in combination with other materials to think in concrete form, to form and thereby grasp ideas. I have seen the story of the nativity 'told' by a class of five-year-olds in a mixture of clay, cloth, straw card and paper. A very large (because important) Mary in clay wrapped about with blue rags, bent over a bundle of straw in which a naked clay baby lay. Over all was arched a bent piece of card and the black paper behind was dotted with silver paper stuck-on stars, of which one, five times as big as the others, was THE star.

Clay may be used as an adjunct to dramatic play, but anything ready-made which lies to hand is more likely to be pressed into service. I have seen clay shaped quickly into a cradle for a tiny doll so that the play could carry on. When play of this kind is being worked out, the child must have to hand the sort of things which will quickly serve his needs, or he is frustrated and the thread of the game is lost. But the time comes in the middle primary years when the urgency of the game is not so great and the making of the toy or equipment is given more attention. The eight-year-old, perhaps, having decided that a clay cradle will not do, will choose a cardboard box for a doll's bed because it will serve and let him get on with the game. A far-seeing child will say —'let's make a bed out of this wood', and is willing to hold up the game indefinitely while he concentrates on the *making*. Sometimes an even more practical strain appears and he announces that once this wooden bed is made it will do for all such future games.

But as the growing child turns more and more from his own private world to the real world he wants to assert his place in that world by real things—not just toys. This is the time when we need to show him that his clay cups and plates can be fired in a kiln and made usable. Some will break in the firing because their shape is unsuitable, their joins too loose, or their section is uneven. Then the child must be shown how to join pieces firmly so that they will survive firing, and soon he will be handling his clay with an eye to the future processes and the future use, not just to express his feeling or to meet his need of the moment. He is adopting the craftsman's attitude to his material and his progress will be followed up in the chapter on pottery.

Stones and bricks may be arranged or combined as adjuncts to dramatic or imaginative play, but they are not usually shaped until some feeling for form as such develops, which is the beginning of serious sculpture (see Chapter X). Wood serves a wider range of purposes. Branches or logs picked up out of doors may suggest a figure or an animal which will stimulate play. Or the child may emphasize by some cutting or painting the idea he has seen in this shape. In progressive schools saws, hammers and nails are provided in the infant days and the child soon learns to use them responsibly. At first two cross-pieces of wood with one nail through will serve for an aeroplane and inspire happy hours of running round and buzzing. But the desire for some furniture for play—such as the doll's bed—or for a trolley or a wheelbarrow, not just of clay or cardboard, but which can really be pushed around, sets him to work on the more intellectual problems of construction. (A wise educationist [1] said that a child should not be given any plaything that he could make for himself.) Here we have a constructive use of material which is a powerful stimulant to *thinking*. A child thinks *concretely*, and with the pieces actually in his hands he can see the relation between the wheel and the axle which would be impossible for him unless we provide the materials, the bits and pieces, and the tools.

Just what does this activity entail? [2] The boy wants a barrow or a bogie to run on wheels. He has first to conceive something of the finished form. He has then to analyse it into component

[1] Ballard, *Handwork as an Educational Medium.*

[2] Several delightful accounts of such essays in construction are given in *The Intellectual Development of Young Children*, S. Isaacs.

parts and find things which will serve as those parts, or pieces of wood or cloth or metal from which to cut them. He must then find ways of joining them together so that he has movable joints and axles for wheels. So he has to be learning some elementary technique. Where the purpose is only to make an adjunct to the imaginative play in progress the child does not really want help, unless he gets into special difficulties, as his imagination is quite adequate to supply the deficiencies of his technique. But when he wants to make a real thing, he has got real problems to solve and he has to try different ways of doing things until he finds a satisfactory method. If he fails he may come for help, and only then can we interfere. The teacher's job until that point is to encourage such projects as will promote these activities. Now all this is a very important educational training, but it must be emphasized that it is a training chiefly of the intellect and of the hands, and if the handwork is *all* of this nature we are missing the opportunity of developing the emotions. One of the early and influential books on school handwork,[1] which contains many sensible and penetrating passages, unfortunately took this narrower view: 'The best kind of motor-work is handwork and the best kind of handwork is that which makes the child think the most, that in which the higher centres of the brain co-operate most rapidly. . . . It is a case of motor activity for the sake of mental efficiency.'

A conception of handcraft which has a more complete picture of the child in view will encourage emotional and imaginative development as well as intellectual. In the light of such thoughts it is now possible to say something about such handcraft as making matchbox furniture which is still frequently seen in schools. If the teacher draws the attention of the children to the fact that six or eight matchboxes gummed together will make a chest of drawers and then a group or the class get busy making chests of drawers, it might appear that they were doing at a lower level much what the boy just described did in putting together a wheelbarrow. But the value of this kind of construction depends on two things: (1) seeing the problem involved, analysing it and finding a solution, and (2) the exercise in the use of tools and the workmanship it entails. Now, if the teacher gives the answer by pointing out the constituents to be used, or even if the child chooses whether to use six or eight matchboxes, the problem

[1] Ballard, *Handwork as an Educational Medium.*

involved is hardly stimulating even to a child of four. The workmanship needed to gum together six boxes the same size is negligible, so this activity as an end in itself has little value.

If, however, a doll's house is being furnished so that family play can be entered into more fully, then the making is *not* an end in itself but a means to a fuller end. But, apart from use in the child guidance clinic, where smashing up the house may serve a diagnostic or therapeutic purpose, surely furniture of a size for the 'house corner' which can really be used is usually better?

The materials suggested included one group leading on to needlework.

The beginnings of needlework proper are discussed in Chapter XIII, but there should be, with infants and young juniors, opportunities for handling cloth in combination with other materials. The use of the cloth with string and handkerchiefs in the nativity described is entirely appropriate. Bright and patterned cloth of many kinds will also be used in the simple types of puppets described in later chapters. Little girls will always want to wrap their dollies in cloths before they can sew clothes for them. An American [1] investigator found that the girls in a mixed group of children who were offered various materials never chose the building bricks. But when bits of paper and cloth were distributed with the bricks the little girls who had not chosen to build with them were immediately stimulated to use them along with those scraps to make tables with cloths, beds with covers, and so on. Most little girls want a doll or a family of dolls. Provided only with an old towel an unsophisticated child will tie a knot in it and henceforth it serves quite adequately as a baby. Provided with scraps of cloth or a bundle of straw or raffia the same child will make a dolly of a different sort. That same wise educationist [2] said back in 1911: 'The value of a toy is not what it does but what can be done with it. Simplicity or even crudeness in a plaything is often more of a merit than a defect. It leaves a wider scope for the imagination and a bigger scope for skill on the part of the player.'

The provision of a wide variety of 'mixed materials' is both stimulating to the senses and the imagination, and it also offers

[1] Phippini van Reesema (quoted in C. Buehler's *From Birth to Maturity*), Chapter V.

[2] Ballard.

11*a*.—DRAGON

'In addition to the known the child will want to express his ideas of the unknown—of giants, witches and dragons. He will want to clarify them in his own mind and to translate them from huge and terrifying beings to small tangible figures over which he has power.'

Here is a dragon shaped by a boy of 8 out of the scrap materials provided. The body was shaped with great speed and pulled out lengthwise with some fierceness, and the bottle tops and wire rings crushed in quickly. For a few moments it served as the channel of a strong emotion, his fear being relieved by identifying himself with the fierceness of the dragon. Then it was thrown aside.

Boy of 9. Teacher: Seonaid Robertson.

11*b*.—CHRISTMAS TREES

The provision of exciting and amusing new materials can itself stimulate the children's imagination, especially in such playful and purely temporary things as these.

Christmas trees and table decoration at the school Christmas party, paper cake cases, steel wool, feathers, hairpins and many scrap materials were employed.

Primary school children. Teacher: Seonaid Robertson.

11*a*

11*b*

III*a*

III*b*

III*a*.—TWO OLD MEN AND A CLOWN

The girls who made these must have seen old men and clowns. Then, their attention caught, looked more intently. When they came to model them they were able to convey the bent-back weariness of the old men, the springing gaiety of the clown, and so to enter, to some extent, into feelings which they have not experienced in reality.

Girls of 10 to 11.

Teacher: Mary Watson,
Hugh Bell Central School,
Middlesbrough.

This central school included modelling and pottery in each year of the four-year course. The girls, being keen, put in extra time in the art room, which was open at all times with free access to materials.

III*b*.—A BIRD

A group of children who played on a derelict bomb site were provided by the author with a box of scrap materials and this was one of the many productions which appeared. It shows how the material provided suggested the subject, feather wings, popping pink-tipped match-stick eyes, but the use of it is almost lyrical. Compare this with the more functional approach of the boy who made IV*b*, p. 60.

the child media which will express his ideas without the necessity for much technique. It is commonly accepted that a child will be excited by the chance to cut or tear bright-coloured papers and that this will actually inspire him to ideas. But it is not as widely recognized that to finger tactually interesting substances, feathers, steel-wool, chamois, may be even more inspiring. Such sensually satisfying things as wood shavings, shells, even bone-rings and pipe-cleaners stimulate ideas which might not occur to the child using only card and paper. The Christmas table decorations (Plate II*b*) show the kind of thing which emerges from just playing with textures. This activity may take other forms, using, for example, the softer materials, combining fur, cloth, beads either in dressing dolls or puppets, or in building up collage pictures by sticking or sewing on bits to a flat surface of cloth or paper. All the 'fancy' papers may serve the same purpose, but on the whole they are less satisfying to the touch and do not continue to provide lasting pleasure, so they are more suitable for temporary decorations and displays. Since the young child will seize any materials at hand to shape his ideas and express his feelings, so we may expect to find strange combinations of bits and pieces from those boxes of mixed materials which should be available in the room. Clay and plasticine may be used for the shaped part to which are added details in card, metal or wood, or they may be used as a seccative to make different materials grip as in the Christmas trees. Once he has come to appreciate qualities such as shininess, furriness, feather-lightness, but has not yet any technique for representing them, the provision of a large variety from which he can select avoids frustration. He can express his intention by a lively suggestion. This is to be distinguished from the sophisticated use of strange materials or unusual combinations which we find in the older adolescent. The child is not choosing his materials *because* they are unusual, but because to him they seem appropriate.

Nor should we expect him to bring everything he starts to a state which seems complete to our adult minds. One such phantasy figure may serve only to start another and so be re-formed or put aside as soon as it is taking shape. The child is stimulated by his own production and may go on following his wandering mind, pouring out one suggestion after another. Such play is intended to stimulate and to extend the imagination and feelings, and producing a well-made, or a useful or clearly-articulated object is none of its concern. The bird in Plate III*b*, with its combination of sturdiness and lightness, and humour, could not have been made in clay alone. Such animals, trees and figures can be quickly and joyfully thrown together still quick with the vitality of the children who conceived them, if the materials are there to hand. Here the *selection* is an important element. This is, I think, a factor that we have too largely neglected in our art and craft training. Almost the only way in which the average adult exercises any æsthetic judgment whatever is in the *selection* of his clothes, his house-furnishings and possessions. Herbert Read said about Paul Nash's 'found objects'—groups of pebbles, bones and shells lovingly arranged and preserved—that selection was as significant as creation. If this is true—and I believe it is—we have at our disposal a source of creative pleasure that we have not fully tapped. From the early years children will put together objects because as a group they make a new whole which is pleasing. If this faculty can be kept alive and encouraged it will provide a sphere of creation at times when the difficulties of technique tend to be too great. And finally it can lead on to just that thoughtful and sensitive selection which makes the job of dressing or arranging a room a creative act. I am not suggesting that in this way the difficulties and discipline inherent in the acquisition of an adequate technique can then be by-passed. I believe no sort of creation is so satisfying as that which takes a raw material and shapes it to the finished form. But for every one of us there are times when this schooling is in danger of being too hard, and the goal seems too distant. Then the more immediate pleasure and the returning self-confidence of making something pleasing is an intermediate satisfaction and provides a new impetus. For many the chief channels of creation will not be the visual arts at all, but they will still need to exercise discriminating selection in furnishing their homes.

The other advantage of making with bits and pieces is that it gives the opportunity for variety of arrangement with the same pieces, and so stimulates from the first a critical appraisal—does it look better this way or that? In painting, in constructional woodwork, in weaving at any level, in carving and other crafts, it is not possible to practise this alternative choice of arrangements of all parts. So it is especially helpful to develop such discriminating selection in the early years before the student is committed to the lengthier working out of his own design.

This can be done in the imaginative work with bits and pieces and scraps which I have described; in the making of built-up pictures in materials and of embroideries which I shall describe in the chapter on needlework; and in the arrangement of natural objects, of which flower-decorations are the most usual type. But we tend to concentrate solely on flowers as decorations for the home, and when there are no flowers in winter to go without or use artificial ones, which chill by their air of dead replicas. In the arrangement of our school at Milltown, described later, we found that shells, brought back from summer holidays, pebbles arranged in glass bowls of water, and a hundred other things the children found around the school or on their walks made as delightful decorations. Large flat plates or shallow bowls could be filled with carefully selected moss, toadstools or lichened stones, wood and bark, snail shells, fern fronds. The stones and the bark were a particular joy both to look at and to touch, and their patterns suggested the search for other natural patterning of animals, undersides of leaves, water ripples, snow crystals. A reservoir of such natural materials was kept at one side of the art room and the garden was a limitless source, so that a child who was self-conscious or dissatisfied with his work could lose himself for a while among them. Very soon he would choose a few to group and find himself creating again. There is another respect in which the quest for 'found objects' may serve a wider purpose, if a slighter one. Between eight and twelve most children develop a craze for collecting. These collections have been studied in detail by several researchers. They seem to be related to the urge to possess, but appear at an age before most children can possess in their own right much that is of value. The commercial value of the collection is of negligible interest. Some children will collect postage stamps, some cigarette cards, some postcards. But *what* is collected seems to be largely a matter of fashion and habit and of adult encouragement. If about this age the interest is directed to shells, varieties of pebbles or crystals, flowers or fossils their collections may well take a form which not only extends their knowledge (as may be the case with cigarette cards or postcards) but increases their apprehension of form and pattern. So a new and more lasting field of interest and pleasure may be opened up for them. It is difficult to overestimate the excitement of putting a new dull pebble in a bowl of water and seeing it come alive and glow, or of examining snail shells or grasses with a magnifying glass.

Paper and cardboard, which are the materials most commonly provided in the handwork lesson, can contribute very little to the kind of development of which we have been speaking. Coloured and textured papers, e.g. doyleys and cellophane, have their occasional use in handcraft, but the texture of plain drawing paper is uninteresting and by its flat stiff two-dimensional structure the type of shapes it can assume is limited. The khaki cardboard normally supplied to schools is in itself horrible stuff, harsh in colour, apt to crack when bent, too tough for youngsters to cut. The frustration its handling causes is apt to inhibit all other feeling. That it is normally accepted as the basic material of handcraft is an indictment of our system. It has its place in the limited fields of model-making and in bookcraft, but it supplies none of the qualities needed to stimulate and satisfy the senses and the imagination.

Since there are many types of 'play with materials' which do meet the needs of the growing child, the enthusiasm for making shown all through the Primary School ages should not be squandered on narrow or educationally fruitless handwork. Whatever educational aim we hold gives us a criterion, and if the development of senses, emotions and imagination are seen as vitally important, any activity can be measured by asking how far it contributes to that end.

I become each year more and more aware of the responsibility we take in the choice of materials we provide and encourage. As the list shows, I believe that in the primary years the choice should be wide. But there is also a criterion of quality. Papier mâché may be a very useful material for such things as the foundation of a geography model. But if small children are given papier mâché for their material for phantasy work the result will be a room full of grotesques. It is practically impossible to make a delicate, sensitive or fanciful object by squeezing papier mâché. It is impossible to convey the kind of feeling shown in the mother duck. If we provide papier mâché we must expect the coarse and crude. Now, in so far as there are times when every child wants to make a grotesque face, this is all right. But there must be alternatives. If we provide prepared pieces of wood and metal which can be fitted together we must expect the emphasis to be on construction, and on problems of *thought*. If we provide only paper and card, and concentrate chiefly on bookcraft and model making, we can hardly expect to encourage imagination and feeling. Almost any material can be used to fulfil a real human need, a child will make little men of bread or orange peel if denied clay; But certain materials encourage certain types of work. We have to decide for ourselves which aspects of handwork are most valuable at which ages, and it is our responsibility to provide the appropriate materials.

MINIMUM EQUIPMENT

Material listed in this chapter.

This should be available (though not necessarily all out at once) in the Primary School.

When any one of the groups of materials suggested is first introduced to the class, it has often seemed to me better that all should experiment together, and that diffident children should be encouraged to explore a new material by the assumption that all will enjoy it. But, of course, one would never insist against a child's will. Later, two, three or all of the groups of materials suggested may be made available in different parts of the room, and children go to the group which attracts them that day.

The order in which these materials are introduced depends on ease of getting them, on the children's previous training, and on the general work they are doing. Thus, in a country district, children can bring pebbles, lichens, flowers from the earliest ages. Since it is important that if possible they should have the joy of gathering these themselves, the city teacher will plan walks, even if only in a park. Clay can be modelled easily from nursery years, bending wire or metal, carving hard materials not till later. Work with needles and scissors must wait till these can be held with ease.

The groups of materials are listed on page 36. Here are the tools and equipment which will be required for their use.

Clay; a bin or pails to hold it, a sack to damp it. Newspapers to cover desks.

Plasticine; a box to hold it. Newspapers,

Dough, papier mâché; bowls to mix it in. If flour paste is used, a pan and heater. Or this can be made at home and carried in a 7 lb. jam jar.

Pieces of wood, chalk, plaster of Paris, etc. Penknives, old kitchen knives. A saw is useful.

Cloth, paper, card, etc. Strong, *sharp* scissors, large crewel and other needles, thick sewing cotton (e.g. Clarke's Anchor), small balls of many colours of wool. Ragbag and boxes of buttons, beads, etc.

Feathers, shells, etc., and miscellaneous objects mentioned, need no special equipment.

Wire, tins. Pliers, metal cutter.

Any of these materials may be used in the sort of activity described in the next chapter, where in addition, wooden boxes, saws, nails of many sizes, hammer will be needed. As these activities expand towards the top of the Primary School they use more and more the normal adult tools of daily living.

CHAPTER THREE

GROUP SESSIONS

A GREAT deal of what we used to regard as 'handwork' springs up naturally in the course of the activities now practised in progressive Primary Schools. The making of a tree-house, of an orange-box motor-car, the dressing and dancing involved in acting out a story, the housing of a family of rabbits, will entail practising skills which need not be taught as class subjects. The 'activity method'—that unfortunate term—has three valuable characteristics: first, the children are physically *active*, which is their natural state; secondly, they learn by *doing* rather than by being told, and in that way learn more thoroughly and more deeply; thirdly, the impetus to master skills comes from *their own* desire to make something, and so has behind it an inexhaustible fund of energy. No longer need any child be compelled to make anything which he does not himself urgently want to make. This by-passes class teaching in the old sense. It puts a much greater strain on the teacher, who must be making a constant readjustment, not only to each separate personality as she moves round the room, but to discovering what each child is trying to make, in entering imaginatively into the child's mind to *see* with his eyes the finished product and steps towards achieving it. But this is the *only* way to develop individuals, with their own ideas and their own experience of working them out in terms of material. The dull bookcraft exercises of uniform size and shape, the woodwork dictated by given measurements on the board, the needlework of a stated size, pattern and stitch, are in a different category from creative craft. One aim of this depressing type of lesson is accuracy in measurement, which is a branch of arithmetic, not art, and the other is the practice of a skill. Now facility in certain skills is necessary too, but any skill can be practised on the piece of work which is the individual choice of the child, urgently desired by him for his own purposes just as well as one dictated by the teacher.

This is clearly shown in the activities which go on in the best of our Primary Schools.

A class of thirty-five eight-year-olds have had *Hiawatha* read to them by their teacher. A group of them are enthusiastic about the poem and want to act it, so they set about this while others, interested in other things, go about their own play. Desks are pushed to the edges of the room, the children choose who shall be Hiawatha and the other characters. These brown their faces and begin to play out the childhood of Hiawatha, while one group of children stand waving their arms and sighing as the pine trees, and another group on the floor sit and chant the chorus when it is appropriate. Billy says, 'We need a wigwam; we'll make one.' So one boy goes out to the wood pile to find a long pole while others collect sacks, which are spread on the floor and stitched loosely together—the boys are just as keen to sew these as the girls. When they are sewing they have to keep discussing the shape of a wigwam and fitting the sacks together to form a cone, which is no simple problem. 'It ought to be painted with Nokomis's name,' says Sally, 'to show who lives there, like a name on the door.' She was remembering:

> *From his pouch he took his colours,*
> *Took his paint of different colours,*
> *On the smooth bark of the birch tree*
> *Painted many shapes and figures,*
> *Wonderful and mystic figures,*
> *And each figure had a meaning,*
> *Each some word or thought suggested. . . .*
> *Sun and moon and stars he painted,*
> *Man and beast and fish and reptile,*
> *Forests, mountains, lakes and rivers.*

So the powder paints are brought out and several of the children try out on sheets of newspaper sign-writing for Nokomis's name —'daughter of the moon'. The teacher discusses sign-writing and shows them examples from different parts of the world. After all the attempts have been pinned on the wall and discussed Alice's is chosen by the class and she proudly paints it on. Now work—or play?—must stop for to-day but the children want to make Red

Indian feather headdresses for themselves, so they are told to bring next day any feathers they have at home. This does not produce a great crop, so they must go out and find some. After coats are put on, they all set off across the yard, and through the fields to the nearest wood. They are looking particularly for feathers, but there are plenty of other interesting things to see, and they learn the names of many birds, greeting particularly those which Hiawatha knew. These will be remembered better when a feather is found to remember the colours by. Having found a few fine pheasants' and wood-pigeons' feathers, they return by a farmyard to collect

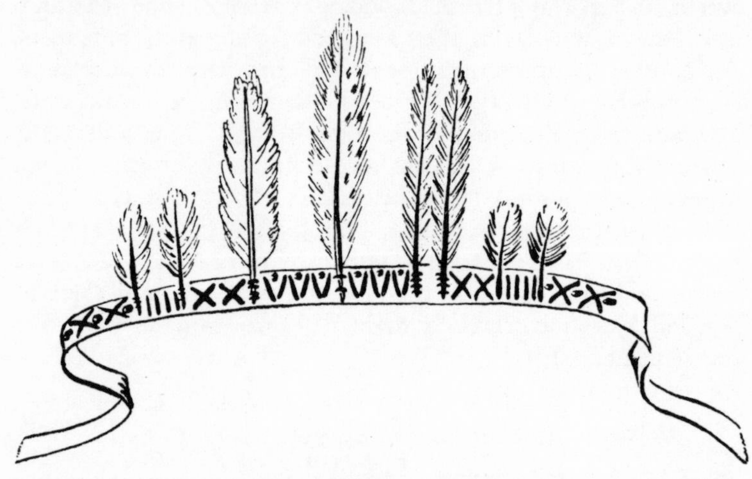

FIG. 2.—An Indian squaw's headband, showing how, from the first, stitches can be learned on something which is wanted by the child. Here the stitches, beads and feathers make a pattern on the coloured braid.

plenty of cocks' and hens' to make up the number. Johnny says he will go and see the poulterer in the town and ask if he can give him more of the long tail feathers. Back at school, everyone starts sewing feathers on strips of brightly coloured braiding, and teacher has to demonstrate stitches which will hold them down firmly and also look decorative. The first to be finished put on their headdresses and strut about declaiming:

'Minnehaha, laughing water,
Handsomest of all the women.'

But the Indian braves need trousers and the sacks are hauled out again. Here is quite a problem for an eight-year-old—how are trousers made? They examine each other's and find the seam running down the back and inside the leg. Two sacks are pinned on to Ronald and the extra bits are boldly cut away by Tom. It would not matter if he made a mistake because the sacks could be used up for something else, so he can afford to be bold. He cuts away too much but the others have taken note and they will do better. Large coloured stitches sew them up, and Vera offers the coloured braid she made into reins for a horse last week to be put up the sides of the trousers, and helps to sew it on. When teacher is reading the next episode of the story the squaws are all threading patterns of large beads on strings for themselves. Next day those who have elected to play the different animals are busy painting masks of Ojeeg the weasel, Ahmeek the beaver, Mishe-Mokwa the bear. Meanwhile some are tackling the problem of a canoe. They learn how this was made of stretched deer-hide over a framework, but since it has to glide over the class-room floor they decide to use an orange-box for the structure, and cut thick brown paper for the covering. This can be gummed along the sides of the box and brought together at bows and stern. Someone is looking in 'the tins box' for four lids the same size for wheels while others set about measuring the box to make sure the paper will cover it. Part of each of the next few days will be spent on making, painting and playing in this 'canoe'.

This purposeful game, then, has included such operations as measurement, acting, sewing, reciting, carpentry, painting, nature study, singing and dancing. It may go on for weeks—so long as the interest persists—gathering into itself many of what would formerly have been disjointed subjects, providing a much more fascinating way of learning about things. But this type of activity, excellent as it is, does not necessarily cover the whole of the child's development. Such activities are a central core which need in addition a certain amount of straight learning, and a certain amount of free creativity, in which children can explore their personal problems. I have deliberately chosen as an example this Hiawatha activity, in which the approach described does in fact stress more the *experience* than the *knowledge* to be gained. It is not to be concluded that the children now know how Red Indians do in fact live. The remoteness in time and distance of the scene encourages imagination to play a part, and the acting of human and animal characters gives scope for that sympathetic entering into the feelings of others. This was an imaginative and dramatic re-telling, but it rouses the interest which can later be directed into factual learning. Activities and projects which are concerned only with acquiring information neglect the child's capacity for a total response. The teacher can do much by wise suggestion, and by not forcing *all* the children in the class into such an activity irrespective of their degree of interest.

CHAPTER FOUR

PURPOSE SHAPES THE FORM

THIS book began by lamenting that handcraft was now apt to be encouraged indiscriminately in our schools. The reasons usually given for teaching it fall roughly into these groups:[1]

(1) To serve as a relaxation from 'serious' work. For instance, painting ready-made lampshades will do this.

(2) To inculcate accuracy, e.g. bookcraft, woodwork, are cited.

(3) To teach skills of immediate usefulness, e.g. lettering for school notices; or of future usefulness in the home, e.g. carpentry, needlework.

(4) To provide pleasant and profitable occupations for future leisure, e.g. embroidery.

(5) To develop the intellect through tackling concrete problems, e.g. bookcraft.

(6) To develop appreciation of sound workmanship, e.g. metalwork, woodwork.

(7) To raise the standard of industrial design through developing good taste in the future consumers.

These intentions in encouraging craft work are all sincerely pursued, and since every craftsman knows that purpose shapes the final form they will inevitably result in different kinds of activity and different approaches. I myself consider the first two reasons too trivial for consideration, the next two too narrow as the same results come as a by-product of a wider aim, and the fifth as mistaken in ignoring the nature of the arts it attempts to use.[2] The last two will be considered in the course of the next few chapters.

[1] Those who judge that this is too gloomy a picture are assured that this list was drawn up from answers given to the question, 'Why do you think crafts should be taught in schools?' given by hundreds of headmasters and teachers throughout the country.

[2] This aim has been expounded in an admirably clear and practical book, *The Education of the Ordinary Child*, by John Duncan. One can be filled with admiration for this record of what has been accomplished while thinking it completely mistaken about the nature of the arts and their contribution to education.

The criterion by which I judge the activities discussed in the following chapters rests on a belief that crafts make their chief contribution to education as a form of the arts, that is, as a vehicle for the revelation of the human spirit, and that they make it in a widely acceptable and tangible form in the creation of a satisfying environment.

This statement of personal belief, far from being a final evaluation of craft activities, is intended to initiate that argument and experiment without which there can be no clearer vision. At least the confusion of values cannot be greater than it is at present.

There is not even any agreement about the meaning of such basic terms as 'craft' and 'handwork'. I shall use the wide term 'handcraft' to cover all those activities in schools of practical work with the hands which might conceivably come under such a heading. 'Craft' is a word with a varied history and a wide range of uses, but there is no other that will serve for the chief subject of this book. There seems to be one antithesis implied in its use in general conversation, in which art as creative is contrasted with craft as skilled use of tools, and another implied in the school use, where art is drawing and painting, and craft is work with other materials. I have tried to preserve something of those two uses. But I myself would like to see the word 'craft' given potency by being distinguished from such terms as 'skill', 'dexterity', 'manual occupation', 'technique', and associated rather with the dignity of craftsmen and craftsmanship where it surely belongs. So I shall use the word 'craft' only for responsible skilled work (usually intended for use and always for pleasure), designed and carried out by the same person and reflecting his attitude to his material and to life. This excludes skilled work put into someone else's design; designing which the originator does not carry out in material; skill put into objects for use with no concern for quality; and dexterity practised for its own sake rather than in the service of a creative whole. But since craft is a word used in such differing senses, it is necessary to define its scope here a little more. Painting is generally agreed to be an art, of the same kind as poetry and music, a creative activity in which the product has no practical use (does not clothe, nor serve as furniture or implement). Now modelling and sculpture are sometimes ranked as arts, and in certain respects they are closer to painting than, say, to weaving. But since they are generally classed as crafts in schools, and since work in clay runs unbroken through modelling and pottery, they have been included in this book. On the other hand, there are some so-called 'crafts', such as lino pictures, wood-engravings, embroidered wall hangings, which might better be called 'picture-making in materials'. But since lino pictures are closely associated with lino fabric printing, and since embroidery is a branch of needlework, it seems more logical to include them as crafts. Most of this book, however, is concerned with work in solid materials rather than on surfaces.

I have left the discussion of the various functions which hand-craft may serve until this point in the book, because I believe that in the earlier years, the issue is fairly clear. Once the importance of the development of the senses, the emotions, and the relation of the phantasy life to the real life through the operation of imagination is grasped, then I think that there can be no question that these are the aspects of education overwhelmingly important at this age, and neglected in too many schools. Since handcraft is or can be a creative activity fostering these, its main function is clear. But occasionally during the earlier years and increasingly

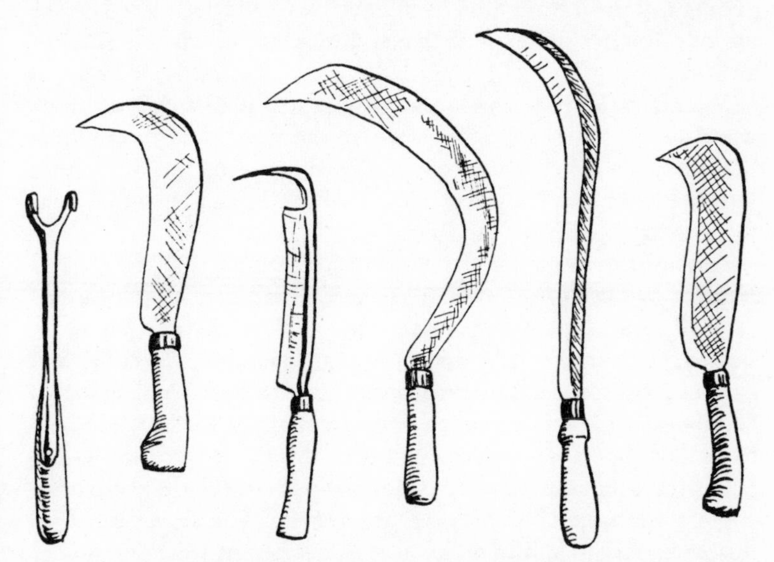

FIG. 3.—A group of billhooks, slashers and drag implements of everyday use in the country, illustrating how the purpose, and therefore the way each will be held in the hand, governs the individual shape of blade and handle, an admirable example of form evolved by purpose.

over nine or ten, there are other needs of the child to which handcraft must minister. The purpose we have will shape the form the work takes.

There are three types of activity generally called 'craft' which do not qualify by my definition, and would better be called handwork. These are work in which the intention is to assimilate factual knowledge; or to learn by experiment how things are made; or practice to gain facility in a useful skill.

The first of these consists of such work as models for history or local studies, the making of dolls and furniture in connection with these, the making of costumes or armour, the imitation of certain techniques, such as those used in early pottery. Not so long ago, children were given a certain portion of information which they might be expected to learn, and were asked to reproduce it in the form of an essay or answers to questions in class or examination. If now they are asked to reproduce it in the form of an Arctic village or of a doll dressed in Elizabethan costume, that does not automatically turn the activity into art or craft. Such teaching is much more likely to be digested and enjoyed if the children are finding out the information for themselves by visits, records, wise use of reference books. But the ensuing piece of work is still not art or craft, if the purpose of the activity is *the reproduction of factual knowledge*. The use of the materials of craft—clay, cloth or wood—does not change the nature of the activity, any more than the fact that a pencil is used to draw geometrical figures turns these into works of art. The *intention* of the work in hand must be clear to the teacher and the children alike.

Perhaps the most popular form of illustrating such subjects as History or Scripture nowadays is model making. Models are of several kinds, and it is necessary to be clear about what is required. A model usually means a reproduction or a copy, and implies a prototype. The reconstruction of a Saxon village or an Elizabethan theatre in which the essential features are derived from illustrations and description is of this type. Since the essential features and the essential relationships between them are to be copied, this cannot be a *fully* creative activity. The degree to which it is spontaneous and to which freedom is permissible determines how far it holds the possibility of being creative.

Of this type too is the 'working model' embodying a mechanism, e.g. of a windmill or a waterwheel, the making of which is a branch of practical science. This may require considerable intelligence to work out and great dexterity in assembly, but so long as the emphasis is on conveying information, it is not creative craft.

Then there is the replica—the small exact copy of a larger prototype, usually to scale, whose making is a source of satisfaction to a certain type of adult. The accuracy required implies a detailed observation of the original, but there seems to be little value in the activity as such.

It must be questioned whether the supposition that knowledge is *acquired* through making models is not a fallacy? Knowledge can be *recorded* in this way certainly. But does the child not need to have acquired the knowledge through instruction or books *before* he can make most of the models seen in schools? The knowledge of how a simple mechanism works *can* be acquired experimentally through attempts to make it, but this is not what is generally known as model making.

Lastly, a model may be the reproduction of a prototype which as yet only exists in someone's mind—the model of a new town which will be translated into actuality. Here it is not the making of the actual model which is creative (this may be done by a technician) but the conception which exists in the town-planner's mind.

Through the use of the word for a small reproduction in clay or wood which is intended to serve as a 'model' for a larger statue in stone or metal, the word had come to mean anything moulded in clay. In schools, however, direct modelling is rightly treated as an end in itself.

Why are the making and use of constructed models so popular with children? It is perhaps natural that small things should have an endless fascination for the small child. After all, almost everything with which he is surrounded in the normal home (though not in the good nursery school) is out of his scale altogether. It may be that this is compensated for by an excessive pleasure in tiny things. Small objects give a child a sense of power which he needs. It must be very frustrating to stumble through the adult-scale world unable to move a chair when one wants it in another place, unable to see on to the top of the table, or to reach the things in the cupboard. Small replicas or toy objects of those can be moved and rearranged, which gives him the feeling of being able to order his world. While the making of replicas (exact

IV*a*.—FEATHER BIRDS

A group of birds, made of clay with feathers stuck in, by a group of 8-year-olds. Some of the birds have beaks of the end of a quill cut off. This whole class made birds on this day, and then they spontaneously ran about holding them at arm's length 'flying'. The obvious follow-on from this would have been a bird dance composed by the children, but on this day no large enough space to try this could be found.

Boys and girls of 8.

Teacher: Cliff Murray,
Student of Bretton Hall,
Snapethorpe Primary School,
Yorks.

IV*b*.—THE DIVER

On this occasion a class of 8-year-olds were given a great mixture of materials—feathers, corks, beads, shells, clay, wire, string. This diver proved a most interesting example of the way in which children 'think with materials' or 'in materials'. This little boy seized a piece of rubber tubing which suggested the diver and built the whole round that. The last addition of shells under his arms full of 'jewels' (beads) was association of ideas with treasure under the sea.

Boy of 8.

Teacher: G. Bridge,
Student of Bretton Hall,
Snapethorpe Primary School,
Yorks.

IV*a*

IV*b*

IV*c*.—THE INVADER'S SHIP

Made in wood with a striped cloth sail on a sea of blue paper and cotton wool.

Boys of 10.

Teacher: Mr. Sully,
Nash Mills Primary School,
Hertfordshire.

This is a small country school which enters widely into the life of the surrounding district. The children dig up clay nearby with which to model and fire in their own primitive kiln. They absorb much of their history in visits to local churches and historic places and record their knowledge in models which show an imaginative use of materials.

models) of furniture or utensils is hardly creative, the imaginative games which the child plays with them may be. Such small furniture is a part of the play material of every good clinic and play centre, and in the form of house furniture and toy vehicles, is accepted as necessary through the primary years. But by the middle of that period the child is usually wanting objects—still light enough to handle and not necessarily fully adult sized—but 'real' things belonging to the grown-up world. Playing at keeping house and at shopping gives way to a desire for a little basket to go real errands, and toy utensils no longer satisfy the need to do real cooking.[1] Tools of his own are demanded to make a real barrow. So, while the model has its place, its purpose and limits must be clearly seen by the teacher. Often, I feel, its function could be better performed by the actual thing. Why should country boys not try a hand at thatching when a thatcher is in the district, or erect a beam and cruck hut just big enough for them to creep inside, rather than make a model? Why not improvise a form of Elizabethan stage for a performance rather than many models? It might be taken as a general principle that it is more satisfying to make something like the real thing, using the same material and same methods if that is possible at all.

These activities with materials, models of Viking ships, history friezes, scale models of new town plans and so on, which we have called handwork, are concerned with learning about. There is, however, another type of learning, learning how. To learn facts *about* swimming or skating is quite a different thing from learning *how* to do it. This is only learned by *doing* it. The growing curiosity of the child about the world around will lead him to ask, not only 'When did men first weave cloth?' but also 'How did they do it?' Not only 'Where do our cups and plates come from?' but 'How does soft clay become so hard?' Between about nine and twelve in especial he will be asking those questions and he should be finding out the answers through his own experience. To learn how the short wool on the sheep's back becomes yarn and then cloth is a

[1] Dewey and Susan Isaacs showed in practice that it was feasible to let children do this much younger than we had supposed. The Secondary School Report, 1931, suggests that it would be more valuable to teach children housecraft in the primary ages when they are thirsting to be allowed to be so grown-up, than to postpone it to thirteen or so when there is frequently a revulsion against it.

part of his general education, a part of the handing on of the traditions of Western Europe (an Indian or a Chinese child would be asking first about cotton or silk). Either in a project or in the history lesson each of those processes should be practised by some of the children in the class. If enough time cannot be given for each child to carry out each process, he will still learn a great deal from seeing others and hearing talk about it.

I believe we largely neglect the education of children by each other, which by making use of their enthusiasm and of their natural way of behaving puts less strain on teacher and taught. If a form is divided up into groups and one group sets out to dig local clay, build a kiln and fire pots, while another makes moulds for lead and melts and casts it, and another collects wool, spins and gathers dye plants, then at the end of a year or even a term each one will not only know a good deal about the discoveries of his own group, but will know something of the discoveries of all the others. The interchange of talk coming to and from school, the attraction of exciting things going on just across the playground, the sharing of problems and discoveries in class and out, all add up imperceptibly to a surprisingly wide knowledge.

It might be argued that since the world in which these boys and girls are going to take their places is a world of machines and mass production in which few people dye with plants or shape a jug by hand they would be better employed visiting factories where these things are done by machinery. This so-called realistic attitude implies that the child can arbitrarily be fitted to the system without regard for his capacities at that age. In the first place, it is exceedingly confusing for a child of nine or ten to be taken round a factory if he knows nothing of the essential processes involved. The complexity, the large scale, the fact that so many of the steps in the series—in a foundry, for instance—go on behind doors or in circumstances where they cannot be watched, frustrate the purpose. The time for factory visits is about fourteen to sixteen, when they can better be digested and when in addition they may have a direct relation to choosing a vocation. But it is in the earlier years that the child asks 'how' and that he must be assisted to find out. Secondly, knowledge acquired by doing oneself is very much more lasting and deeply imprinted than that acquired by seeing other people doing. In all the industrial arts mentioned and most others the *essential* process is the same as the hand process. It has simply been geared to a greater source of power and multiplied many times. The machine cannot invent an original process, nor can it discriminate. The first mould, the first pattern had to be made by somebody, somewhere. I am neither repudiating nor underestimating the value of the machine, but the machine cannot be used until the fundamental process is understood. Only then can endless variations of that be arranged and the process multiplied indefinitely by machine power. Nor am I suggesting that children should be altogether kept away from machines. That would be quite artificial. They may be a powerful stimulant to intellectual development, and a part of the furniture of their world. But a child must be introduced to exploring them at a level he is capable of understanding, the scales used in cooking, the pulley and ropes, or the tricycle. The understanding of a complex mechanism must still be approached by way of understanding the simple, but each generation seems to cover the steps more quickly if given the right opportunities. This understanding of the processes by which things are made is usually conceived as an intellectual activity. But there is more to it than that. A child can understand when told that in spinning, the thread is twisted so that the scales on each fibre grip one another, and that the fibres are pulled out till they terminate in different places so that the weakness of the breaks is distributed. But this is very different from the understanding which comes when he has spun even a little. This is an understanding of the body as well as the mind, of the senses, of the muscles, closely linked with, not deliberately detached from the emotions. Half an hour with a loom under his hands, or even a sheet of card, a needle and some string, will, with some demonstration, teach a child more about what weaving is and how it is done than many hours of description. So, if it is considered part of a child's general education to learn the simple fundamental processes underlying the complexity of machine mass production, *a short course* of weaving going rapidly through different types is indicated. If on the other hand, or in addition, the activity of weaving itself is seen as something valuable to the growth of his personality and proficiency in it a source of pleasure and satisfaction, then he needs a *long* course, chiefly on one, or a few types, so that he has time to gain that depth. In the same way, he can be told that different chemicals affect the way in which wool will take a dye. But he *knows* in different terms altogether in a different dimension when he has actually seen wool mordanted with alum, with iron, with copper, dipped in the same dye, and when he has come to distinguish the peculiar quality of all colours treated with the same mordant. This is again something which cannot be adequately described. It has to be experienced.

If the aim is to understand processes, then trying a hand, as interest arises, at weaving, baking clay, beating metal, will be most useful. The later years of the primary school will probably be the time for this, and it is not so much proficiency that is to be looked for as comprehension. This is in contrast to adolescent craft where a longer period of time must be spent in order to learn to make well. The teacher must be clear about what each particular child needs. Is he asking how it is made? Or for help in making a good job of it?

The third aim of handwork teaching mentioned was the acquisition of useful techniques. There are a number of practical skills useful in daily life which the school is quite rightly expected to teach, in which not only understanding how it is done, but gaining a certain proficiency and ease, is desirable. This implies spending a certain amount of time in practice. Knitting, even where it is taught with bought wools to a dictated pattern—as it almost invariably is—is one such undoubtedly useful skill. But why should it be only that? Why should children not be taught to knit with wool which they have spun and dyed themselves, and taught knitting as a constructional subject instead of following a pattern? They can be shown how to knit a straight strip, then how to knit a cylinder, how to widen slowly or sharply, till they have all the *elements* with which to build up any shape they wish. Later they can themselves create both surface patterns and structure from the simple elements they command. And so one of the most routine of feminine skills can become a source of excitement and any woman can truly *create* a garment for herself. I do not necessarily suggest that every woman should go on spinning and dyeing her own wool for the family knitting (though why should she not, if she wishes to?), but an understanding of wool colours, of knitting construction, and a satisfaction and pride such as is never glimpsed in the normal knitting class, results from such an approach.

So, learning a skill may, if taught in this way, be the preliminary stages in practising a craft. But that name must be denied to much of what goes on in the 'handwork period'. Any production which has to follow the essential features of a prototype, or in which the size, form and method leave the child little scope for his own interpretation, cannot be fully creative. Any activity in which the emphasis is only on the acquisition of knowledge (even practical knowledge such as how a coiled pot is constructed) or on the acquisition of skill without concern for the quality of the finished product must also be termed mere handwork, not craft. This last type is close in approach to the old 'manual' training. Unfortunately most bookbinding, and much woodwork and metalwork, as they are in fact taught, must be so classed. Much needlework, too, but we shall speak of that later. The demands these make on the student are those of accuracy, neat manipulation, and conscientiousness. But every one of these could better be approached as a real craft when full possibilities of the subject are seen. Cutting uniform slices from a hollow roll of plastic for napkin rings, or putting a border of dictated stitch round a cotton tray cloth of given size, will give some small sense of satisfaction to the child who has no legitimate opportunities for real creation. In the same way a woman knitting a jumper from a shop-bought pattern gets an undoubted satisfaction. But how infinitely greater is the sense of achievement and the strengthening of the personality which results from a beautiful piece of work consciously directed at every point of its making with colour, form, texture all devised for this individual thing.

In this connection it is helpful to distinguish clearly *making* and *decorating*. Just as a pseudo-craft may be carried out in material which is already imprinted with another's mark either in colour (e.g. plastic), or in pattern (e.g. ready printed paper for endpapers of books), so the larger part of the satisfying job may be taken out of the children's hands by giving them ready-made objects to decorate. Ready-constructed boxes or candlesticks of whitewood to paint; ready-made lampshades to paint; the made-up and stamped teacloth sold with the silks all selected—none of these can rank as crafts in our sense. Decoration should never be something superimposed on an article made by someone else. All live satisfying decoration springs (1) either naturally from the process of making as does the alternation of lines or checks in weaving, or (2) is the final flourish, the overflowing exuberance in the love of his medium of the maker-craftsman, as is the slip-trailed decoration of the potter excited by the surface of wet clay. Somehow or other, in a community which is frustrated in its desire to make, that small part of making which is decoration has become separated off and elevated to the status of a craft. The part has usurped the place of the whole. It is as though the sweet were served up as a meal, and since it is not really satisfying the tendency is to go on consuming sweets repeatedly. So one gets perverted decorators who cannot buy a plain blouse or see a cushion or a curtain without lusting to embroider on it. Our responsibility in school is a far bigger one than teaching them an adequate number of stitches to do this with some skill. It is to teach them to *make* first, and to let the act of making flower into such decorating as the materials, the form and the purpose of the whole may suggest.

CHAPTER FIVE

THE VALUE OF CRAFTS IN ADOLESCENCE

THE baby who is born into this complex world lives by entering into relationship with two sets of factors which make up his personal environment, persons and things. These two relationships interweave and the success of one influences the other, but here we are chiefly concerned with the relationship to things. The stages by which the human infant enters his full relationship with the material world can be traced fairly clearly. The new-born baby grasps an object which touches his hands but this may be purely a reflex action. Before he is half a year old he stretches for and grasps things within his reach, and then moves them about and rubs them against any handy surface. Through the next few months objects are shaken, or rubbed together, or hit together, or thrown down, but all objects and substances are treated alike. But all the time the baby is becoming more aware of the nature of things by sucking, biting, grasping, knocking them. Before he is a year old he is probably placing objects down more carefully, which shows that he is aware of himself as having some effect on the object. But for some time yet, he will not be aware that he can in some cases actually change its form. Some time in the second or third year he will notice that soft materials such as clay and plasticine can be squashed by banging with the fist, that a push of the finger actually leaves a hollow, and later that the lump can be formed into a ball or roll. For the first time in his life he relates his own activity to the shape of things. Alongside this growing consciousness of his power to shape materials another acquisition is recognized. When handling blocks one may accidentally be placed on another. The immature child takes no notice of this, but somewhere round one and a half years, he suddenly becomes aware of it and looks with wonder at his first construction. For a time he may concentrate on this new activity with great satisfaction. Spasmodically, from now on, in contrast to random play, his *intention* determines what is being done. He builds towers with increasing numbers of blocks and knocks them over with great enjoyment. His feeling of power grows with each achievement. We can early distinguish some difference between those whose forceful tendencies incline them to build upwards, and those whose retiring nature leads them to build enclosures with protecting walls. Soon all sorts of structures are tackled—houses, bridges, castles and other complex arrangements. In well-equipped nurseries this building will be done with coloured blocks, but other children will equally use real stones, scraps of wood and bricks, and get along very well.

The first remarkable discovery that he can *mould* soft materials may in itself give sufficient satisfaction for quite a long time. But eventually, the child begins to express ideas through them, making little men, loaves, houses and animals. Soon too, if the materials are provided for his use and not snatched away from him, he will find that wire will bend, that cloth, like paper, can be torn, that straw and wool and paper can be bunched, twisted, even plaited. The next stage is the discovery of tools. Probably the first tool is usually a *material* with which he is playing—a stick is used to scratch on clay, or a piece of metal to break something up, or a brick to press plasticine flat—but soon he discovers knives and scissors and many tools which are specially designed for their purpose. So the possibility of expressing ideas and feelings is enormously widened. It can truly be said of these early years that the child thinks in materials. In fact the materials, either in themselves or in his playful manipulation of them, are the inspiration of his activity. The act of making stimulates the flow of ideas.[1]

[1] Charlotte Bühler, in *From Birth to Maturity*, speaks of creation as 'a specifically human pleasure experience which first appears with the construction of an object. In contrast to the pleasure of activity, in which we pour forth our energy in movements, we have in the pleasure of creation the characteristic satisfaction of transferring our energy to the material, and of impressing upon it the stamp of our individuality. We generally express this by saying that we express ourselves in the material. And in this expression of ourselves we expand beyond our limits and leave a more or less permanent impression of ourselves in the material. With this are connected three important experiences characteristic of mankind: while he is active with the material, man surrenders himself to it, masters it, and puts something new into the world. Surrendering one's self, mastering the material, and producing an object are, one may say, such definitely human experiences that

Between about four and eight years we find a sublime confidence in his power to form. In front of an easel, with a sand tray or in a garden, whole worlds are constructed. In play on the sea shore the elementary upheavals of the earth are—albeit not consciously—repeated every day when mountains are heaved up, rivers are diverted. So in the garden, farms and houses are built in an hour, or railway stations laid out complete with bridges and trains. The whole is manipulated with the power of a god. What happens to this sublime confidence in his will to form, which is displayed by all young children? How is this divine belief in the power to create so minimized, so frustrated, so destroyed that we get the ugliness and disillusion of Milltown?

We can say two things for certain. First, the power to create—and to create harmoniously—does exist in every human being, and survives frustrated and distorted where it does not get a proper outlet in childhood. Secondly, the creations in material of the young child, however lovely as evidence of what he would wish his world to be, crumble eventually in the face of material difficulties. The tide comes in and destroys his city, the rain washes out the colour of his painted clay figures, the wooden structure falls apart because it is not properly fastened with nails, the clay cups dry and fall to pieces.

The whole of craft teaching lies in the span between these two worlds—the idea which, while it must assuredly develop in complexity and subtlety yet enshrines the original harmony for which we all strive, and the persisting reality of Milltown existing at this moment in England. If the Milltowns of the future are to be built with the confidence and idealism of the child's play, then the practice of crafts must teach the maturing child to embody his ideas in

---

without them one is not human. These experiences . . . have normally fallen to the lot of the six-year-old child.

'Without such a surrendering, and the capacity to make such a surrender, normal emotional and character growth cannot take place. Children, deprived of adequate opportunities of constructive play, are children who later grow up deficient in constructive imagination, and are inhibited in experience.'

Charlotte Bühler is of the opinion that the passage from the use of material as an instrument for phantasy to the use of even the same material for construction is a definite stage in maturation. While the age-limits she suggests and the fixity of the lines she draws cannot be entirely accepted as universally applicable, it is without doubt that a desire to construct makes its appearance in all healthy children at a definite period.

a material which can take its place and perform its function in the physical, practical world in which we all live. Thus play with materials leading on to crafts can serve as a focal point in which the world of ideas and feelings and the world of material things are united within the child's and the adolescent's experience. Before he can understand anything of philosophy or politics he can know with certainty from his own experience that man can mould the physical world.

The years which stretch from the seashore castles to Milltown are the years of education. How much of the proper confidence in his own powers which is natural to the child lives on in the adult, and how much of the unreality of his wish-fulfilment is translated into the reality of brick and mortar, will be largely due to us, his teachers. In so far as the people of Milltown—or anywhere else—accept, in making or buying, the pretentious or inappropriate, their childhood's purity of idea and feeling has become distorted by other factors—snobbery, fashion, undefined purpose. So far as they say 'folk like us can't expect to have good things' they have lost their childhood's confidence in men's power. The things we make or buy are governed by the nature and the amount of the materials available on this earth, but inside these limits man can create his environment, his cups and chairs and playgrounds and towns, to the shape and form he desires.

It is because men must keep their belief in this, that we must teach crafts in schools. The only way I know to keep this belief is to give them three things: first, the realization that everything made has its own particular form, colour and texture because *somebody* conceived it so; secondly the acquisition of skill to translate their own conceptions into tangible form; and thirdly the experience of entering so completely into the nature of this particular material that they can think in terms of it. And the only way I know to attain these three is the practice of a craft for years.

'The practice of a craft' implies a very different attitude to things, from the young child's exuberant play with materials. How does this come about? The activities discussed in the last chapter—that is, forms of handcraft arising from (1) an interest in gaining knowledge (e.g. of History); (2) a curiosity about ways of making things (e.g. baking pottery, or making cloth); (3) a desire for useful skills (e.g. knitting)—may go on through the upper primary and secondary years *alongside* fully creative work which grows out of the younger child's play with materials.

But, some time in early adolescence, usually round about the twelfth or thirteenth year, a fundamentally different attitude to making will develop in almost all children. This is not a sudden break, but rather a change of direction in a steady curve which may appear slight at first but leads to a totally different outlook. It appears spontaneously, is little influenced by previous training, and apparently can only be explained by maturation. This concept of maturation or ripeness is one of immense educational significance, but its implications have hardly affected our teaching because where research has been done on our specific problems it is not readily available. Very little educational research has been done on these, and that is locked away in unpublished theses or volumes not often in the hands of the ordinary teacher. A good deal of isolated experimental work has been done in schools in various parts of the country, but the writing up of such experiments and their correlation is usually beyond the individual teacher. A centre for the collection and consideration of such material is urgently needed.

Maturation is a recognized phenomenon in physical growth, and can be contrasted with that type of growth which is the result of exercise or training. In physical maturation there is a *differentiation of the functions of various cells*, as when the identical early cells of the embryo develop, some into the brain cells, some into liver and heart, some into simple muscle cells. In contrast, the growth due to training—as later when these same muscles are used and exercised—is due to *a multiplication in the number of the same sort of cells*, not to a differentiation in kind. The stimulation of the embryo to growth appears to come from the interaction of the parts themselves, whereas the growth of limbs and muscles due to their exercise seems to come from their directed activity. It is obvious that the important bodily changes of puberty and the menopause are due to maturation from within the organism, but many of those activities which we had previously thought to be induced by exercise and training have been shown to be dependent first on a spontaneous bodily maturation. For instance, the ability to walk, to climb stairs, to do up buttons is not developed earlier by persistent training, but matures at a certain time in each child's development. Before that time exercise is not only useless, it may be actually harmful to his final performance.[1] It has always been found better to exercise fully the ability to talk when that is already present rather than to press on to reading lessons before the child is ready. Many researches in the acquisition of skills suggest strongly that the essential thing is to find the point at which it is *natural* for a child to enter on the new activity, the time when the capacity for entering into it matures spontaneously. This is just what we do *not* know in almost every educational problem. A painstaking headmaster who objected to the freer methods of painting encouraged in these days said earnestly: 'I find that I have to make the children use rulers for their drawing from seven onwards because it takes them all that time to learn to use a ruler accurately by eleven.' One immediately wants to ask him whether he had tried starting them at ten and a half to see whether they did not get to the same proficiency by eleven. The introduction of subjects or demands—such as that for mechanical accuracy—at the wrong age is not simply a waste of time and energy on the part of teacher and pupil. It is positively dangerous. It destroys those qualities which *should* be developing at that age. As Herbert Read insists throughout his book *Education through Art*, if *undue* intellectual or mechanical skills are encouraged through the primary years the child will arrive at puberty worse off, in lacking the rich emotional life which has been inhibited by a mistaken emphasis on merely factual accuracy. Maturation on the emotional and social levels is as important as on the physical.

I do not, however, want to press this idea of maturation beyond reasonable limits. It is better used as a limiting concept to explain growth which cannot otherwise be explained. But I believe that its significance for the art and craft teacher has nowhere been realized. Handcraft syllabi are almost always planned to an adult and intellectual scheme, not to wait for and meet the needs of the child as they actually arise.[2]

How does the child's attitude to material change? The earliest type of play is bodily activity, stretching, kicking, grasping. At this stage activity is directed towards materials without any clear appreciation of the differences in their nature. Then about three to

[1] C. Bühler, *Birth to Maturity*, Chapter VII.

[2] One even finds a handbook for teachers with an Introduction by Cyril Burt (*Art and Artistic Handcrafts in the Infant School*) stating: 'Surely the best place to begin perspective is at the beginning, in the Infant school.'

four we find the realization that materials can be formed into shapes which stand for something, into symbols such as he uses in his drawing. But the young child's creation is swift, spontaneous, transient, and rather loosely thrown together. Later comes the persistence and the acceptance of the intermediate steps required to gain a desired end.

One observer [1] instances the behaviour of two little boys, three and a half and seven, with their mother's clothes pegs. The younger calls them 'loaves' and pulls them about in his cart, offering them for sale. The elder takes his pegs and puts several together to make a horse, then a house, an aeroplane, a motor-car. The younger can start and finish his activity at any point. He is unperturbed by the evident dissimilarity of his pegs to rolls. Stones or balls of paper would probably have done just as well. They serve as rolls for him. The elder is trying to represent something to others as well as himself by his artifact, and asks for each object to be identified in turn and is glad when the adult guesses right. He is trying to *convey* something. Also, he has set himself a task and will not stop till it is complete. We have here two threads which we have to disentangle. One is the use of material to create a thing and the patience and perseverance shown in working through to the end ('work maturity' in contrast to that play in which the activity is itself the end). The other is the effort to represent the form even in this very elementary way. The younger child might as well have taken a clothes peg for his game and said it was a horse. The elder boy attempted to construct of his unpromising material a horse which would be recognized by others and satisfy himself by *some* similarity to the original. This *hint* of similarity is enough for several years after seven. The boy of seven sees that his horse of pegs has a body, long neck, head, four long legs, and that is sufficient to indicate that it is a horse. But before eleven or twelve he would begin to see that its legs did not end in the proper sort of hooves, that its head might as well be the head of a giraffe or a cow, because he has begun to *look* at things in a new way. The change of vision which takes place in early adolescence has been discussed at length in books on education, so I shall content myself with saying that—if it has not been previously forced—a closer and more acute observation appears then, an *outward* turning to attend more intently to

[1] C. Bühler, *Birth to Maturity*, Chapter VII.

the *appearance* of things. This usually results in a period of faithful representation in drawing and representational crafts such as modelling and carving. Now this may deteriorate into mere naturalism if a strong enough interest in pattern, in colour and in feeling has not been built up in the previous years. Or it may find new subject matter in the locality, new interest in the familiar streets and occupations, the crowded dockyard, the grey canal, the pattern of factory roofs or red brick houses. It is as though a young child's eyes were fixed so far away that he sees inwardly, any fantastic, remote and (to us) extravagant vision being related to himself. Then his seeing is gradually turned outward and the near comes into focus and is found to be full of its own fascination. Many of the great artists have experienced such an alternation and achieved a synthesis in giving to their vision the reality of careful observation, or in giving to the homely and near the quality of magic. But some like Blake were all vision, and some like Holbein all observation.

This careful observation of detail, which usually appears for the first time at adolescence, may, with the child who turns not *to* representation (in meticulous drawings of natural objects or people) but *away* from it, be an inspiration for craft. The loving study of a group of moss-covered stones may lead to a desire to paint the stones, but it may equally lead to a desire to capture the combination of colours and textures in weaving. Or the poring over and handling of smooth boulders of sea chalk or of the tusks of animals may produce a desire to enhance these by elaborating them. This interest in looking at, in attending to, the objects of the world around is to be encouraged—though not wholly at the expense of imaginative work—as a healthy and wholesome entering into the objective world, and as a balance to the intense subjective experiences of this period. Probably the *looking* is itself the most important thing, but when it can be related to creative work either directly in studies of actual objects or indirectly in the inspiration of a remoter kind, the two worlds, the inner and the outer, are made one.

So there seem to be four main forms of creative work to which this change of seeing may lead. In representational art there is (1) the loving portrayal of the appearance of things, and there is (2) the new discovery of the interest in the immediate, even though drab, environment. In the less directly representational

V.—SEA CHALK WOMAN

'The careful observation of detail, which usually appears for the first time at adolescence, may, with the child who turns not *to* representation . . . but *away* from it, be an inspiration for craft. The loving study of a group of moss-covered stones may lead to a desire to paint the stones, but it may equally lead to a desire to capture the combination of colours and textures in weaving. Or the poring over and handling of smooth boulders of sea chalk . . . may lead to a desire to enhance these by elaborating them.'

Here is a sea chalk carving by a girl of 17, in which the original ovoid shape and the natural striations of the stone have been the inspiration of the subject. This carving shows a beautiful appreciation of a simple and humble subject in a humble material picked up on the sea-shore outside the school.

Girl of 16.

Teacher: Miss Errington,
The Girls' High School,
Bridlington.

This is the school which pioneered in the carving of sea chalk, which can be picked up on beaches along much of our east coast. The teacher was a painter who experimented in carving along with the girls, until a tradition grew up over some years. This suggests how a school—whether offering other crafts or not—may gain greatly by building up a fine tradition in one.

V

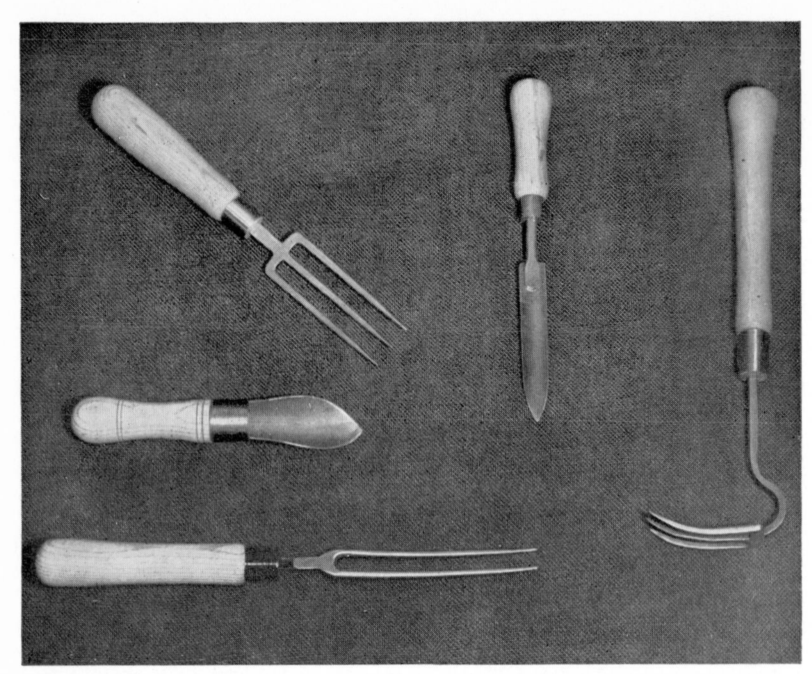

VI*a*

VI*b*

VIa.—METAL TOOLS

'The adolescent wants to be trusted with a real job of work.'

These gardening tools were made by the boys of a small country school which specializes in rural science. They probably represent the most purely utilitarian objects of the craft work shown in this book; but how beautiful they are to look at, and how satisfying.

Boys of about 13 taught in a mixed age group.

Teacher: the Headmaster, B. V. Coates,
Bronington All-age Rural School,
Whitchurch,
Shropshire.

Experience in gardening and rural life combined with the available skills in wood and metal have led to the evolution of these tools, for specific gardening jobs. Mixed age groups of 10 to 13 are taught together so that beginners and experts are doing completely different jobs. There is a small workshop fitted simply for wood and metal, with a forge. This is open with help to old boys once a week, and boys in their last year are allowed to use it out of class time (two hours per week) when they have finished other work.

VIb.—MUG AND BOWL

'If it is a good jug it will fire well, hold water, pour neatly and be comfortable to hold.'

In adolescence, when authority is sometimes felt as an unwarrantable imposition, and resentment turned against the person who wields it, the material exerts its own impersonal discipline out of its own nature.

Here are two useful simple pieces of pottery in which the makers have accepted and used the limitations of their material.

Boy and girl about 15.

Teacher: Louis Jones,
Wennington School,
Wetherby,
Yorks.

This is a co-educational progressive school in flat farming country. Interest in pottery grew up through the teacher, primarily a painter, forming a close liaison with a small local pottery where he went to work on odd days and holidays. This sound practical background has resulted in an emphasis on simple wheel pottery almost of the rural tradition. The boys and girls built themselves a wood-firing kiln and now have an electric one. The pottery is a wooden hut equipped with kick-wheels and three wheels running off a half-horse power motor.

crafts, there is (3) the discovery of strange forms, colours, and textures, unnoticed before, the inspiration from them to create in wool or clay, and also there is (4) the discovery of the beauty of stones and wood which can be accentuated by working them.

But since all children are surrounded by naturalistic representation in magazine illustrations, in posters, in pictures in the home, there is always a strong pull through the pressure of public opinion to regard naturalism—however much the art teacher may throw her influence the other way—as the criterion of good art. Familiarity with the works of artists who obviously did not accept this criterion but developed different modes of representation and a different system of perspective, such as the Persians, the Byzantines, and many of the moderns, will break this down in time we hope. But, too often in spite of all efforts to show him the validity of other modes of working, the young adolescent is dissatisfied because he cannot achieve the standard of naturalism he has adopted from these external sources. If this does happen, he can escape from his frustration into a sphere where there is no possibility of this standard of naturalism being set up, into the weaving crafts, or pottery, or wood-turning. In those, the elements which the art teacher would wish to emphasize—form, composition, colour, texture—are presented uncomplicated by representation. All the stress is on these and on a real achievement in three dimensions, instead of an endeavour to represent three dimensions in two and the consequent confusion of perspective.

So craft may prove a valuable channel just at that time for the same artistic urge which earlier found its outlet in painting. The Norwood Report (p. 126) speaks of 'craft, which for many pupils is the more natural form of expression and a more natural approach to the study of design'.

Thus the child's *seeing* changes. Now we can return to the changing attitude to *making* and see how this is influenced. We had traced the 'activity with materials' through aimless playing, through shaping into an indeterminate form enlivened by imagination, and on to a more determinate form where the intermediate steps are undertaken towards a preconceived end. This attitude persists through the primary years, showing increasingly more care given to the making so that the finished product may function better. But the next development appears to be the maturing of a quite new attitude. The desire to do a thing well *for its own sake* appears. It is no longer enough to tack a skirt on to a doll so that it does not fall off, to nail two pieces of wood crosswise and hurl it into the air for an aeroplane. The developing pride of craftsmanship leads to a very different attitude. There is real satisfaction in making well, in making something which will last and in which each part is skilfully fashioned. This satisfaction is not achieved at once. Some skills take years to learn. But the different *intention* has emerged and will continue to be an important factor in all art and craft work.

At first this genuine interest in technique (which is usually quite absent from the young child's make-up) is apt to lead to technique as an end in itself. This shows itself as skill increases in an adolescent elaboration of method—the newly acquired ability is enjoyed for its own sake and flourished in the face of observers. Some of the great civilizations have not developed their crafts beyond this adolescent stage where facility in technique is an end in itself. But having gained ample self-confidence and passed beyond the need to show himself and others how well he can do it, the artist craftsman can afford to be more restrained and select his method and his decoration as they are appropriate. This cycle is the experience of most sincere craftsmen. The stage of rather unrestrained exuberance is not to be frowned on by any adult appeal to good taste. The adolescent needs the satisfaction it gives him, the feeling of having mastered a medium sufficiently to be clever with it. He needs the resulting self-confidence and, if given a chance, he will pass through it himself to a far more stable and certain standpoint of his own. But this will only be reached if he is given time to outgrow it at his own rate. Faced with a group of sentimental or crudely exuberant adolescents any good teacher, by the quiet, firm insistence on the virtues of restraint, or by the appeal to the outward pressure of accepted good taste, or by the provision only of those materials not capable of the wilder extravagances, can draw out a set of work showing a restrained maturity which is, in fact, the maturity of the teacher. This temptation is perhaps especially strong under the pressure of time in the training colleges or for scholarship examinations. But are these students, reared in such a forcing house, so firmly based on their own convictions of what is satisfying, that when they leave the influence of their teacher and the studio environment they can not only maintain that standard but go forward on their own? The sad falling away of the standards of students whose own work at training college was charming, and the choice of dress, furnishing and amusements of my own students in Milltown, suggest that this is not so.

This interest in acquiring skill which is the characteristic of adolescent craft work is closely linked to the most fundamental need of the adolescent—that of acquiring independence. His situation has been summed up in this way: 'In all ages of the world and in societies of widely differing culture, adolescents have had five main problems to solve. These are (1) adjusting to their own physical growth and development; (2) achieving emancipation from the family and attaining emotional independence and maturity; (3) accepting their own characteristic sex role and adjusting wholesomely to the opposite sex; (4) finding and entering upon a suitable vocation and (5) developing a philosophy that will give them meaning and purpose to life. The solution of these five problems seems to depend not so much on the internal biological and physiological changes in the adolescents themselves as upon the social forces that affect teen-age boys and girls in the particular environment in which they live.' . . . Our modern adolescent has a much more difficult time of it than his counterpart of a primitive community. Legal maturity is delayed until he is twenty-one years of age, and other forms of social maturity may be delayed to an even later age. At thirteen, fourteen, or fifteen years of age, when a great number of our girls and boys reach puberty, they are still in school and may remain there for many years. They are economically dependent on their parents—often until twenty or twenty-five years of age.' [1]

[1] S. R. Laycock, *Adolescents' Problems—Growing Up Emotionally* (Home and School, p. 64, Nov. 1948).

He goes on: 'Because of this fact, every effort is made by many parents to belittle the adolescent's physical growth and development, to keep him tied emotionally to his home and to delay, as long as possible, his interest in the opposite sex. He cannot marry for many years after puberty. He is either not ready for a job or a job is not available for him. As a result he must continue to be supported by his parents. Added to this is the fact that his parents, in many cases, have no sure philosophy of life of their own. Consequently, they are often of little or no help to an adolescent who is trying to understand what life is and how he should relate himself to it.' What constitutes this process of growing up to emotional maturity? 'He begins life entirely dependent, egocentric, irresponsible; he should become fully independent, altruistic, responsible. He has to pass from the completely filial to the completely inde-

Since he can in fact achieve comparatively so little in the adult world because of the set-up of our society, the great need for the adolescent is to achieve something. If he cannot achieve something creative it will be something destructive. There are many ways in which this dependence can be lessened by responsibility in the social sphere. In crafts he can be given the opportunity to tackle a job and carry it right through which will add to self-respect. Therefore it is essential to guard against insulting adolescents with trivial forms of handcraft. It is well that the bodily movements should be pleasant and agreeable, but adolescents will accept hard and continuous work for an object they value.

I have not discussed craft as vocational training because I take it as axiomatic that we are not in schools concerned directly with vocational training at all. But craft work is one of the very few school subjects which if well taught may occasionally be carried straight on, passing imperceptibly into training for a craft or trade. Here is a source of real independence, the knowledge that one is preparing for a satisfying and socially valuable job. The serious adoption of one group of media at adolescence has, too, a settling effect, with the implication that there is enough to discover here to provide a serious occupation for a long time.

In addition to all the practical problems to solve, a growing self-consciousness is one of the almost invariable concomitants of adolescence in our civilization. The desire for self-revelation and close emotional bonds alternates with periods of secretiveness and a desire not to 'give oneself away'. This desire not to expose oneself is apt to lead to inhibitions in painting, especially of the more expressive kind. At this time, therefore, the young person often finds the impersonal quality of craft work a relief. When a sometimes terrifying range of emotions is discovered within oneself without adequate means of expressing or controlling them, to have definite limits set by the nature of the material and by the

---

pendent attitude. From being the victim of circumstances and environment, helpless in the face of these two factors, he should end by being independent of both and the captain of his own soul. Lastly, from being first unconscious of himself as a centre of attraction, he should attain to the completely adult attitude which includes readiness to be ignored. . . . If one of the major objectives is to lead a child from dependence to independence, many difficulties beset the path of the child and adolescent. The chief danger lies primarily in the attitude of his parents and secondly in the attitude of his teachers and comrades.'

possible processes of making from it, is to know better where one is. In addition the very familiar and almost homely nature of such substances as wood or wool gives a foundation of stability to the whole work. There is here a parallel to the new way of seeing. The ordinary and familiar things are found to have within themselves infinite variety and fascination which is worth exploring.

If we are agreed about what we hope the practice of a craft will do for adolescents, then there are a number of occupations generally referred to as crafts which we can leave on one side. One of the possible reasons suggested for teaching crafts in schools was the provision of leisure occupations for later years. I think there is no need to make this a direct aim because, in fact, if we choose our crafts to develop the senses, the feelings and the imagination, we shall find that a fair number of pleasant and relatively undemanding leisure occupations will have been acquired by the way. But these will have been acquired *related to a craft* which is seriously practised to a rewarding standard. They will be, as it were, on the fringes of a creative occupation, and so they will be enriched and will themselves enrich this core. Such is patchwork, which can be built up of tweeds or velvets for a stool or chair seat, or silks or cottons for a cushion or bedspread. Here the art is all in grouping colours and textures within the formal framework of the whole. One would not want to spend much time on this in the precious craft period in school. Yet the suggestion might well be introduced in the needlework lesson since it takes its place as a branch of the subject closely allied to constructive work in scrap materials. In addition experience in both the selection and the joining of the pieces contribute to more creative forms of needlecraft.

Quite apart from the æsthetic value of the finished article, I would prefer not to introduce at the age of serious craftsmanship an activity which is isolated from the main stream of the crafts we have chosen to practise, as, for instance, barbola work or plastics. There is not enough breadth or depth in such materials to provide the experience of delving deeply over a number of years which has been found most conducive to the growth of personality. Nor would I introduce an activity such as rug making, even though it is a sound traditional craft and can be linked to the main stream of needlework or weaving. It entails so much monotonous work to accomplish one article that the school student cannot get enough experience of seeing how his designs work out. He has not time to explore even one branch of the craft fully enough to be able to design in terms of it.

This seems an appropriate place to say something about those activities which I have no hesitation in calling 'bastard' crafts. There are a great many ways of employing the children during the craft period which are little more than just keeping them busy; ways which make few demands on their sensibility, their intellect, or their gift for creation, which are no more than a harmless time-wasting employment. But there are some which by borrowing the name and prestige of a real craft, teach false techniques and get a quick and easy result just when the adolescent is willing to tackle difficult materials and wants to be trusted with a real job of work. The making of 'stained glass windows' of coloured cellophane, or even by painting on real glass, the making of 'paper mosaics', produce superficial effects with insidious results.

It is the confusion of values which is so dangerous. This imitation of the technique of one craft in the materials of another is a pernicious deceit. Its products are on a level with electric bulbs set in mock candles or ceiling paper stamped to look like plaster work. It scorns the possibilities of honest workmanship in simple materials. How shall we help the young craftsman to search for the essential qualities of wood or clay in order to express those as much as himself, how shall we teach him to seek the method of working which will draw out the latent qualities of the material, if we contravene our own principles in this way?

This is perhaps the most essential distinction between work suitable for the young child and the young adult in craft. The young child might legitimately use coloured cellophane to stick on collage pictures or make Christmas lanterns. This is fun rather than craft. His phantasy will invest any material with the qualities he needs at the moment so that each idea can be given form from what lies to hand, and then discarded or turned into something else. But the adult must work with things as they are, with the limitations of the materials he has. These very limitations are of the nature of this world, and to accept them and yet have the vision to use their possibilities to the utmost is true maturity.

These qualities of the basic craft materials are in fact an important element in the contribution of crafts to the education of the whole person. Every real artist knows—though this seems difficult for the layman to believe—that the practice of an art or craft is the sternest of disciplines. Perhaps so much talk about the need for free expression in art and craft has tended to obscure the persisting need for self-discipline. There is no evading the fact that a period of concentration of energies on a purpose accepted by the whole personality is the only way to achieve a satisfactory piece of work of any kind, including a work of art. Let us consider each of the three parts of this statement separately. I say 'period' because I believe that the balanced life is an alternation of day-dreaming with periods of concentrated energy directed to working out some of the possibilities glimpsed. I stress a purpose which has behind it the *whole* personality because if there is conscious opposition to the set purpose the result will be resentment for the authority which sets it, and if there is unconscious opposition the two will work against one another and result in repression or illness. Hence so much emphasis on finding activities which are welcomed—in our particular sphere that means giving a choice of crafts. A 'satisfactory work' is one which is firstly satisfying to the maker, satisfying both in the doing and in the final product; and secondly is acceptable to the more discriminating section of his society. But to be needed and to be wanted are so much a part of the normal make-up that these two are usually closely bound together. One thoughtful writer [1] says that the artist needs praise more than any other man just because—since there is no objective test of art—he cannot see with certainty that his work is good and makes a contribution to society. The engineer need not wait on the verdict of others to know if his bridge is good, it proves it is good if it stands firm and takes the strain. The craftsman has a similar criterion in the work itself. For this reason, for the adolescent whose values are probably in a state of flux, and who is uncertain whose opinion he shall trust and respect, the practice of a craft is often a factor making for stability. Painting may be an outlet for strange, not fully realized emotions which are apt to overwhelm at this time, but craft opens up a field where standards are a little simpler and not so dependent on the values set by other people. If it is a good jug it will fire well, hold water, pour neatly and be comfortable to hold. If it is a good stool it will stand firmly, take the seated body at a comfortable angle, feel smooth and bring out the quality of the wood from which it is made. In

[1] William MacDougall.

dealing with this age when authority is apt to be felt as an unwarrantable imposition, and resentment turned against the person who wields it, the material exerts its own discipline out of its own nature. If clay is not treated with due respect as clay it cannot be formed into a vessel. Wool hastily joined in spinning snaps and itself demands persistence till the technique is mastered. The teacher need not condemn—the work condemns itself, the thread is broken. But when that happens and help is asked for, there is so much that the teacher *can* do. I deprecated the teaching of technique in the years (under ten roughly) when the child is largely content with his own method and finds it is sufficient for his purpose. But after a desire to make seriously has matured, then we are bound to teach technique. It is unhelpful to leave children of this age to struggle on alone. They soon become disheartened. And there is a great deal to teach them in any craft we have really studied. Human experience over a great period of years has gradually crystallized into ways of doing things which can save disappointment and waste of energy.

While there is certainly something to be said for the adventurous attitude of teacher and class embarking on a new craft together, the only way to teach a craft thoroughly is to be so familiar with its material that one thinks in terms of it, and to be prepared to demonstrate the processes to any student at any stage. But is there not something fundamentally wrong with our system? If the only way to teach a craft is by practising that craft in front of the children then the obvious inference is that there should be a practising craftsman in the room working through all the successive stages whom the pupils can watch and question when the need arises. Now this may well be the teacher herself, because the old apprentice system was in the past found the only way to train craftsmen and it is probably still so to-day. But the workshop did not consist of one master craftsman and some thirty or more apprentices. Even in a time when the necessities of life were much more pressing, this would not have been considered an economic outlay of the craftsman's time. For us there seem to be two possible solutions, (1) to have considerably smaller classes (it would, for instance, be reasonable to ask for the same number in a secondary school craft class as in domestic science), or (2) to have students at different stages of mastery of the craft working side by side. This last has in fact proved to be an excellent

VII.—WOODEN SPOONS

Some of the feeling for a shape which is related to the hand, apparent in the old wooden corn-scoops, ladles and household spoons, is seen in these wooden spoons and knives made by boys and girls of 12 to 13. See how beautifully the graining of the wood has been revealed in the bowl of the spoons and the obvious pleasure in this natural form of decoration.

Boys and girls of 11 to 17.

Teacher: Mr. Mann,
Michael Hall,
Kidbrooke Park,
Forest Row,
Sussex.

This is a Rudolf Steiner co-educational boarding school. All the work is closely bound up with this particular educational philosophy; but these spoons, usually the second sort of work undertaken in wood, are close to the traditional rural craft in this country.

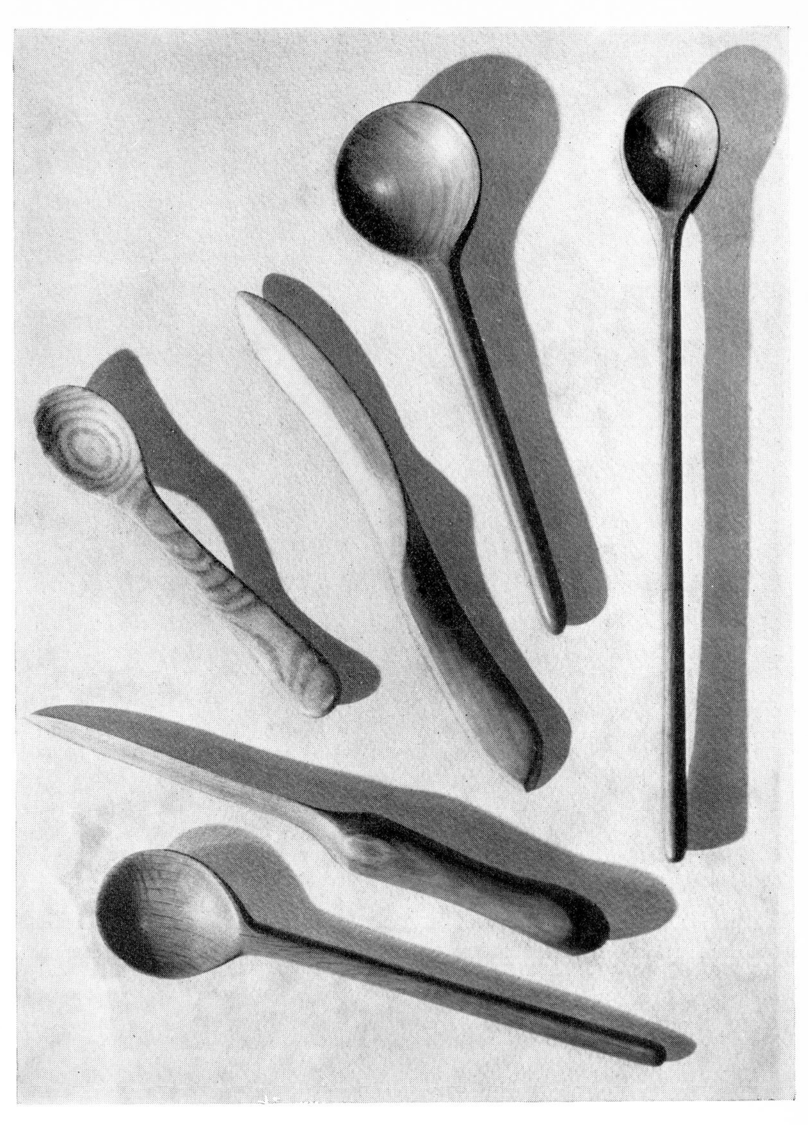

VII

VIII

VIII.—WOODEN BOWL

'Lathe turning presents its own problems, the balance of inner and outer shells, using the grain to full advantage, the problem of the edge.'

This turned wood bowl was done in a class of forty in the 45-minute periods of wartime, and an evening once a week when the workshop was open.

The whorls revealed by the sensitive use of the grain call to mind rhythms other than those of growth, the receding wave, or the striations of a hillside seen from the air.

Boy of 16.

Teacher: Mr. Dyke,
Southfield Grammar School,
Oxford.

This school holds a five-year course in woodwork for School Certificate. It has a fully-equipped workshop open one night a week with help to seniors and old boys.

arrangement. The seniors feel an added incentive to a better standard of work and develop a sense of responsibility. The beginners and middle-stagers seem to absorb largely without direet teaching the additional techniques they need. The atmosphere of serious constructive work created by the senior students sets a workshop tone, and the practice and quiet discussion of the advanced workers is in itself an almost unconscious education for the juniors. This, after all, is the most fundamental mode of education. Perhaps our strange system of rather rigid age divisions is only useful in strictly limited departments of education. It should not be difficult to arrange that classes work in age groups for a part of the day at the more formal subjects where class teaching is necessary, and for another part of the day divide into interest groups, each covering a wide age range, for practical activities. Such activities as dramatics, swimming, singing, orchestra, are parallels to craft in this respect.

As well as such an age range in the craft workshop it is a great help to have a practising craftsman on the premises or near at hand, working continuously at his trade while the teacher concentrates more on helping individuals. This is a constant stimulation and source of inspiration to the children, as well as inculcating by suggestion and example a serious work attitude towards the job.

Those schools are fortunate which have in the district working craftsmen whom the children can visit. There are all too few of such left to us. But fortunately potters, joiners and cabinet-makers, tailors, basket-makers, bookbinders and sculptors are not quite extinct.

CHAPTER SIX

THE PRACTICE OF CRAFTS IN ADOLESCENCE

All the really successful craft teachers I know have come to the conclusion—which is borne out by my own experience as a craftsman—that, once the stage of serious craftsmanship is reached, much more is to be gained from working at one material, rather than taking up a new craft each year, far less each term. There is so much to know about any one material before one can use its potentialities to the full. It needs constant and continuing practice with many of its forms, with oneself exploring different possibilities in different moods. It is necessary to establish a close and intimate relationship with it as with a person, going so deeply that one finds an understanding which does in fact illuminate everything else. This is the essential experience of craftsmanship. Possibly any work, probably any art, can at this deep level provide such an integrating experience. But none of the craftsmen I have known thought this could be gained by a superficial contact with several crafts. After a certain familiarity with one material has been gained, and when there is enough confidence and skill to be able to design in terms of it, then a second material can be tackled, and the one experience will illuminate the other.

If a sound pre-craft training in free imaginative work and in practical knowledge of the basic materials, clay, wool, wood, etc., has been given, the work of the craft teacher in the secondary stages will be much easier. The child will probably know which materials interest him most and which crafts he wishes to study at length. If this is not so and students come fairly new to the materials from which they have to choose, I have found that the best preparation is a few weeks of something resembling the 'playing' of the junior years, handling the stuff in different forms, getting the feel of it, seeing from the work of more advanced students what can be done with it, and tackling some small job not demanding a degree of skill in its execution. Several materials should, if possible, be provided in this preparatory period so that the young student can choose his medium. I am convinced that the 'instinctive' liking or dislike for certain crafts depends to a considerable extent on the student's reaction to the physical properties of the material, and so can be discovered more quickly if attention is not distracted from those. Some students dislike intensely the soft, squelchy feel of clay, and even though their attention may later come to be concentrated on throwing shapes, they will never be able to give themselves up to the material and accept it completely while this repulsion is suppressed. To the potter, this very quality is a continuing source of physical pleasure which helps him over the long uninteresting periods of mastering technique which come in every job. Similarly the noise of hammered metal is so distressing to some people that even when they think they have got used to it they still cannot relax in the noise of a metalwork shop sufficiently to enjoy thoroughly the job they are doing. Now, if we set the student at his first encounter to solve a problem in his material or to make a definite object, his attention may well be so absorbed mentally by the new task that he may hardly be conscious that something is worrying him physically. So the best attitude for the first few weeks is, I believe, a loose, relaxed one, without much pressure of a task. This should be a wandering exploratory period for picking up and handling the material and the tools, getting the feel of the whole field rather than the knowledge of one corner. This is in contrast to the attitude which is encouraged once the student has chosen and settled down to the material of his choice. In considering the work most suitable for the adolescent, that is the 'crafts proper', it is useful to distinguish two types of craft: (*a*) those made from manufactured materials such as cloth as in dressmaking, or paper, card and leather as in bookmaking, and (*b*) those made from the raw material, as clay, wool in the fleece, or wood, and carried right through the process of making. Many craftsman-teachers have come to the conclusion that using raw materials is most rewarding of all, but there are many activities which form such a valuable field for creative making that it would be perverse to refuse to recognize them just because they start with a manufactured material. Because the running of a home is such an individual activity so little amenable to the methods of factory mass-production (though one waits eagerly for more heavy-labour-saving devices, and more adequate centralized services) it happens that more girls continue to use the home-crafts or -skills learned in school than do boys. So I propose to consider in some detail needlework, the commonest of feminine skills. In this group of work with manufactured materials will come, too, bookcraft, treated from the angle of young children's work with their own patterned papers and lino cuts, rather than as traditional bookbinding. Fabric printing will be linked with dressmaking or upholstery. One of the advantages of teaching these crafts in school is that they are skills which the adult will find extremely useful. Capable of being practised with a minimum of equipment, they may well provide part of that education for leisure which is increasingly asked for. But adolescence, like childhood, is not only a preparation for adulthood. It is a time when the growing personality in its own right has certain needs and desires, and any teaching must never concentrate *solely* on the preparation for a future state, but provide opportunities and satisfactions in the present. Rousseau surely meant this when he spoke of childhood ripening to its own maturity.

Within the group of crafts which are practised with materials in their raw state and taken right through to the finished article, are work in wood (sometimes including basketry), in wool from the fleece (sometimes including rugs), in clay, metal, stone. If cooking, which is more ephemeral, fell within the normal scope of handcraft in schools it would be grouped with these. In a world in which everything is increasingly pre-processed, in which few of us see any of the processes of making—far less the original raw material of the common objects we use—why, it may be asked, advocate the use of raw materials at adolescence when the student is entering more fully into that world? If we are concerned in schools only with turning out the largest number of useful articles, we had better drop crafts, and turn over to technical and mechanical education. But surely we are still, at this stage, concerned with the developing personality, which needs opportunities to become more sensitive to quality, and the satisfaction of being fully creative. The conviction that work with the raw material best provides these is born of experience and has three foundations.

First, sensitiveness to quality, especially physical sensitiveness of touch, appears to be developed by handling the *raw* material as in no other way.

Secondly, the preparation of the material is an essential part of the making. To by-pass this by the provision of partly prepared material, e.g. to weave baskets or trays from cut and prepared cane on prepared wood bases or to weave entirely from ready spun and dyed wool, may save much time, but it deprives the student of several essential experiences which are integral to the whole. First, it deprives him of that loose relaxed period of preparation which comes at the beginning of so many craft processes, e.g. the preparation of the wool, or of the clay. During this, one is adjusting gradually from other activities—in our day so often hurried and tense—to the physical looseness of muscle, to the tactual awareness (which takes a little while to reach each time), and to the mental attitude necessary for working with this material. This entails first a state of diffused attention, almost a dreamlike state, induced by the rhythmical action. In spinning, this frame of mind is induced by teasing, and in pottery by wedging. Then comes a rather more directed attention, in which the conception of the finished piece influences the shaping at this stage of the work, as in carding wool, or the early treatment of clay on the wheel. Then a mounting tension directs the shaping more explicitly, till a deep but still relaxed concentration narrows on the more delicate operations and brings the final form to its completion. An exact parallel cannot be forced and the length of time at each stage varies, but something like this cycle in shaping seems to occur in most crafts which use raw materials.

The third reason for using raw materials is that control is exercised at every point. The wool can be dyed to normally unobtainable colours; it can be spun for worsted or for woollen, thick or thin; the colours can be combined at the spinning stage or at the weaving. The stool or bookshelf can be not only of the size needed, but of the shape and wood desired. The clay can be mixed with grog, or sieved fine, wedged lightly or thoroughly, whichever is demanded by the process of working and the finished object. The final conception is thus directing all the intermediate steps. But the material is also directing. The slow tempo gives time for the idea in the mind of the craftsman to interact with the feel of this particular batch so that one is adjusted to the other. The material is prepared and shaped so as to be suitable to take on the imagined form, and that form is adapted to the physical state and variety of this batch of material. Since natural materials such as clay, wood, wool, leather vary with each batch, and the practised craftsman does not sit down before a new piece with a rigidly defined pattern of what he is to make complete in all its details in his head. If he *has* a clearly defined idea, then he has to look about for the piece of material which is just right for that—which means having a wider range to choose from than is usually possible in school. But more usually the quality of the material is 'sounded' in this preliminary preparation and the idea is adapted to what is most appropriate to this particular piece. The idea itself of course may almost be said to be suggested by the clay or wood in that what we call 'clay shapes' or 'metal shapes' are those to which the material takes most kindly and in which its qualities are used to best advantage. No craftsman tries to force his material. He who has not been trained to appreciate this by the playing with materials which I advocated during the primary years, often comes at first to the craft class with a firm idea or even a sketch of what he wants to make. If gentle discussion on the part of the teacher does not redirect him he goes ahead and usually he fails completely. He probably thinks more determination or persistence is needed and then tries again and again with increasing force, till he is trying to batter the material into his shape. Failure may result in such discouragement that he gives up. But if he is more humble—as all mature craftsmen are—and approaches the material with a ready awareness and desire to understand it, he will learn its ways and will be able to use those to shape his purpose. The materials of the craftsman are strangely like people—or animals. One has to know their characters and their possibilities before one can work with them. It is no use trying to impress or to bully. And one has to know the point beyond which they cannot go. The master craftsman, who has served his long apprenticeship and knows his material intimately, works always within its limits. Then, once in a hundred years comes the genius who, having served and understood his material, suddenly by an act of faith extends those limits, shows us that this material is capable of a use undreamed of. Such an advance was the soaring stone of flying buttress, the springing arch of steel, the space-poised architecture of Lloyd Wright. But for us who live in the wake of an age when nearly every material was prostituted to imitate some other, when clay was twisted into tortuous coils and metal pressed into sugared cake forms, for us, the most difficult thing to learn is that appreciation of the material itself, which must precede the design. For designing must be in terms of the material. Any talk of 'designing for a craft' at the student stage is inadequate and misleading. Designing can only be *in* a craft, and expressed *through* that craft. All work on paper as a test of ability to work in another material —the form practically all crafts examinations take—is fantastic. The ability to conceive entirely in the mind and transfer to paper, an interpretation which must then be mentally transferred back into the material to convey the idea, is only attained at an exceedingly advanced stage. No wonder school designs on paper for metal or claywork are depressing and often ridiculous. The increased awareness, the growing sensitivity comes only through handling the material direct and can be judged only through its imprint on the material. It comes through a synthesis, sensory, emotional, and mental; through a continuous but ever-changing rhythmical relationship with the material, a sinking of oneself in it, in absorbing its nature, alternating with impressing form on it and the expression of the self through it. Yet these are not two processes but one. And it is a slow pensive process lasting necessarily over a number of years. The germ of understanding is, for long, frail and fugitive. But once it is rooted firm it binds and strengthens the whole personality.

Just because this relationship is so difficult to build up in the midst of the varied and pressing demands of education to-day, it is advisable that once the stage of serious craftsmanship is reached, its growth should not be disturbed by the claims of too many different materials at once.

Finally, the qualities which we value in painting, good composition, colour, line, interpretation (of a subject in painting, of function in craft), ought to be found equally in both. But in a civilization which is predominantly verbal and visual, I would stress that the strength of craft lies not only, in fact not chiefly, in its *visual* aspects. Each must speak from the enthusiasm of his practice but I have found that the experience peculiar to craftsmanship is the relationship (I am almost tempted to say mystic relationship) of man to material in making a thing which then stands as an entity in the world of men, offering them in its turn a new experience in its acceptance and use.

In this way a piece of craft work may be a work of art. I said that art influenced first the maker, and ultimately the beholder because it distilled experience. The quality of focusing or distilling is something which is common to all the arts, but the experience is less closely related to everyday life in an abstract art like music, and more closely in what might be called the utilitarian arts, or the crafts such as metal work, wool or pottery. In these all the features of past experience which have a bearing on the problem of 'what shape shall it be' are sifted out and seen in relation to one another. The musician is bounded by nothing except the sounds his instruments can produce and the length of time people can listen. The painter is bounded only by the shape of his canvas and the possibilities of his medium, paint. But craftsmen making for use have chiefly to consider something quite other, the function. Suppose the potter is going to make a beer mug. The shape his mug will finally turn out is determined (1) by the nature of clay, (2) by its purpose to hold beer, (3) by the fact that it is to be handled by a human being. He will consider not only the different clays, in weight, texture, colour and so on, but also the shapes which clay takes in its plastic state on the wheel, and the best shape and section to stand up to the strains and stresses of firing. The shapes clay takes naturally on the wheel vary from the hollow pillar to the wide bowl. But this is a vessel to contain liquid so it must not be so wide as to slop over or so tall and narrow as to be impossible to clean out by hand. Then, the lip must not curve inwards or it will be awkward for drinking, nor outwards so far that the beer will gush out, and it must taper a little in section. In addition, since it will be held horizontally to the mouth, there should be a hollow into which the dregs will fall each time it is lifted, and which will trap them at the last draught. All our associations with fullness, with pregnant richness, lead us towards the elongated sphere shape which liquid assumes at its moment of greatest pressure, the pear-shaped drop of water, the plum, the udder, the breast. So by employing this type of shape we are not only using the economy of material seen in nature but enriching the subject with deep-seated human associations. But this mug is intended to be held in the hand, and by those impatient with the finer reactions required to balance an afternoon teacup, so it must be prepared to take the whole fist and give a comfortable grip to it. In this position of the hand the smaller fingers will lie below so it is quite practical to bring the handle inwards there to fasten on. It is comfortable, though not altogether necessary, to have a rest for the thumb on the upper curve. The form of the handle will depend on the strong simple curves of pulled clay which take the greatest strain in firing and lifting, and on the methods of smoothing the handle ends into the body of the mug to make them grip. Now we are left within the limits of this main structure a certain range of possibilities, perhaps all equally functional, from which the craftsman will choose that which he considers most pleasing to eye and hand. But the joy in his material and the pride in making may lead him to add something which is not purely functional, a bit of decoration in clay, or scratched with the handle of his tool, or painted on the glaze. He may want to balance the handle with something on the opposite side, or, more likely, to give the drinker a motif on the side facing him to look at in his pensive moments. Perhaps he will embellish it with the name of the pub, or some visual allusion to the contents of the beer, or a vision of the happy life which is near in such moments. Any of these may be an enrichment so long as they do not add a burden to the potboys by introducing knobs which are easily knocked off or hollows where the dirt can lurk.

This then is the way the craftsman sets about one small job—but it is in essence the way any craftsman sets about any job, drawing on his knowledge of his materials, the process of making and his knowledge of human beings, their physique and their habits and their associations. And occasionally this serious and responsible attitude is peppered with a little frivolity and lighthearted fun, but that has its value only against a background of serious work.

CHAPTER SEVEN

WOOD

I HAVE said that many of us have come to believe that, after the earlier exploration with many materials has indicated which will be satisfying, it is more rewarding later to explore fully the possibilities of one. But this does not mean being confined to such a narrow range as might be imagined. I am concerned to show that there is a certain range of work, with the emphasis either on technique or on creativeness, on the impersonal or the expressive approach, which is possible in all the materials we shall consider. It is so even with that which in the past has been most limiting, most confined by a strict technique—wood. Within one school, within one craft, these are some of the possibilities which will attract differing personalities, and provide a considerable range during the school life of any student who becomes so attached to this material that he wants only to go on exploring its varying forms.

Leading on from the whittling of sticks and the making of catapults and bows—all of which gives some practice in judging the strength, weight and pliability of various woods—cutting and shaping for a definite purpose can be attempted. The English countryman used to make most beautiful corn scoops, grain ladles and household spoons, which in weight, balance and texture are a delight to handle, and perfect for their job. Some of the same feeling for shape related to the hand is to be seen in those wooden spoons and paper-knives made by twelve- to thirteen-year-old boys and girls in Plate VII. See how beautifully the graining of the wood has been revealed in the bowl of the spoons and the obvious pleasure in this natural form of decoration. These were made with no other equipment than gouges and sandpaper and wax to finish the surface.

Surely it is beneficial to begin formal lessons in such a craft by shaping something for the human hand, so that the feel of it can be gauged as one works, rather than to begin by making separate parts which require to be put together before the adequacy of the whole for its job can be seen? Such an immediate test relieves the pupil too of the necessity of constantly asking 'Is this right?' and leaves much of the teaching to the craft itself, to the absolutes of material and purpose. Then, too, such training keeps in the forefront of his mind the necessity of relating all human tools and furniture to the shape and scale of the human body. Much senior

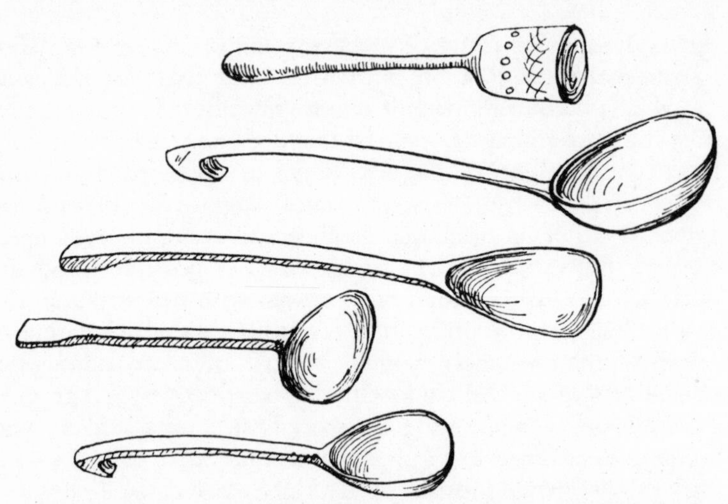

FIG. 4.—Shapes of traditional wooden spoons, and potato masher, showing how the purpose—to scrape a flat-bottomed pan, to ladle, to scoop—determines the satisfying finished form. These are designed for use by the human hand and fit it comfortably.

woodwork and many modern furniture designers have lost sight of this permanent factor in a search for novelty.

Such work is best introduced through the gouging of small bowls, ash-trays and so on, from flattish blocks of wood, perhaps an inch deep (Plate IX). The main shape of the bowl part, circular or oval, is roughly pencilled on the flat, and the gouging begins straight away, cutting always radially towards the centre. The conception of the bowl grows as it is cut, and through the constant handling, the meeting of the grain this way and that, the child is learning directly, intimately the nature of his material, and the shape evolves in this learning. The making of a spoon introduces two essential elements in a simple form, the hollowing of the bowl, and the shaping of the long straight piece for the handle. Here the balance and a clear conception of the purpose are constantly kept to the fore by the fact that the spoon is actually handled all the time in the making. The cutting of fruit and nut bowls of deeper shape, round, oval or boat-shaped, develops a feeling for hollow forms and the balance of inside and outside shape. The tool marks themselves and the use of surfaces to show up the grain of the wood are the most appropriate 'decoration' and illustrate how the most natural form of decoration is not added but arises from the working of the material itself.

Or the rounded form may be developed in the sphere of lathe turning. This presents its own problems, the balance of inner and outer shells, using the graining to full advantage, the problem of the edge, which must be thick enough not to dry and split and thin enough to be definitive. Some will prefer the wider varieties of the irregular form gouged in the hand; some the clean harder lines of the machine-turned bowl or vessel. The shaping of the handle and its relation to the bowl of the spoon leads on—perhaps after practice in planing on cheese and bread boards—to simple furniture. Whereas the conception of the spoon grows and becomes clear as it is being shaped, even simple furniture does demand a preconception of the final form and an analysis into component parts. If we are concerned with craft as the attainment of skill or technique, or in order to teach appreciation of sound workmanship, it will not matter whether this analysis is done by the master and handed out as measured drawings or taken from a book on the subject. But if we are concerned with an individual undertaking a responsible piece of work, the conception of the finished work must be the student's own and the steps towards it must be worked out by him. That this can be done from a comparatively early age has been shown in those schools where a free responsible approach has been used.

So boys can be encouraged to work not from lists of predetermined measurements or from measured drawings by the master or in some book on woodwork made easy, but from their knowledge of the requirements of that thing they have chosen to make. If they are going to make even a teapot-stand or a breadboard each child can settle his individual size and shape. When he comes to make a bookrack or shelf its size should surely be decided by

IX*a*.—Tools for wood gouging, and the first cuts made in a block of African walnut.

IX*b*.—Gouged bowls and a spoon made by gouging with only these tools. These are the first attempts of adult students.

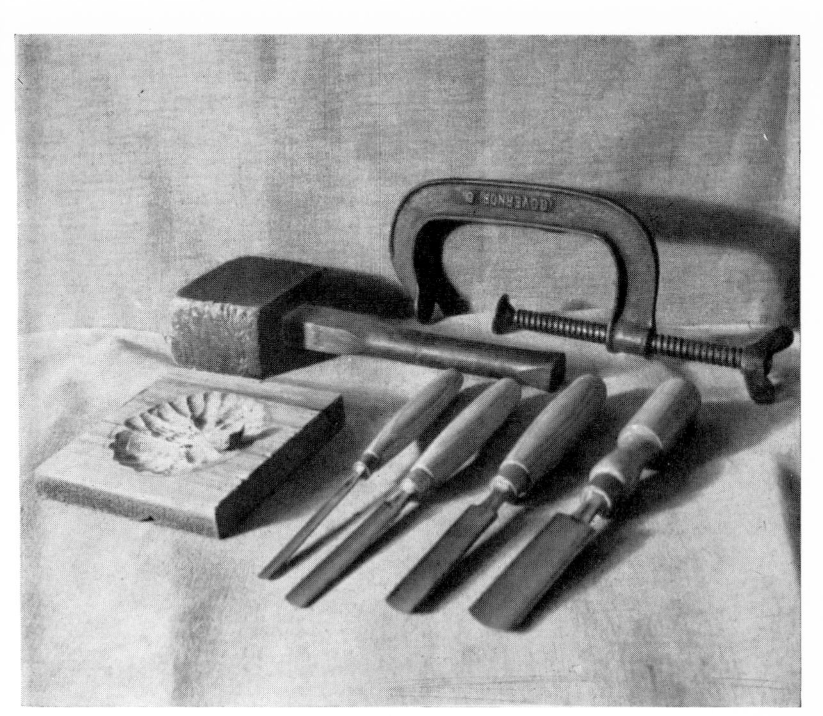

IX*a*

IX*b*

X

X.—HEAD OF DEER

'Wood by itself can provide the material for a range of crafts from the predominantly utilitarian to the purely æsthetic.'

This carving shows how the conception is realized within the shape of the block, the whole neck, head and ears growing upward as a tree grows. The solid pillar of the neck gains in interest and intricacy as it rises till the antlers spring like branches swelling with nascent buds.

Boy 17.

Teacher: Donald Potter,
Bryanston.

This is a boys' boarding school with wooded grounds which provide much of their raw material. The teacher is a metal worker and carver trained under Gill, and a potter by adoption.

the width and height of books it is to hold, rather than arbitrarily by a class recipe. So that when a boy progresses to making a stool for his little sister, he decides the height, and he alone, by deciding the height from the ground comfortable for her legs and sawing off his second support to match his first. This more imaginative designing in the hand comes *before* designing on paper is possible, and leads to a more personal and thoughtful approach. A boy who has worked, however efficiently, through a series of exercises is not necessarily at the end able to create anything of his own, but one who has had to think at every stage how to make each part more fit for its ultimate use is both more adaptable and more critical. All the joints can be learned, just as the stitches in needlework can, by skilfully encouraged individual work, as and when the need for them arises, without the drudgery of making useless specimens, which waste wood and labour.

Another extension of the play with saplings for bows and arrows, and the building of those withy houses which give children such endless pleasure, is the making of baskets. This may also develop out of coiled or plaited raffia work, which is usually introduced at too early an age, being very repetitive work and offering no scope for play of imagination. Basket-weaving is a traditional craft providing many links with daily living in the making of shopping, pet, garden, log baskets, and may be well taught by a local craftsman. But it is very hard on the fingers, rather limited and hardly offers great scope for creative work.

Since the beginnings of art and craft are in play, the things children choose to make in play can suggest several other lines to follow. Give a class of ten- to eleven-year-olds pieces of wood and penknives and leave the subject to them, and probably three-quarters of the products will be boats. Some schools which have a river, a lake or canal near enough to make the scheme a feasible one have developed their woodwork lessons on this inspiration. Progress might be from the rough flat-bottomed toy ship—possibly alongside all sorts of other wooden toys at the pre-craft stage—by way of the working model yacht, which teaches a great deal about draught and balance, to the making of a real dinghy and so finally to a sailing-boat.[1] Conrad said that of all the works of mens' hands they have put more of themselves into boats than

[1] Weybridge School, in the Isle of Wight, has a tradition of boat-building.

into anything else. The making of a boat of one's own or among a group arouses a passionate intensity of enthusiasm even among the boys most lethargic to all other school subjects. And the connection between good workmanship and subsequent happiness is such an obvious and immediate one that it is borne in on those who cannot grasp this relationship in other forms. If the boat is well made, we can go sailing in it. If not, it is no use at all, we shall be left behind. The need for independence in adolescence is a real need which our lengthy education tends to frustrate by not providing opportunities which meet the interests and excitements of that age. Going off for a day or a weekend in a boat one has helped to make oneself, being entirely responsible for one's own safety, one's comfort, one's progress and return, is an experience which is unrivalled for developing self-reliance.

Some progressive schools have shown that expeditions and even quite considerable voyages can be undertaken by schoolboys trained to responsibility over a period.[1]

But if boat-building is a craft which can admittedly only be practised by a limited number of schools—though perhaps many more than have tried it?—there are other ways of using wood which are open to all schools and which require comparatively little equipment.

We can go back and pick up the thread in the suggestion that children should be encouraged to find odd and curiously shaped pieces of wood and work on them. A boy or girl to whom this appeals will begin to gather quite a collection and will be seen to go over them repeatedly, stripping off the bark, and stroking the branch, turning it this way and that—just as many sculptors do—waiting to see what it suggests. Many of those pieces will, of course, prove too green or too rotten to do much with, but all the time the youngster is learning about woods, which are hard, which are soft, which smell pleasantly, which crack easily. By the provision of blocks of various kinds and sizes picked up from a working carpenter this attention to the wood as such can be carried on to the early stages of carving proper. It is best to emphasize the three-dimensional form by cutting straight away in the hand. Others will want to draw the shape on the sides of the block as a guide before cutting. But all the time the shape and marking of the wood itself should be the decisive factor in the design. The

[1] e.g. Gordonstoun, near Elgin.

child who comes to this straight after cutting a spoon like the smallest in Plate VII may well see that a flat piece straight in the grain suggests the back of a tortoise. The paper-knife in the same group might lead on to seeing an elongated curved human body in a long grainwise block.

So simple gouging leads naturally to wood carving where the centre of interest is in conveying an idea rather than serving a function. The head of a deer, Plate X, has been chosen to illustrate wood carving in preference to other more mature pieces from the same school because it shows so admirably how the conception is realized within the shape of the block, the whole neck, head and ears growing upward as a tree grows. The solid pillar of the neck gains in interest and intricacy as it rises till the antlers spring like branches swelling with nascent buds.

So wood alone can provide the material for a range from the predominantly utilitarian approach to the purely æsthetic. In a studio where such is the practice any one mode of thinking and constructing in wood is freed from a narrow viewpoint and illuminated by the work of others with different angles of approach. Here is an education which touches life both material and social at many of its facets.

These pages of suggestions for minimum equipment which are added at the end of most chapters are not in the least intended to be a ready-made requisition list. A teacher will only know precisely what tools he needs for the particular types of work he hopes to do, by working with the tools himself. But it is hoped that they will serve for those thinking of opening up some new branch of craft, as an indication of the amount of equipment and room which will be needed. The firms mentioned are those from whom I have obtained satisfactory materials and are certainly not exhaustive. Whereas with younger children, it was suggested that it usually worked better to introduce a whole class to a new material, where tools are expensive and to a great extent particular to the scope of work undertaken, it seems better to begin a new branch of craft in a small way, getting a few tools and perhaps trying different firms. Using these with small groups within larger classes, or with voluntary after-school groups, the teacher is able to decide whether the work he has planned is suitable for his students, and which tools are most satisfactory before ordering on a larger scale.

Minimum equipment for some of the types of woodworking suggested in this chapter.

For the gouged bowls:

Gouges of $\frac{3}{4}$, $\frac{1}{2}$, $\frac{1}{4}$ inch sizes, and one or two bent gouges. One set of these between about four children.

G-clamps—one each. Sandpaper.

For spoons and larger bowls it is convenient to have a wooden vice. Spoons such as those in the photograph can be made with gouges only but chisels will speed up the early stages of the work.

Strong tables or woodwork benches are necessary.

For the turned ware a lathe is the essential, and this requires a good light, preferably right in front of a window, and is a fixed object which slightly limits the adaptability of the room.

For the structural woodwork, the more orthodox equipment of the school woodwork room, saws, planes, chisels, etc., is necessary.

For wood-carving again, after the whittling in the hand stage for fun is passed, a vice and an assortment of gouges are required.

Gouges are not easy to obtain. The firm of Tiranti, Charlotte St., London, W.1, supply wood-carvers' tools, but gouges are in short supply. The best source is a local carver or auction sale, as the pre-1940 steel is much better.

For polishing: Beeswax melted in turpentine.

For the bowls and spoons hard wood is necessary, but quite small pieces, off-cuts from furniture, can be used first. The wood is always better to be seasoned, but for carving really well seasoned wood must be used. Obviously, this is best seen as a long-term policy in a school, and each generation of children can be using the wood 'laid down' by a previous class, and in turn laying down a supply for the future.

CHAPTER EIGHT

MODELLING

No other substance is a substitute for clay. No other substance responds so intimately to the contact of the fingers, or can be shaped in so many ways both to stimulate and embody imaginative experience. But much has been said already about its value, so the first part of this chapter will be concerned with the practical difficulties in schools, and the second with methods of firing and glazing.

Clay is not expensive if obtained from a local source, and modelling and non-wheel pottery need little equipment. With young children, there is no need to keep the work for long, it is the *experience* that is the valuable thing. But with older ones, permanence and usefulness are important so the question of firing must be tackled. It is the 'messiness' of clay which is usually the stumbling-block to its introduction into schools. Of course, the same used to be said about powder colour, and only a conviction about its value for every school will encourage us to fight for its recognition. But why not begin by introducing modelling as a summer-term activity out of doors? A shed or a Nissen hut where there is freedom to be really messy is the ideal thing, but a great deal of satisfying clay work can be done in the ordinary classroom, with newspapers spread over desks. The children come to see that all scraps of clay can be kept above desks and rolled up inside the papers at the end. Tables are obviously more satisfactory, or four desks can be turned inward so that the modellers can discuss one another's work, or occasionally, perhaps, make their individual contributions to a group work. It is much better to let the children be messy in overalls and gym shoes (which can be wiped with a damp cloth before they leave) and to let all help in the clearing up, than to fuss over tidiness, which destroys the atmosphere for work.[1]

[1] We are trying the idea of having everyone slip coarse socks over his shoes while in the clay room, so that no clay is tramped round the building.

It is much better to order clay from a local source if such is available, because the children can go to see the clay pit and learn something of the influence of soil on the industries, the agriculture and the plants of the district. A few enterprising schools have located clay nearby and made excursions with a barrow or cart to fetch it. But the heavy work of obtaining the clay cannot often be left to the children and such surface clay usually needs sieving to get rid of the pebbles. A brick or tile works, or better still, a pottery, will supply clay ready sieved and pugged (that is, worked till it is fully plastic), and this needs only to be emptied into the bin and kept damp. Three cwt. will fill a small ash-bin, but it is better to keep a good supply in a heap outside in the yard from which the bin can be replenished. 'Weathering' in the frost and the sun will improve its plastic qualities. The Japanese families of potters used to preserve their maturing clay from one generation to another, as Englishmen laid down vintage wine for their grandsons.

The plasticity of clay varies from the dense and plastic ball clay of Dorset (so called simply because it was transported in football-sized lumps) in which the particles are packed so closely that gases cannot easily escape in firing, to the 'short' sandy clays found in hollows in most parts of the country. Clay is decomposed granite and is washed down and laid in the beds of rivers or under the loam and sand of low-lying fields. The very plastic type can be stretched, pushed in and out of shape, plaited or coiled, but it must be pressed thin and even and fired slowly under careful control, or it will warp or crack as the gases inside escape from the dense mass. A sandy clay will not stand so much handling nor hold together so well but it can be fired thick, with a less even section, and it will better stand up to inexpert firing. Between these extremes lie many variations. If the local clay is too sandy to model with, it can be mixed with a ball clay and the two wedged well together. If it is too plastic to fire well, the best thing to add is not sand (unless the composition of this sand is known) but grog, that is, clay which has been fired and ground down, which performs the same function of opening the pores and letting the gases out. The colours of raw (unfired) clay are due to mineral and vegetable deposits, and only firing will reveal its final colour, which in any case varies with the amount of oxygen present in the kiln.

If the new clay arrives in a hard solid lump, put it in the bin, cover with a wet sack and a waterproof, and sprinkle with water at intervals for a few days till it can be cut with a wire. But if it has been allowed to go 'white' hard, as potters say, so that scratching with the nail produces a white dust instead of a sliver of clay, there is nothing for it but to break it up with a hammer or an axe, and put the pieces to soak in water. If clay is ordered from far away it may go white hard on the journey, which is another reason for using local clay. When the clay has crumbled down to the bottom

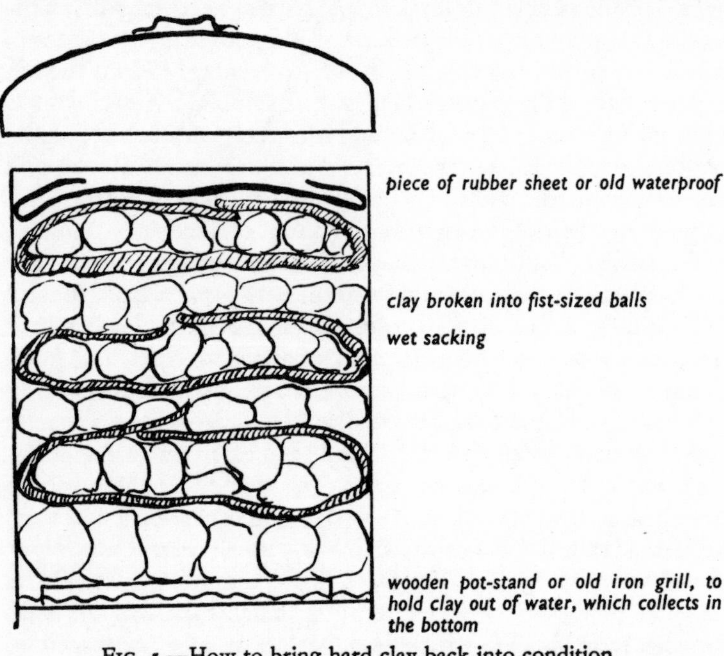

FIG. 5.—How to bring hard clay back into condition.

of the bath or tub, the surplus water on the top can be siphoned off with a rubber tube, and after the wet clay on the bottom has been allowed to dry a little, it must be brought back to plasticity by pugging. This can be done by squeezing it repeatedly through the hands, but is much more effectively done by taking off shoes and stockings and treading it up and down in the traditional way. I have found that many children get the greatest satisfaction from this, and I have had girls in their teens return day after day, when school was over, to ask if they could pug the clay. If the clay needs further drying, a slab of plaster of Paris is useful. The method of mixing this is described in the chapter on Carving. If an old table is available, it can be given a permanent plaster surface by building up 6-inch wooden walls round the top, and pouring plaster in. Stretched metal, wire-netting or scrim laid on between pailfuls of plaster will reinforce this, and when the plaster is level with the walls, a metal bar or yard-stick can be used to smooth the surface. A movable plaster slab can be made by pouring it into a shallow box, or by building walls of clay to hold the plaster till it sets. Such a movable slab has the advantage that when it is damp it can

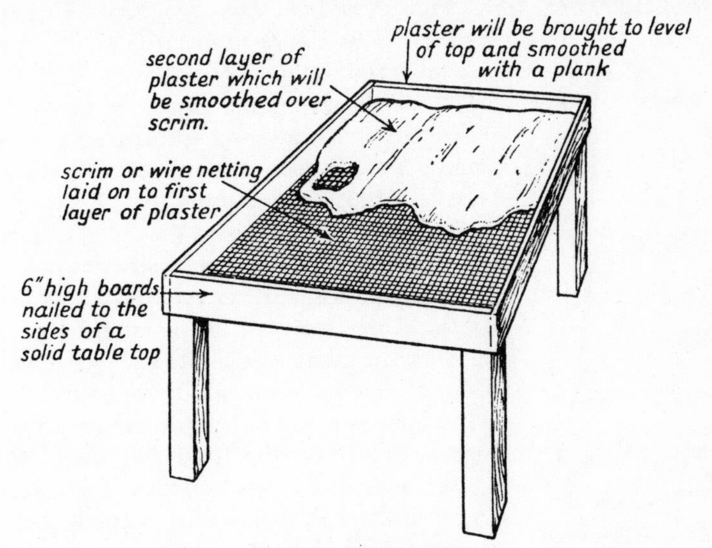

FIG. 6.—Plaster table.

be leaned against a radiator or stove and so serve again sooner for drying the clay.

It is helpful to know how to treat clay when it gets 'out of condition', but by carefully keeping the clay always damp in the bin, it is possible to work all through a year without any of these troubles. It is a mistake to buy clay in powdered form. It is ultimately more expensive. It means a great deal of hard work damping and squeezing it and it does not get into really plastic condition for a long time. It is claimed that it is easier to store in this form, but once the principles of keeping clay have been grasped, it needs only a little care to keep it in condition.

Since one of the advantages of clay is that it is three-dimensional, I think it better to begin clay work at any age by modelling not on modelling boards but *in the hand*, where the work is constantly turned about and more sensitively *felt*; much of the point of using clay with young children is lost if they are provided with tools. The direct pressure of the finger-tips, the pressing and squeezing out of projecting parts, and the discovery and use of the shapes clay assumes in working, the ball, the roll, the pancake shape, are all encouraged by this way of working. The illustrations of little clay models from eighth-century Cyprus, which could be paralleled from India four thousand years ago, from Central America, from Egypt or Early Greece, show how universal is this way of shaping clay.

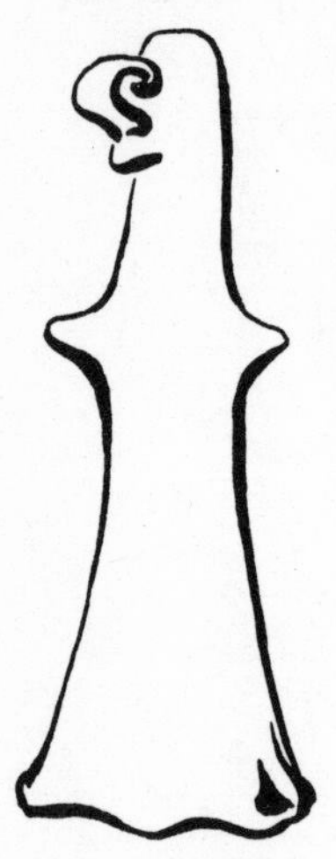

Fig. 7.—Human figure in clay of the eighth century from Cyprus.

The simple clay figure from Cyprus shows one of the most primitive three-dimensional conceptions of man, with pinched-out arm 'buds' like those of the four-year-old's model in Fig. 1 (ii), but it has the monumental quality found in some of the earliest work of our children. Some people will tend to work by using one lump of clay and pulling or pinching the parts out of it, and some will make separate parts and add them on.[1]

The interest in the little figure on horseback is concentrated on the head and arms—the legs are quite unimportant, which is also seen clearly in the right-hand king of the Nativity group on Plate XI*b*. The deer shows that no misguided striving after naturalism has spoiled the essentially *clay* forms of the legs and horns. But that the forms which clay assumes naturally can be used to *convey* an idea comes out clearly in the sheep's wool by a primary school child in the Pottery district. The little group from the same school (Plate XI*a*), of a woman taking her baby to a church topped by a great bird, is a delightful thing, full of feeling in its portrayal of the big arms encircling the small baby, and full of liveliness in its treatment. The decoration by strips of clay and incised lines is in the direct tradition of mediæval European pottery, and its gay colours and shiny surface give it the appearance of our own 'Staffordshire' cottage pottery of the eighteenth and

[1] Victor Lowenfeld's book, *The Nature of Creative Activity*, casts interesting light on this.

nineteenth centuries. This model is coloured and glazed, and fired in the brick kiln built by an enthusiastic master and children in the school playground.[1]

When children begin to feel the need of boards for their modelling, they can usually find flat pieces of wood about 5 to 8 inches square which are suitable. After they have themselves begun to use the handle of a brush or the blunt end of a pencil to decorate their model they can be encouraged to trim their own few tools from wood with a penknife. In the upper years of adolescence one or two modelling stands and proper tools may be useful for more

FIG. 8.—Two animal figures of the eighth century from Cyprus. They show the same characteristics as children's work in clay.

considered work, but even then the sensitive finger-tips are best to capture impressions and record feelings.

A large model can be made in 'open' clay and hollowed out a little, or it can be built hollow round an open core (though this requires considerable practice). With a very slow firing it is possible to fire models several inches thick. At the school level, I see little place for building on an armature and casting, especially as the cast will not be made in metal. Apart from the fact that it is very difficult to keep the mess within bounds in casting, it has serious educational disadvantages. If a one-piece mould is made, only one cast can be taken, and it would be better to model direct and keep that model rather than taking risks and spending time on

[1] At Summerbank Primary School, in the Potteries.

XI*a*.—A WOMAN TAKING HER BABY TO CHURCH

The complexity of this subject is resolved by the simple direct conception, and the importance of the figure and the bird emphasized by their size. The church is decorated with strips of clay and markings incised with the pencil stub.

Girl of 10.

Teacher: Mr. Rolley,
Summerleas Primary School,
The Potteries.

This Primary School is in a crowded industrial district, with no special facilities at all. Many models, such as this one, are turned out each week in an ordinary class-room and the work in hand stored in a wall cupboard.

With technical help from the local Art School, the class teacher aroused this great interest in modelling among the children. He and they together built a brick kiln on the playground, where these models were fired. This school was the first to break down the traditional objection of the pottery workers to their children doing clay work in school. It is another example of a school which has adopted one craft and, in the last primary years, concentrated on it.

XI*b*.—NATIVITY SCENE (GROUP WORK)

Here is an early effort at modelling by a group of girls of 11. Each figure, sincerely and directly modelled, contributed gravely to the atmosphere of the whole scene. Two radically different ways in which children model are apparent here. Some *pull* such projections as they need—nose, hair, etc.—from the main ball of clay, some *add* these details as balls or flat pieces laid on.

Girls of 11.

Hove Girls' County School.

XI*a*

XI*b*

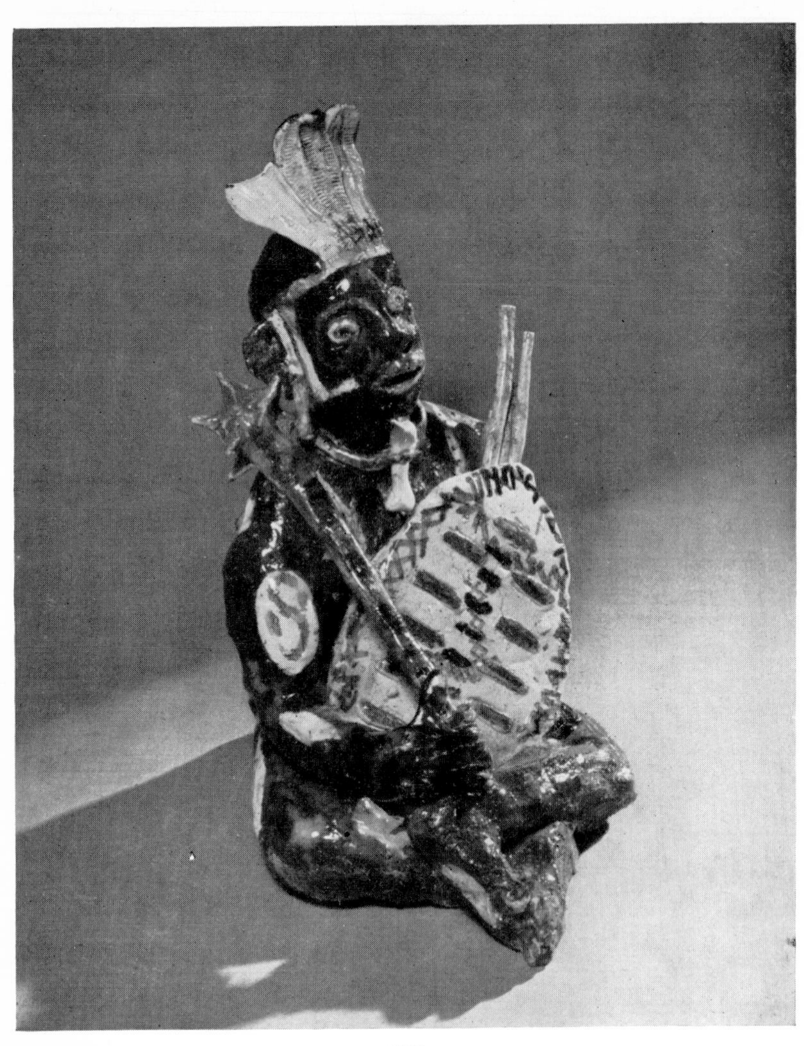

XII

XII.—AFRICAN CHIEF

This model shows a nice appreciation of the subject and is carried out with some of the methods of decoration for models and pots suggested in this chapter. The figure is in dark clay, but the headdress, shield, knuckle-bone tied round the throat and arm-bands are in buff clay. The decoration on the shield is laid-on strips of clay of different colours with some brush work added, and the texture of the feathers in the headdress is suggested by tool work with a piece of wood. It is not often that so many types of decoration can be used together, but they have been successfully combined in this rather exotic subject.

Boy of 16.

Christ's Hospital,
Horsham.

This school of very ancient foundation provides very good facilities for modelling and pottery.

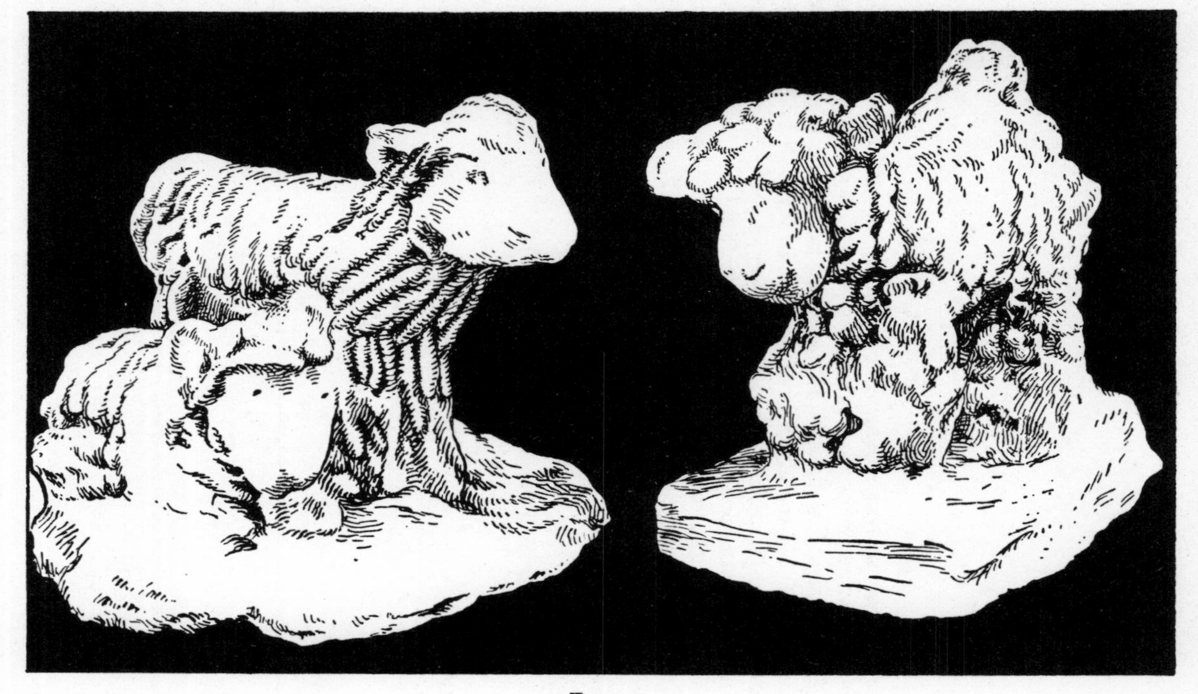

Fig. 9.

the casting. If a multi-piece mould is made, the child must spend a relatively long time on the technical (not creative) process and the only advantage seems to be that one can reproduce the identical model many times, surely a doubtful educational policy.

So modelling seems to be most fruitful when it is handled direct, and with older students this can be encouraged by modelling blindfold at first. Many children will be all ready with a subject to model, the butcher with his basket and apron, the family having a picnic, animals they have seen or imagined. When a subject is suggested to a whole group, it should be wide enough to allow every child to find some aspect or variation of it which pleases him. Occasionally the whole class, or groups within it, can make separate contributions which are finally brought together in a procession or a gathering on a central table. Such subjects are a fairground, with the roundabout, the helter-skelter and the caravans, the fat lady and the strong man; or nearer home, the town market with stalls heaped with fruit and ironmongery, the shoppers and the horses, perhaps, tethered behind. Such a group is the Nativity scene (Plate XI*b*), in which each figure, sincerely and directly modelled, contributes gravely to the atmosphere of the whole. This group shows too, how, as very young children will sometimes dress up their little clay figures in paper or cloth shawls and aprons, so they soon find that clay itself can be rolled, patted and wrapped into garments and accessories.

The modelling of younger children is usually sincerely felt and unaffected. But under the constant influence of debased commercial 'ornaments' and in the absence of a sound tradition of hand modelling (of a common or popular nature) the adolescent often loses his way. There is in this country a tradition of fine china figures, delicate and sophisticated, but too remote and refined to relate to schoolchildren's work. And there is a tradition of popular 'china' (in fact earthenware) figures and dogs, which have a simple unpretentious appeal and are often very good of their type, but they are press moulded, that is, shaped so as to be easily reproduced in numbers out of a back and front mould. But as well as the primitive modelling from all parts of the world, the smooth rhythmical figures from China and the curled and frilled Etruscan tomb figures, we have a small but fine tradition of essentially *clay* modelling in this country. The eighteenth-century salt glaze horsemen and pew groups, the occasional humorous potters' 'dolly',

FIG. 10.—An eighteenth-century horseman showing the traditional use of a second colour of clay used in decorative additions.

show the same use of impressed clay and contrast of clay colouring as we find in our pottery. Here, I believe, is the sanest and most rewarding approach to modelling in the Secondary School. It grows along with pottery—if that is practised—using the same materials in the same sorts of ways. The absence of a confusing range of underglaze colours to rival cheap commercial ware will direct energy away from that dead end, to the excitement of the clay itself and the full exploration of a limited field. The shapes the clay assumes, and the uses of rolls, pats, coils and incised marks, will soon be discovered by anyone using it imaginatively. The making of the coloured clays will be described in the next chapter.

With young children, the experience of making is the essential thing and there is no need to worry if the models cannot be preserved. I have found that if the children were allowed to keep their little figures and animals in the classroom or to lay them out in a landscaped pit in the garden for the first two or three weeks, they gradually accepted the fact that there was always more clay available and cheerfully broke them up to go back in the bin at the end of the period. But as they grow a little older they want to keep their work and then it is necessary to tackle the problem of firing. If clay is obtained from a local brick or tile works it is sometimes possible to start by having them fire one or two models for each child in odd corners of their kiln. A neighbouring school or a pottery 'centre' for the district, such as Hertfordshire provides for its schools, may solve the problem. But quite soon, I believe, the children must be *involved* in the firing, either by going to see it done (and the time it takes is a problem) or by doing it themselves. Of course, the best thing is to build a kiln, and for unglazed models in an open modelling clay, a very simple firing arrangement is feasible. Earthenware is fired at about 1000 degrees centigrade, stoneware at 1250 to 1350 degrees, but over 500 degrees will change most clays from their fragile unbaked state to a hard permanence. Before firing, clay should always be dried off very thoroughly (three weeks in a normal atmosphere will do it, or a shorter time in a dry or slightly warm cupboard).

The essentials of a kiln are, a place to feed the fuel in, a firebox with a good draught, and a chamber to hold the ware. One of the simplest types is a trench 3 to 4 feet long, 1 to 1½ feet deep, sloping down at the feeding end, and 1 foot wide. Old iron bars are inserted to keep the wood fuel up and allow a draught under, and to let the ash drop through without clogging the fire. The kiln chamber may be an inverted flowerpot where the hole lets the hot air out, or a brick-built box with a piece of old pipe for

Fig. 11.—A trench kiln with iron bars inset to form fire-box, and flower-pot chamber. The flower-pot is packed with ware, held in with an old grid or three iron bars, inverted and rested on the edges of the trench end. The sods removed before digging are heaped up all round to conserve heat.

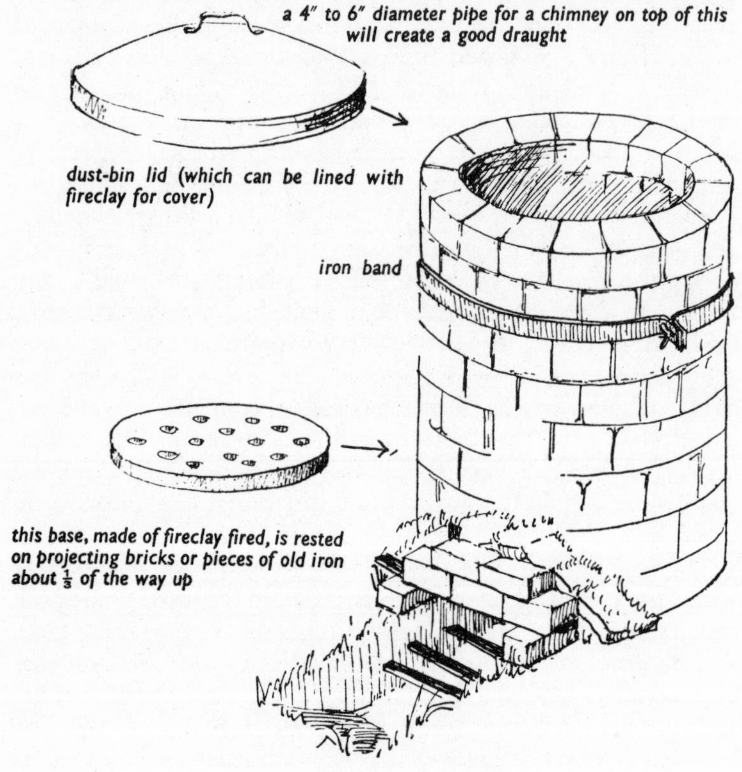

Fig. 12.—Circular brick kiln.

chimney, but unless the whole kiln is to be built afresh each time it must be possible to get inside it to pack the ware.

Circular bricks will make a good cylindrical chamber, which gives a more even firing, and by leaving four bricks projecting one-quarter or one-third of the way up, one can rest an iron or fireclay grid for a floor, and pack the ware over this from the top (which is closed over last). This can be done by stepping in a few rows of circular bricks to form a cone, or more simply by covering with a conical dustbin lid pierced in the centre and well insulated by a covering of fireclay and sods. In building a kiln, a mortar of fire-clay mixed with waterglass works well, and since brick structures expand and crack with the heat, these kilns hold together better if bound with one or more iron bands. To preserve the heat in the chamber and raise it to a good temperature it is necessary to insu-late all round, and after filling all cracks and interstices with fire-clay mortar, dry sods are a convenient way to do this. Increasing the height of the chimney increases the draught. The fire must be begun slowly with chips or brushwood or twigs and stoked regu-larily, working up to big logs and usually taking a whole day.[1] It is also possible to get up a good heat with an oil drip on coke. Since the cheapest method of making these primitive kilns is to use what materials are available, no exact instructions or descrip-tions of particular kilns have been given, but rather an outline of general principles. The firing chamber may also be built square or rectangular with bricks. The trench may be dug into a hillside. In those types described the flames pass up through the firing chamber, licking the pots (and often darkening their colour in the process); it is a tricky business to glaze with them. In a 'glost oven' the glazed ware is protected from the flames inside an inner wall, and the flames run up between the inner and the outer to meet at the chimney, so that a greater heat is required. This protection can be given in a primitive kiln by the use of a sagger (a fireclay oval box used in the potteries to protect glazed ware in the older type of oven) inside a brick wall, or the inner chamber may be built of thin fireclay slabs, but it is necessary to get up more heat. But several schools have built themselves a fair-sized workman-

[1] Kilns can, of course, be fired with coal, coke and oil, etc., but wood, if available, is best to experiment with. Master and boys of the George Salter School, West Bromwich, built themselves a gas kiln. We have built about thirty small primitive kilns for different fuels.

like brick kiln with proper chambers and chimney from the blue-prints obtainable from R. W. Baker,[1] who knows far more about kilns than anyone else in this country.

In a biscuit firing the ware can be packed as close as it will go, but glazed objects must all stand free, resting only on an unglazed base or on small stilts or fine sand spread on floor and shelves. A new kiln tends to absorb the glaze off its contents, but this can be avoided by giving the inside walls a coat of glaze before the first few firings.

For the school or centre which is buying a ready-made kiln, I advise gas as being cheaper in initial cost, less likely to go wrong, and much more adaptable in use. The essential point to watch in its installation is that a large enough gas pipe (1½ to 2 inches) is put in in the first place. There are several good makes listed at the end of this chapter. An electric kiln is clean, and in some ways more fool-proof, but the elements go quickly under the strain of high temperatures and cost a lot to replace. In addition one cannot get such a wide range of different kiln conditions producing all varieties of oxidized and reduced firings. In an oxidized firing, air is circulating freely through the kiln producing a 'clean', even, but less exciting range of glazes. In a reduced firing, through stopping out the air at strategic moments, or by burning resin chips or other fuel in the kiln, the oxygen is drawn from the colouring compounds of body and glazes, leaving varieties of pure metal and reduced oxides which produce many of the lovely effects of stoneware. But there is a great field of lower temperature effects to explore, more suited to schools.

The temperature of any of the kilns mentioned can be known by the use of cones, which are compounded to flux and bend over at a certain temperature. So, by putting two or three of these marked for different temperatures in a kiln, and leaving a spy-hole to watch them through, the firing can be stopped at the appropriate temperature. If the clay is fired too high it will lose shape and finally sink down in a pool, but this is not likely to happen with home-made kilns.

A glaze is really a glass, and the purpose of glazing is primarily to give a smooth clean surface to vessels for use, but it also gives

[1] Formerly Professor Baker of the Royal College of Art, now retired.

sensuous pleasure in itself. There are an infinite number of combinations of materials which make a glaze, and it would simply be confusing to try to condense the elements of this tremendous subject to a few pages. Those who want to understand more will find it in the pages of Leach and Binns.[1] All I propose to do here is to give the beginner the simplest method of glazing for schools and beg him to find a teacher and pursue the subject for himself.

Pottery is usually fired once (the biscuit firing), then glazed and fired again (the glost firing), but it is a great saving to glaze the 'green' pots and fire once. A few clays will stand this if glazed quickly and not moved for some hours. Glazes consist of a fluxing part, a stiffening part and sometimes an opacifying part. The best introduction is to start by mixing a flux e.g. lead sesquasilicate, with your clay body in differing proportions, fire, and study the results. One child can mix 20 parts silicate with 80 parts dry clay, by weight, another 40 silicate to 60 clay, and so on. We have found that 80 silicate to 20 clay made a glaze, which was much improved by 5 parts of whiting and 5 of china stone. In this way the children will discover by experiment which mixtures flux into a glaze, and what effect each ingredient has. The dry ingredients are put through a 120 mesh sieve with a potscrubber and plenty of water. When it settles the extra water can be siphoned off. One comes to know the right consistency of a glaze by the feel of it, but a useful measure is that one pint of glaze should weigh 32 ounces. Glazes should be stirred frequently with a wooden baton while in use, to keep them mixed. Some clays[2] have the very useful property of taking a glaze when they are bone dry before the first firing. But most clays need to be once fired before they will take a wet glaze. If the first firing is too low, the ware is 'soft' and absorbs so much glaze that it flakes off as it dries, or else crawls in the firing, leaving gaps. If the first firing is too high, the hard surface will not absorb enough glaze to cover it adequately.

These glazes are of the clear, slightly yellow type familiar on traditional English slipware and are the most suitable for clay

[1] Bernard Leach, *The Potter's Craft*, a fascinating book every potter must read, with philosophy and technique rubbing shoulders all the way. Binns, *The Potter's Materials*, a useful practical handbook.

[2] Hartley's of Castleford, Yorkshire, is one such.

decoration. But an opaque white glaze (which opens up possibilities of majolica decoration to older students) can easily be made from the basic recipe given by adding up to 10 per cent of oxide of tin, demanding a higher firing temperature. Here are some suggestions for producing from that basic glaze coloured opaque glazes. But it must be stressed that with children the *clay* stages of the craft are the most valuable and clay decoration itself holds endless possibilities, so it is misguided to rush on to complex glazes which they cannot understand. If the colouring oxides are used at all, it should be only the basic two or three, and those with great discretion.

To the opaque tin oxide glaze, may be added—

To make blue: 0·05–1·5 per cent cobalt oxide.
To make green: 0·5–8 per cent black copper oxide.
To make a purplish-brown: 2–10 per cent manganese oxide.
To make a reddish-brown: 2–8 per cent red iron oxide.

Another range of low-fired glazes is based on borax frit. One difficulty of using this is that its fluxing temperature lies within a narrow range and once it starts to melt it goes quickly and runs off. This quality can be used to positive effect in a method derived from Japanese Raku firing which is described in Leach's The Potter's Book, but I would suggest building up a glaze by experiment with different proportions of ingredients as with sesquasilicate. It is necessary to use a very open, groggy clay to withstand the extremes of temperature. I have found that nothing gives students the sensuous appreciation of glazes like the excitement of waiting for the exact moment to draw the luscious, dripping pots from the muffle with tongs, to catch the glaze in the very act of fluxing and fix it in cold water. It is a magical experience, a kind of alchemy in which art and science meet in the transformation of matter. No regulated electric kiln—however necessary for industry—can give the *educational* experience of being involved and being in control, of working *with* the fire in this way.

Nevertheless, before this stage is reached there is a great deal which can be done in pottery without glazes, playing on the quality of the clay itself by incising, slipping, burnishing plant-pots, nut and fruit dishes etc. Burying pots in a sawdust or peat kiln produces beautiful varieties of clay colours.

The fundamentally wrong approach, I am convinced, is to order ready-made-up glazes with fancy names and attributes from a commercial firm. The children will not know the composition of what they are using, they will not be able to reproduce it and make variations on it. There is for all of us a kind of magic about the effect of fire on substances, but if children are to feel that this is a field in which they can create, ready-made complex mixtures will not help them. They must use a few simple substances which they can understand and manipulate so far as possible.

MODELLING

Suggestions for minimum equipment and materials. (Obviously, quantities must vary with numbers, type and amount of work done. These are only rough suggestions for the novice.)

For modelling:

Plastic clay; a bin to keep it in (dustbin or pails with lids); an old sack and piece of waterproof.

No tools; no boards at first.

Later, odd pieces of wood will serve as boards, brush handles or whittled sticks as tools.

For glazing:

A wire sieve, 80 to 120 mesh; a pot-scrubber; several enamel or aluminium bowls or pails; a pair of kitchen scales.

Later, access to chemical balance.

Sesquasilicate or alternatives (perhaps three stones for the first order).

White oxide of tin (1 stone); black oxide of cobalt (1 ounce, this is very expensive); black oxide of copper (1 lb); oxide of manganese (1 lb); red oxide of iron (1 lb). All these come from Podmores, Stoke-on-Trent, who are helpful in suggesting glaze alternatives.

Kilns:

Gas: Gas, Light and Coke Co. (their Vyse Kiln is one of the best).

Oil: John Askam, Avenue Road Works, Aston, Birmingham 6.

Electric: Grafton Kiln, from the Applied Heat Co., Elecfurn Works, Watford By-pass, Watford, Herts; Catterson Smith, Exhibition Grounds, Wembley; Cromartie Ltd., Stoke-on-Trent.

Kiln furniture:

Kiln shelves may be made by a local fireclay works or from Acme Marls, Hanley, Staffs; props of different sizes to hold them up, from Wengers, Stoke-on-Trent, or Acme Marls; cones, for measuring temperature, from Wengers.

Ware glazed right down to the bottom will stick to the kiln floor unless propped up on three-legged stilts, or on a layer of fine sand, both from Wengers.

Since this book was written twelve years ago the author and many others have experimented widely in building home-made kilns. There is now a fund of experience on this subject which can best be shared in practical work on short courses.

CHAPTER NINE

POTTERY

Pottery is one of the oldest and most universal crafts practised by the human race. The methods of making have varied at times, but almost all of them still serve for some artist potter or rural craftsman as valid ways of making things which people need. The rural potteries of our country—which from the Middle Ages had kept alive an unbroken tradition of hand making, many preserving some typical shape of jug, or form of decoration, or way of fixing a handle—were sadly reduced in number during the war. But, historically, geographically, and culturally pottery has still links with a very wide field.

While no serious educationist who has practised it doubts the value of clay work, there is a misconception abroad that pottery is not a feasible craft for the majority of schools because of the great amount of expensive equipment it needs. This is quite untrue and arises, I believe, from selecting, out of the whole history and tradition of pottery, inappropriate methods to practise in schools. Out of the many forms which pottery has taken at different ages—the Japanese slab-built jars, the Central American thumb-pressed pots, superb Renaissance thrown and painted majolica, Neolithic coiled urns, Greek vases, Chinese stoneware, English slipware, cast and enamel-painted china—out of all these one method must be chosen to introduce pottery to the children, and from that one some other methods developed. I believe this choice cannot arbitrarily be made by the teacher from what she considers the highest achievement of pottery, stoneware perhaps to-day, as she would have probably favoured Greek vases two generations ago. Nor do I think it can be made on grounds of historic sequence. It would be interesting to follow the development of one form out of another from primitive times, if we knew it, but in fact the sequence appears to vary in different

XIII.—NON-WHEEL POTTERY

This group illustrates several of the types of non-wheel pottery described, and also ways of decoration in the clay stages of the work.

A tile stands on the left decorated with two colours of slip put on with a stiff brush and emphasizing the thick opaque nature of the slip. In front of it is a thumb-pot, and in this case the ridges formed between the rotating fingers and thumb are left as part of the final shape. To the left again is a finer pressed-out thumb-bowl joined again on opposite lips with a little slip and turned into an amusing bird by the addition of clay feathers. The others are mould-pressed dishes showing (*left*) how the edge or (*right front*) the base can be cut to give interest. They are all decorated with slip trailing, showing how this can be very formal (in the rectangular dish) or very free (the large plate) with a motif suggested by the first blobs of slip.

Students' and children's work. Teacher: Seonaid Robertson.

XIV.—BUILT POTS AND ONLY TOOLS USED

A small polished thumb-pot set beside three hand-built coiled pots of which the largest is 17 inches high. The only tools used were found in the yard—a smooth pebble and a piece of broken flower-pot to smooth outside and inside respectively, a stick the end of which is used in two different patterns (*right* and *left*) for decoration, and a shell used to work together the coils of the centre pot, giving the striated surface. The illustrations in this book are by children and adolescents, but since no other photograph was available at the time, these shown are the first attempts at coiled pots by adults.

Teacher: Helen Pincombe.

XIII

XIV

XV*a*.—SGRAFFITO POT

This pot, an early effort at throwing on a kick-wheel, is dipped in white slip and a straightforward child-like pattern scratched out with a finger and a piece of stick.

Girl of 15.

Teacher: Louis Jones,
Wennington School,
Yorks.

In this school the pottery is a converted stable, and the clay a local one prepared throughout by the children. Mixed groups, boys and girls of about 15, work two hours per week, and come to the pottery when they can out of class time.

XV*b*.—BROWN POT WITH SPIRAL INCISIONS

Here is a fine example of wheel-throwing about 13 inches high, from a school where the boys have opportunity to practise sufficiently to achieve such skill. But it is more remarkable for the maturity of its well-conceived neck and the supremely appropriate spiral incisions, bold in scale, which give emphasis to the shape without detracting from it. This potter has arrived at the point where he can design *in* his material.

Boy of 16.

Teacher: Donald Potter,
Bryanston School,
Blandford.

parts of the world. No, the selection of what type of pottery to practise in schools must rest, as does the selection of any other craft, on its educational value. So, following the general principle of this book, we can ask which forms of pottery can, within the practical limits of the class-room, develop the senses, the emotions and the imagination, and can give the adolescent a sense of real achievement?

The development of touch and muscle senses obviously comes through direct contact with the clay rather than in the manipulation of tools. The imagination is more stimulated, I think, by modelling rather than the more pedestrian work involved in pottery, and for that reason should be kept up alongside it. But the decorative use of the forms which wet slip, for instance, assumes, and the practical use of the objects that lie around as elementary tools, foster imagination. The satisfaction of achieving something complete at an *early* stage is a proper encouragement, and is a reason for not starting with wheel work. And fortunately enough, I believe the best types of pottery for schools all lie within our own English tradition, so that we can more easily see and handle examples of them—I mean thumb-pots, coiled pots, tiles, and mould-pressed dishes. And all those—which will start a school a long way on the road to understanding pottery—can be made (apart from arrangements for firing, which were discussed in the previous chapter) with equipment costing from nothing to a few shillings for a whole school.

Since modelling is the form of clay work most likely to be familiar to the children of a good Primary School, thumb-pots, which are most similar in the use of the fingers, form the easiest transition to class teaching in pottery. In addition, the children will have been making little cups and jars for their own games and will be aware of how these break at the thin edge and crack where the section is uneven, so they will be ready, probably about ten or eleven, to learn how to overcome these defects. If I had a small group, I would show them all together how to make thumb-pots, probably for fifteen minutes, at the beginning of several consecutive modelling lessons. But since most of us work with groups of between thirty and forty, I think it better, since the children need individual help in *feeling* the thickness and in adopting an easy rhythm, to take one quarter of the class to begin with while the others are modelling or making tiles.

Clay which is to be used for pottery needs to have all the air bubbles driven out of it, and to be in good plastic condition, and this is done by kneading or wedging. But to watch someone do this for two minutes explains far more than any amount of description. A reminder to look at the clay the night before and put it on a plaster slab if it is too wet, or between damp sacks if it is too dry, will save much energy and irritation in the morning.

To make a thumb-pot, a spherical ball (an orange suggests a possible size for the first one) is cupped in the left hand, and with

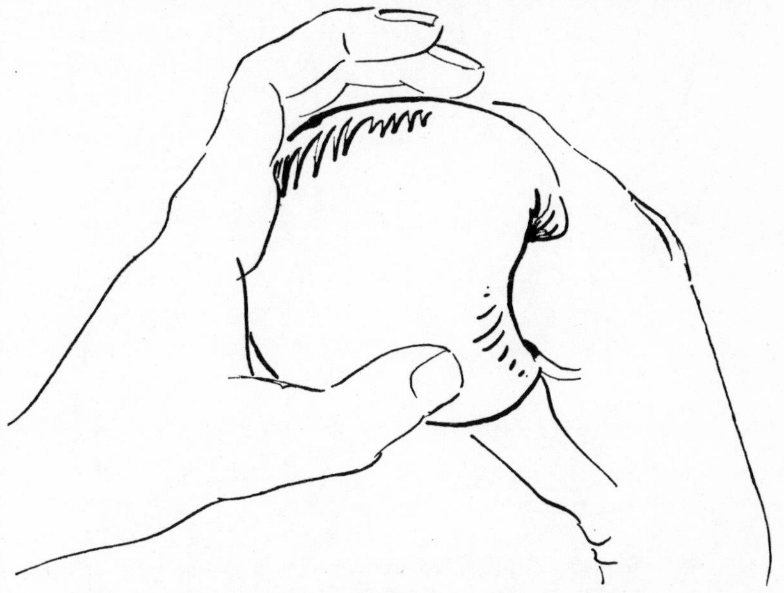

FIG. 13.—The position of the hands in making a thumb-pot.

the right thumb resting on a slightly flattened top, it is rotated with the right hand. The thumb is gradually sunk into the centre to about three-eighths of an inch from the base. Still with a rotary movement (the rhythm is the important thing in getting evenness) the walls are pressed either out in a slope for a little bowl, or upwards, keeping the neck small, for a honey-pot shape. The pressure is made between the ball of the thumb and that of the three fingers outside, and it is carried up in a spiral, keeping the section even. The upper edge must be kept thick till the end or it will crack, and if it begins to get dry, the pot can be inverted

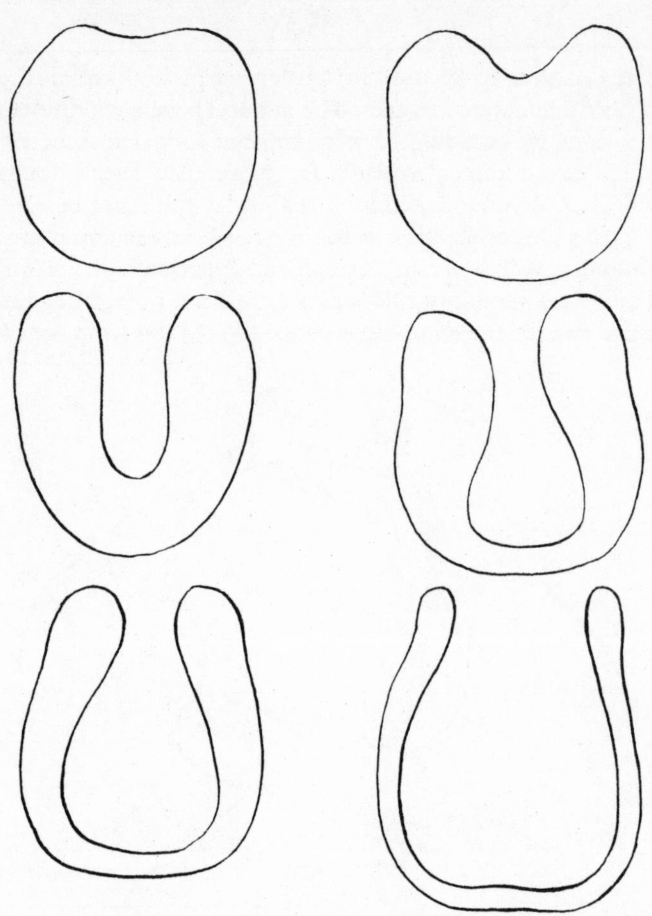

Fig. 14.—Progressive stages in one method of making a thumb-pot, showing the section.

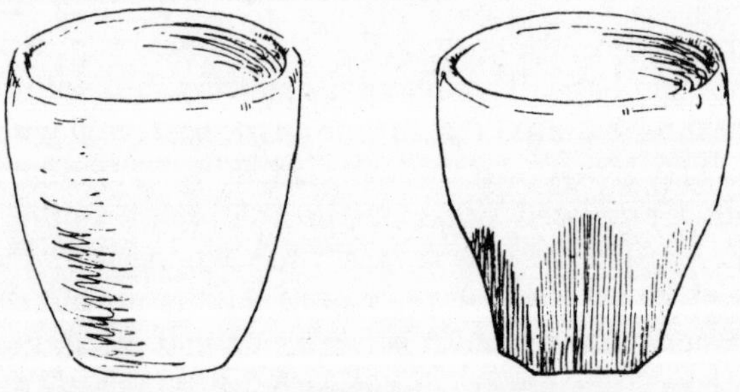

Fig. 15.—A thumb-pot with its thick base trimmed away in planes, contrasting with the round top.

on a damp cloth for ten minutes, and then worked again. By this method, little bowls, egg-cups, ash-trays, butter and jam dishes, and finally quite fair-sized pots can be made. They may be knife-trimmed at the base if that is thick, offering a contrast of round and flat sides, or they may be lined with another colour of slip, or incised as will be described.

Coiled pots are often ragged lopsided efforts, quite unsuitable for any useful purpose. While the coils or the thumb marks which are an essential of their making *may* be part of the inherent decoration, many who made them for practical use in their homes(including the Neolithic potters of this country and the Pueblo Indians of Central America) thought fit to smooth the surface as much as they were able and even to polish it to shining cleanness with pebbles.[1] These pots should be built on a piece of brown paper or on a small board for easy lifting, or they will stick to the desk or table till they begin to dry. On to this surface a round pancake of clay flattened between the hands is patted and the edge of it is turned up all round. A number of coils should be prepared so that the rhythmical work once started can go on without a break. The coils are made by rolling balls of clay into thick sausages (two or three times the diameter of the finger) with a long rolling movement, using the whole length of the hand. Begin rolling with both hands, thumbs together in the middle of the sausage, and move them towards the ends. The first coil is placed round the base just inside the turned-up edge and fastened well down to the base with thumb strokes inside. It is joined to itself by nipping each end to an oblique point and fitting them together. The next coil is laid about half-way down inside that one, and pressed to it by the pads of all fingers outside, and the thumbs inside, moving evenly round the pot. The join is made each row in a different place for strength. The thickness of the overlapping coils gives room for enough pressure to bind them together without thinning the walls too much. With good thick walls left to support it, a large pot can be made even at the first attempt, which will give a satisfaction and sense of achievement denied to the first efforts with thumb-pots or on the wheel. The walls can be built fairly straight up, as they will always tend to swing outwards, and from

[1] I must here acknowledge a debt to Miss Helen Pincombe of Guildford School of Art, who showed me how much more effective was the Pueblo method of laying the coils inside rather than on top of one another.

time to time the inside can be smoothed off with a curved pebble or the right finger-tips while the whole left hand is held outside to give support. The walls inside should be smoothed in this way before the shoulder is brought in, and the angle should not be too

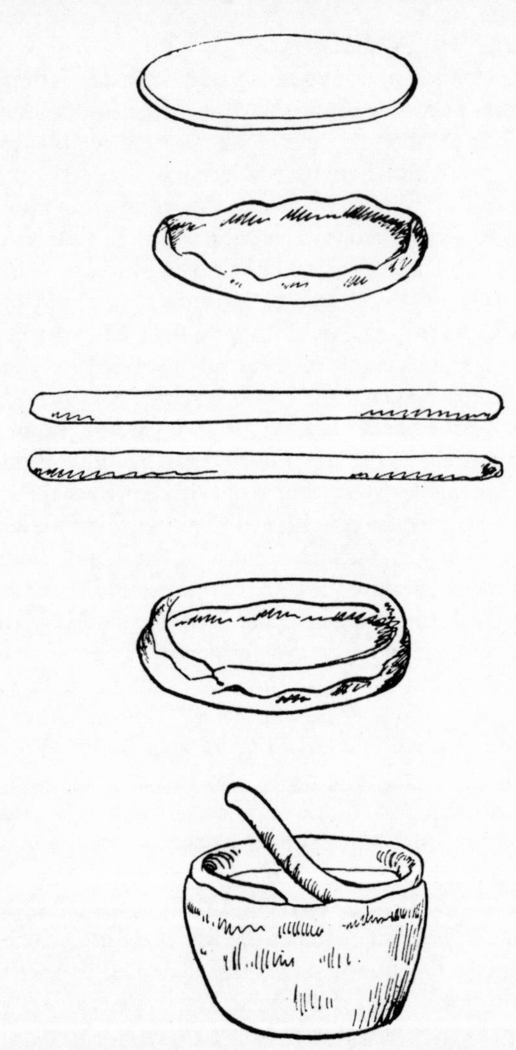

FIG. 16.—Stages in making a coiled pot by the Pueblo method, showing flat pancake, edge turned up for the base, sausages, first coil laid inside the turned-up edge of the base, and a later stage with a coil laid inside the smoothed wall already built.

suddenly flattened or the damp clay will not support the weight. If it tends to sag, a few hours' drying in the air will harden it up. The neck must be studied in relation to the base and the curve of the walls, and finished with some definition. These fine monumental pots may be decorated with incisions, with bold slip brushwork, or left with the marks of the smoothing tool or polished (see Plate IV). They need a slow even firing.

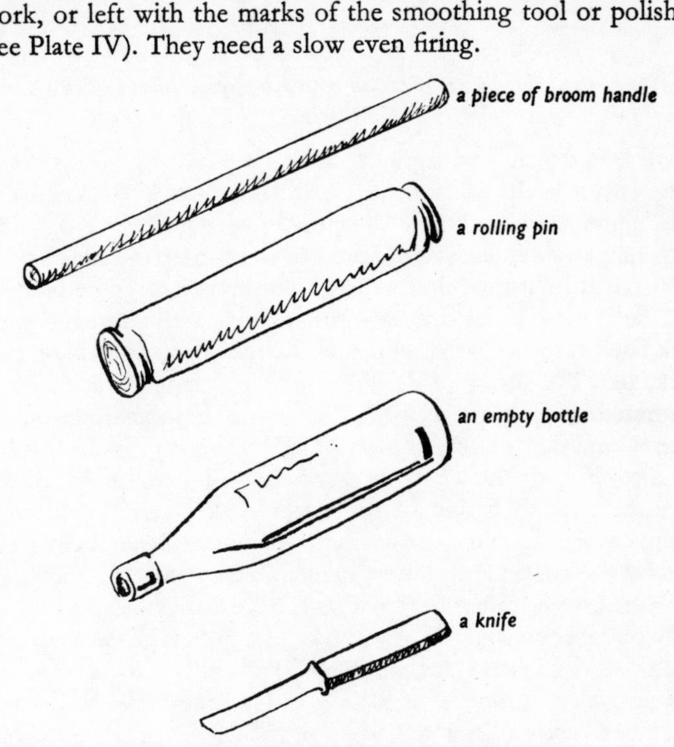

FIG. 17.—Equipment for tiles.

Tiles and press-moulded dishes are made from wedged balls of clay, patted flat and rolled out, on a piece of brown paper or cloth for ease of handling. An empty bottle serves well as a rolling-pin, but a broom handle cut into lengths is better because a 12- or 18-inch length can be handled with ease. If two flat sticks, $\frac{1}{4}$ to $\frac{3}{8}$ of an inch thick, are placed parallel on each side of the pancake and the roller rested on them, it gives an equal thickness all over and it also compresses the clay well. From this flat piece, tiles square, six-sided, rectangular or round can be cut by the children, possibly from their own paper patterns. Tiles, being thick and flat, tend

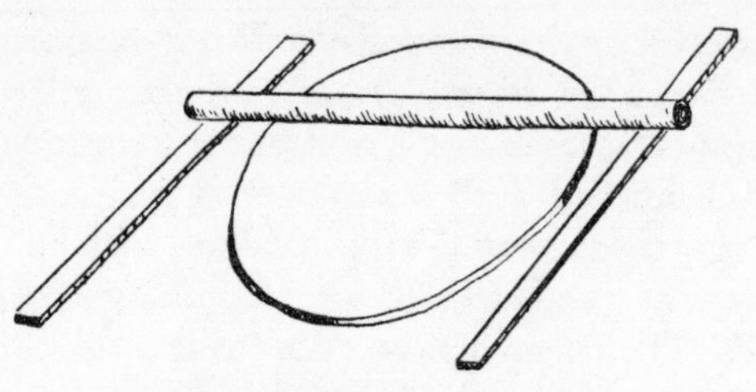

FIG. 18.—Ball of clay being rolled flat with broomstick roller resting on two sticks to keep thickness even.

to crack in drying and firing, so it is often helpful to mix some grog with a batch of clay for tiles, or for each child to sprinkle it in as he prepares his lump. Since the upper surface will dry first in the air, it will contract and pull up the corners a little. So the tiles should be turned upside-down during drying to counteract this. Such tiles can be decorated by incising with a brush-end or stick, or given a coat of slip and incised through that or slip decorated. They are another of those simple things which a child can make for his home at the first attempt. He should be encouraged to find out the size of his mother's teapot to make a teapot-stand to fit it, or the length of a window-sill which holds plants to make a set to fit into it for easy cleaning. All clay shrinks slightly as it dries and again as it is fired, but the behaviour of any particular clay can only be learned by experience, so that it is advisable to find the most suitable clay available and stick to it.

By the provision of tile boxes, tiles of a given size can be made quickly and efficiently. A plaster of Paris tile box is made by putting a clay prototype of the tile in the centre of a board and building a clay wall round it to a height of ¾ to 1 inch and about

FIG. 19.—Making a plaster tile box. The cut clay prototype stands in the centre. About 1 or 1½ inches away is a wall of clay and the plaster is poured in and over the tile and allowed to set. The hollow formed by this first tile can be used repeatedly.

1 inch away all round. Into this mould plaster of Paris is poured, allowed to set. As the first tile shrinks and drops out it leaves a hollow mould into which any number more can be pressed. This is done by pushing small sausages of clay into the corners and on to the base and building up more on them, being careful not to trap air between, till the heaped-up top can be scraped even with

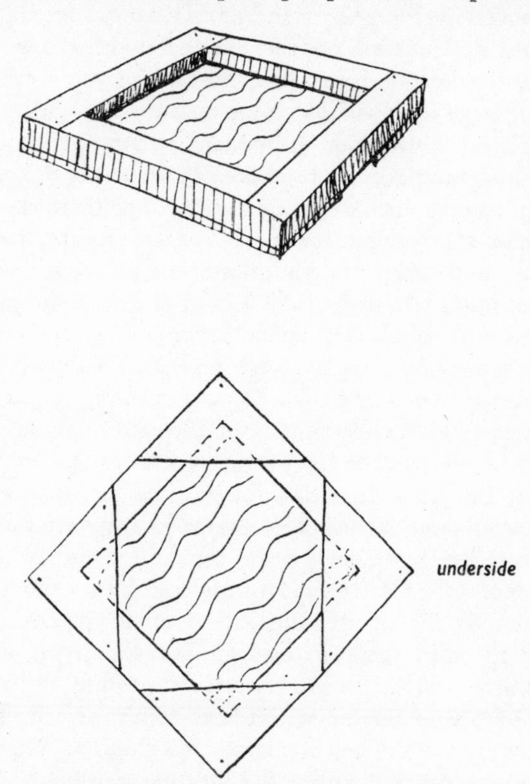

FIG. 20.—Making a wooden tile box. The detachable base (of three-ply wood or, better, asbestos, with the rough side up) rests on corner pieces and can be pushed upwards to take out the tile.

a wet ruler or a piece of metal. A similar wooden tile box with a detachable base is easily made and if a layer of paper is put in before the clay, the tile can be pushed up and removed at once and the box used again immediately.

Plaster of Paris is used for several kinds of equipment in pottery because of its property of absorbing the moisture from clay.

A plaster of Paris slab was advocated for drying clay, and bats on which to build coiled pots or which fit on to a wheel head are useful. Plaster of Paris poured into flat-rimmed sandwich tins makes good circular bats as they spin round easily and the edges do not chip off. Plaster varies from the roughest plasterer's type to fine dental plaster which carves best but is more expensive. It can be spoiled in storage by standing in a damp atmosphere or on a cold floor so that it will not set. I have found that a wooden box (a tea chest) raised on four bricks near a radiator serves well to store it. A large bowl is filled three-quarters full with cold water and the plaster is sprinkled in by hand, stirring gently to keep it from forming lumps on the bottom. The feeling of the plaster just beginning to set comes with experience. Then there is no time to be lost. It must be poured at once. The basin and spoon should be soaked in cold water, and the plaster should never be washed down the drain, where it may set hard and stop the pipes. Any equipment made of plaster benefits from storing in a warm place, and a shelf above the radiator can be kept for this. It is almost impossible not to make a mess with plaster, and I suggest choosing a fine day to make such equipment in the yard or an outside shed. If it must be done in the clay room (where tiny pieces of plaster in the clay can be an irritation for months) I devote a week or two to plaster alone at the end of a term (perhaps after thumb and coiled pots, before starting press moulding) and make all the equipment and the plaster slabs for carving, for the months ahead.

The moulds for pressed dishes are made professionally by throwing the dish shape in clay *upside-down* on the wheel and making the reverse mould from it, or by 'turning' the mould out of a bat of plaster on the wheel head before it sets. But these techniques are too difficult for almost all children. We make our moulds much more simply by collecting cardboard boxes or salvaging the two pieces of broken pie or Pyrex dishes, or misfired pots. By exchanging from the collection each child gets a shape something like the shape he envisages, and by pouring in plaster and taking the mould out (in from five minutes to half an hour) while it is set but still soft, he cuts it to the shape he wants. Rubbing the inside of the dish with thin slip or soft soap prevents the plaster from sticking. Several of the dishes moulded in Plate XIII came from moulds of this type. By exchanging moulds, by re-trimming, and by cutting afresh the large pieces from moulds which break in use, we get quite a selection. The dishes are made by rolling out a flat pancake of clay, on a brown paper or cloth, as described for tiles, and putting the dried mould curved side down in the centre. With a deft flick the whole is inverted and the mushroom put down on a box, bowl, plaster bat, or turntable—anything which holds it up off the table. With the wrist over the centre the mushroom is rotated while the fingers pat down the clay evenly all round. The overlap is cut off by sliding a knife horizontally along the flat base, and the edge can be pinched like piecrust in the traditional manner, or rounded with a damp cloth. In a few hours the drying clay will separate from the plaster mould, which can be dried off and used again indefinitely. A little flint rubbed on a tile or dish mould prevents the clay from sticking. If the dishes are now to be slip decorated they should be lightly sponged inside and supported with a ring of clay to buttress the curve underneath.

The rhythmical action of patting, and the experience of making an even section by pressing between hand and mould, are related to thumb and coil building, and to throwing on the wheel (where the section is formed between the two hands). But admittedly the shapes which can be made by this method are limited and children —like the country potters who until very lately produced pie-dishes and plates by this method—love to finish with a flourish of decoration. The decoration of one colour of clay with another was mentioned in connection with modelling. The same slips are used in pottery and two or three colours in addition to the body clay will give a range for great variety of decoration.

The slips should be made from the body clay sieved (as for glazes) through a 60- to 80-mesh sieve with some of these oxides.

The oxides I suggest for colouring clay are those which are found giving to clay its natural colour in different parts of the world. But few of us are fortunate to live in a district which has two or more colours of clay, so we can use our body clay and make other colours by adding these to it. Amounts are only approximate, and must be discovered for each clay by experiment.

To make red-brown: 5–10 per cent red oxide of iron.
To make dark brown or black: 12–40 per cent black basalt (which contains manganese and other oxides).

To make blue :	0·5–2 per cent black oxide of cobalt.
To make yellow :	4–10 per cent yellow ochre.
To make white :	Ball clay.
	Ball clay alone may 'fit'—that is, cling to the body clay used and expand and contract with it—or china clay and flint may be mixed in proportion with it to achieve purer whiteness and adjust contraction. About 5 per cent felspar will help the slip to cling by fluxing into both slip and body.

I suggest beginning with one of these contrasting slips, which can be used to line a dish or bowl or painted on in a simple design of brush strokes. To line a pot or jug, an egg- or a tea-cupful is poured in, the whole is swivelled round in the hands and poured out. The outer rim or shoulder may be dipped by holding the pot upside-down and *level* in a bowl of slip. But both inside and

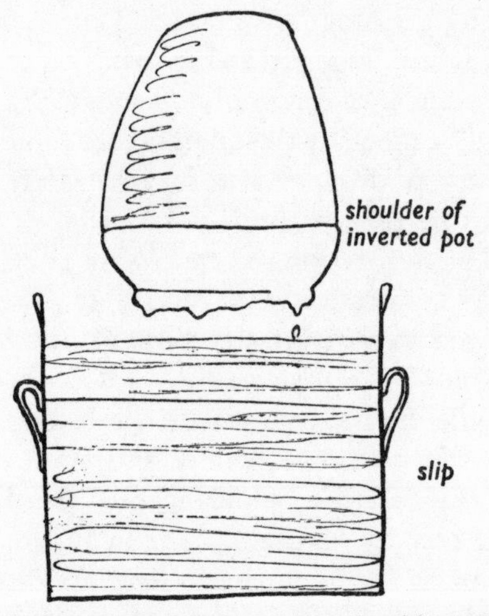

Fig. 21.—Dipping a pot in slip as far as the shoulder. The pot should be given a slight shake when lifted out to flick surplus slip off the rim.

outside should not be dipped because the pot tends to collapse with absorbing so much new moisture. All slip dipping and decorating is done when the ware is 'leather-hard' (finished some hours but not yet dry). The slip does not hold but flakes off in firing when the ware is too dry. Tiles are best dipped in slip and glazed by sweeping them down on to the surface of the liquid and up again, and trimming the sides with the downward movement of a ruler or knife.

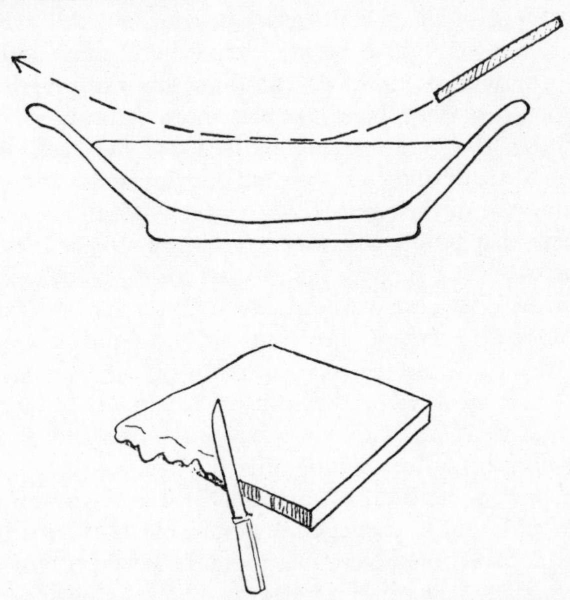

FIG. 22.—The sweep taken in dipping a tile, and the downward movement of the knife in cleaning slip or glaze off the edges.

Dishes are lined by rotating them with a small quantity of slip inside (having buttressed them outside as suggested), and the silky surface that results may be incised through to the body colour, or decorated with a further slip. This is squeezed on to the wet slip surface through the nicked corner of a paper bag, or a large rubber thumb-stall, or a baby's bottle, or a professional slip trailer, which is a rubber bag, convenient to the hand, with a nozzle. Slip trailing exerts a tremendous fascination and I have seen children and adults who could not be torn away from this fascinating activity with all its possibilities of pattern in feathering, drawing with the trailer, and sugar-icing. The extreme mastery of decorative work in this style is displayed in the plates of our English Thomas Toft. Schoolchildren often reach the same kind of intoxication with their own skill and want to decorate everything to show themselves and others how clever they are, and be confirmed in their sense of achievement. I believe that instead of being crushed by reference to canons of good taste, they should—if it is a form of achievement which holds out possibilities of further development—be allowed time to work through it, as a natural stage in the growth of craftsmanship, and they will eventually emerge secure enough to be more critical and more restrained. In any form of decoration with clay (in contrast to superimposed decoration in glaze, which is much more difficult to manage successfully), they are learning more about the basic material itself, and the patterning—as in wood gouging and tabby weaving—is arising out of the nature of the material itself.

The fact that pots and dishes have to dry for at least a few hours before being dipped in slip may create difficulties where classes come only once a week. One solution is a really airtight damp cupboard, perhaps lined with an old blanket which can be kept damp, or simply put instead in plastic bags and store there till next week when they can be decorated. But a pottery club in mid-week or twice a week is a solution and each child takes responsibility for looking after his own work.

Wheel pottery has been left to the last not from any conviction that it should not be practiced in schools, but because it is more common and yet less practicable there. One wheel in a school which practises only wheel pottery must be a tantalizing frustration to the majority. It takes some time to master a wheel and little can be accomplished without regular practice twice a week or so. Yet the sensation of throwing is such a satisfying and thrilling one that it is good to have it as the privileged culmination of the sound but slower methods I have suggested. The early stages of co-ordinating hands and feet on a kick wheel may be reached by way of working in pairs, one child kicking while the other throws. I have no more inherent objection to the power wheel than the power lathe or sewing machine, so long as children are *introduced* to pottery in one of its simpler forms. The making of a thumb-pot is in essence the same as the throwing of a wheel pot. While the ball of clay is rotated the section is pressed out in a spiral between the fingers. But at the thumb-pot level there is *time* to feel physically, and to appreciate mentally, what is being done—if one does not put the thumb down exactly in the centre one side will be thicker than the other. If one presses too hard a hole will be made. On a wheel all these happen so fast that they are more difficult to understand. Since the cost is the greatest objection to power wheels in schools, it is good to know that one enterprising pottery teacher[1] has fixed up three or four wheels to a half horse-power motor running at one slow speed. Two of these wheels are connected up with the belt just by pressing a foot pedal and disconnected by its release, so that they have one slowish speed only for learners.

The beginner on the wheel can learn more from five minutes with a good teacher than in a multitude of books. The continuous and concentrated work of two weeks at a summer school is only the very beginning of learning to throw, but in some ways it is more useful than occasional nights at a crowded class, where the physical co-ordination acquired one evening is apt to be lost after a week has passed. But the only way to learn is to find a good teacher and opportunity to practise and persist through the early difficult stages. At long length there does come that miraculous feeling of complete control and ease in which one's thoughts and feelings are transmitted from the balls of the feet through the muscles of the back and shoulders, the taut elbows and relaxed wrists, and the whole being shapes, through the mobile fingers, a finished pot.

When it comes to teaching children, it is often helpful to hold one's hands over their hands, especially in the early centring stages, or to draw up with your left and their right hand doing the work, and then your right and their left. I think no tools should be used in throwing at this stage—one must develop the greatest possible sensitiveness of touch. The base can be finished by being thumbed down as the mediæval tankards often were, or trimmed when leather-hard with a pen-knife. At a later stage turning with a tool can be shown, but this is harder than throwing, and less valuable and satisfying as an activity itself.

From the days of making doll's teapots, children will roll little handles and push them on. But these fall off as they dry, and when they come to the stage of wanting to make things properly they will want to make handles. A mug or small jug will take a wire-pulled handle (formed by pulling a wire twisted to the desired shape through a wedged lump of clay), but a bigger pot will need a handle which will take a strain, a handle in which the clay has been coaxed into the greatest plasticity in one direction. Such a

[1] Louis Jones of Wennington School, Yorks.

handle is traditionally made by taking a pear-shaped ball in the left hand and with the right hand, which is constantly dipped in water, stroking the small end of the pear into a 'tail' of the requisite thickness. The section of the handle—round or rectangular—is made by the ring formed by the right thumb and first finger as they stroke. As for all handles the top is broken off

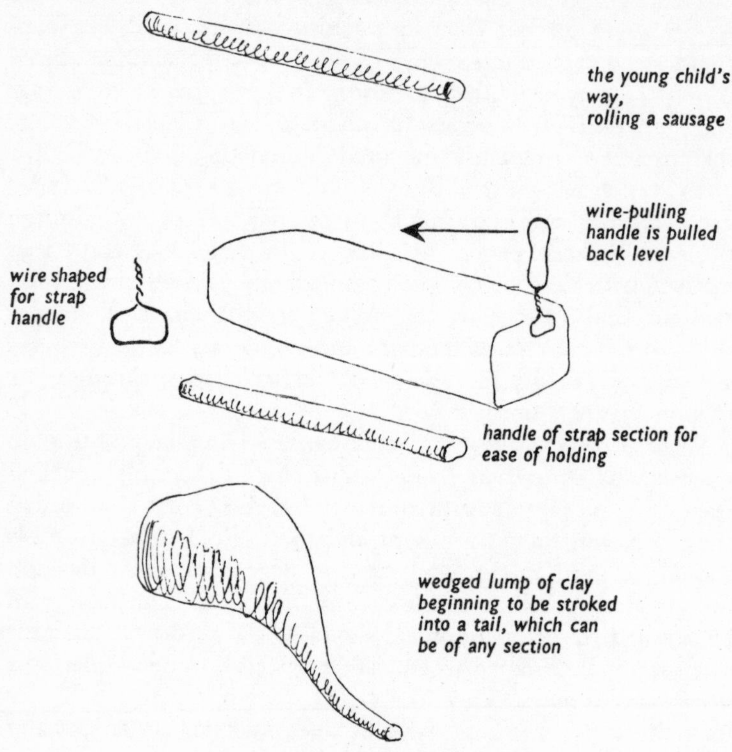

FIG. 23.—Ways of making a handle.

in a point between finger and thumb, and when a place has been cross-hatched on the pot and dabbed with a little slip to receive it, it is firmly and neatly pressed down and the edge worked into the pot. The other end of the 'tail' supported in the left hand can then be curved down and the right place to join studied before the surface is prepared as before and the join made with a few decisive strokes. It is well worth while to study the jugs of the traditional rural potters, of such artist craftsmen as Bernard

Leach and Michael Cardew, whose handles are primarily clay shapes, designed to fit the human hand, and related superbly to the pots they serve. When our children begin to consider handles in this way, they are well on the way to being craftsmen.

Modelling and pottery, I believe, offer such a varied range of experience to so many different types of children, with only one set of materials and limited equipment, that they should be more widely accepted as school crafts.

POTTERY

Minimum equipment for introducing each new type of clay work. Flat desks will serve for almost all purposes, but tables with washable tops are obviously easier.

Non-wheel pottery:

Thumb-pots and coiled pots: No special equipment at all, presuming there is clay and a bin to keep it in. The pebbles or potsherds used to smooth the coiled pots can be picked up on a rubbish heap.

Tiles: A knife, and rolling-pin between two or three children (an empty bottle will do, but a piece of broom handle and rolling sticks are better). A piece of brown paper or scrap cloth each.

Tiles can also be made in tile boxes.

Pressed dishes: Boxes for plaster of Paris moulds; a knife each.

Wheel pottery:

Kick wheels, Potters' Equipment Co., Brittania Rd., London, S.W.6; Tiranti, Charlotte St., London, W.C.1; Welding Industries, 90 Victoria St., Bristol 1; Specifications for making kick wheels, The Leach Pottery, St. Ives; Electric wheels, Potters' Equipment Co., Boulton's Ltd., Burslem.

Turning tools, home made in metal shop or from Tiranti.

These quantities are only suggestions for novices starting pottery:

3 cwt. clay.
1 cwt. grog.

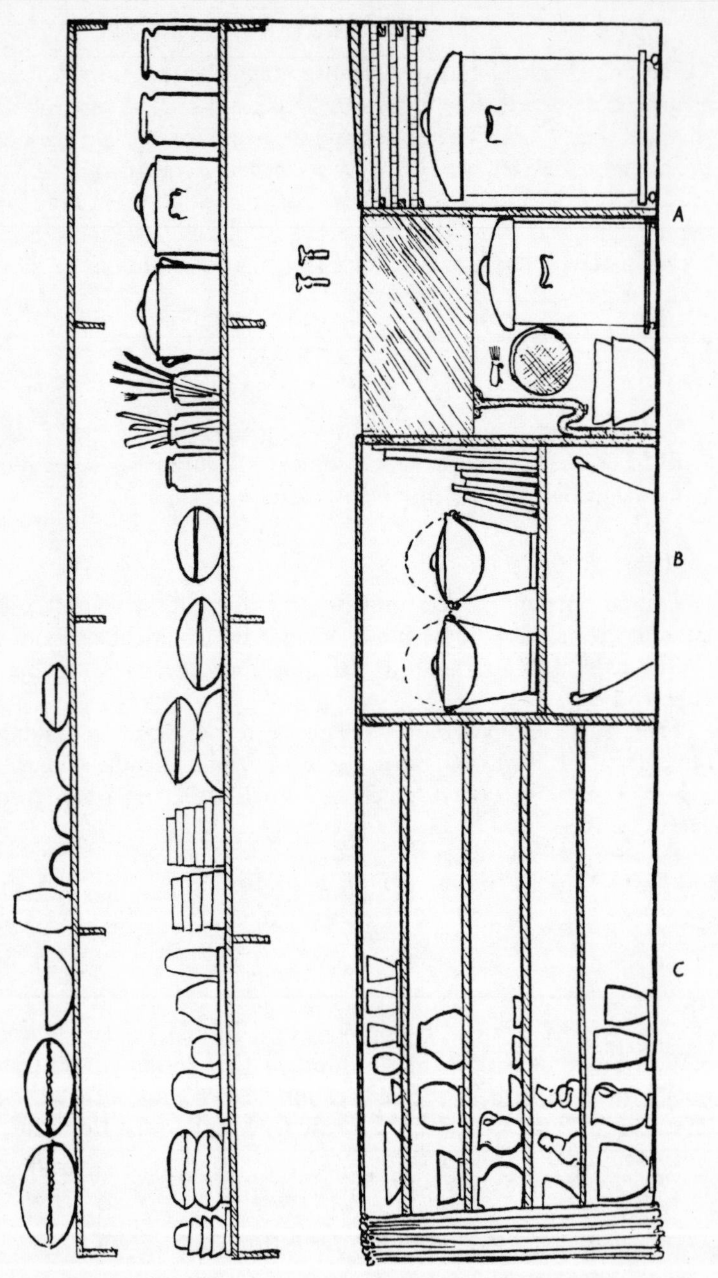

Fig. 24.—Suggested arrangement showing how one part of a wall of the room, round the sink, can be used to store pottery material.

For making slips and for reconditioning clay:

One or more sieves, with phosphor bronze 60- to 80-mesh (from Wengers, Stoke-on-Trent); pot-scrubber; several basins, one at least 18 inches across; 7-lb. jam jars are good for holding slips but pails with lids or small bread bins are better, to allow room for dipping.

For slip decorating:

Several thick soft brushes for painting; slip trailers, e.g. thumb-stall, paper bag, or rubber bulbs. The rubber bulb off a cycle horn, fixed to the metal nozzle off an oil can.

No special tools for incising—anything which lies to hand, or a trimmed stick.

Materials for coloured slips:

To be added to body clay, or to white slip (suggested quantities for first order):

black basalt	about 2 stone
black oxide of cobalt	1 ounce
red oxide of iron	3 lb.
yellow ochre	5 lb.

To make white slip:

white china clay	½ stone
ball clay	2 stone or more
flint	½ stone

Materials for glazes are given on page 123.

A. A large bin to hold plastic clay, and a smaller one to receive dry clay waiting to be repugged. Basins, a sieve and scrubber under the sink. Some drawing boards slip into prepared rack so that there is a space between to store and dry rolled-out clay, or tiles. Above are containers of glaze (with lids) and 7-lb. jam jars for ingredients.

B. A tub for pugging the clay and pails with lids for slips and dipping. Odd pieces of wood for boards.

C. Shelves of different sizes to keep ware damp. This is best fitted with doors, but a blanket curtain, kept damped from time to time, will serve. Above is drying ware, and storage space for press moulds, etc.

XVI.—FISH DISH

A press-moulded dish lined with black slip and decorated with a fish, a motif well chosen to fit the shape of the dish. The edge of the dish is finished with a simple finger decoration like pie-crust, and the outside is unglazed.

The white slip in which the fish is drawn is laid on the wet black with a slip trailer (like icing a cake) and the scales represented by 'feathering' which is described in this chapter.

Boy of 16.

Teacher: Donald Potter,
Bryanston,
Dorset.

This progressive Public School affords excellent facilities for several crafts. The pottery is in a converted basement, and has four wheels, some school-made. It has a wood-firing kiln built by master and boys together.

XVI

XVII*b*

XVII*a*

XVII*a*.—HEAD OF A HORSE—PLASTER OF PARIS

The value of carving is almost complementary to that of clay. It has a general educational value for two types of adolescents, only a few of whom may want to carry it further as a serious craft. Those whose use of clay is becoming too superficial and clever, and those who are aiming too narrowly at a naturalistic representation, will benefit from a short course of carving.

This head of a horse cut from a box-shaped slab of plaster of Paris shows how the form is determined by the original shape of the material and has constantly to be adapted to this, resulting here in a still, restrained and almost classical form.

Boy of 11.

Teacher: Mr. Lasenby,
St. Paul's Junior School,
London.

XVII*b*.—OLD MAN IN SEA CHALK

'There must be many possible materials for carving lying on our uplands or among the rocks of the moor or the shore.'

The schoolgirls of our eastern sea coast who carved these figures in small boulders of sea chalk, in relating a concentration of carving on one facet to the natural curve of the boulders themselves, have shown a fine respect for their material.

Girls of 15 and 16.

Teacher: Miss Errington,
Bridlington Girls' High School.

CHAPTER TEN

CARVING

SCULPTURE is a craft which has proved most rewarding in those schools where it has been practised. Carving may well be introduced in the primary years, but it was not discussed in detail earlier since this is essentially the introduction to an adult craft rather than a play activity. Since to teach this, like most crafts, to a level at which it can become a fully satisfying vehicle for expression to sixteen-year-olds, requires some training as a sculptor, it is not likely that many schools will make this their chief craft. But carving justifies its inclusion as a craft at some time between ten and fourteen on more general grounds. The teacher who has the adventurousness to tackle this, and has any sense of three-dimensional form at all, will find his or her own work developing alongside the children's. For those occasional pupils who show a special aptitude, some more advanced instruction may be found in the neighbourhood. A local stone-mason may have much to teach about technique even though his work cannot otherwise be taken as a model, or a student may by arrangement be able to take work for criticism to some art school or sculptor.

Carving in some of the relatively softer materials may be introduced at about ten or eleven. But why should this activity have a special justification at this age? Clay, as was pointed out, takes easily the impress of the forming fingers and is the ideal for spontaneous imaginative work in three dimensions. Now the value of carving is almost complementary to that of clay. Whereas clay modelling can sometimes encourage a dangerous facility, carving, because the materials are hard, needs patience, persistence and forethought. For this reason it has a general educational value for two types of younger adolescents, only a few of whom may want to carry it on further as a serious craft. Those whose use of clay is tending to become too superficial and clever, and those who are aiming too narrowly at naturalistic representation, will benefit from a short course of carving. These two tendencies frequently occur in the same child.

For the first of these, carving may be an important element in building up character. The very hardness of the materials discourages facility and gives the over-clever child something to pit himself against. It is less easy to achieve a superficial effect, and less easy to be merely illustrative in carving. Clay, by virtue of the very qualities which were so valuable to the young child, holds certain dangers for the adolescent. There is at this time a growing interest, the careful observation of natural forms. There is a temptation for this observation, coupled with the interest in technique, to result in models which are just reproductions of objects seen. A merely naturalistic representation, however clever, contributes no new experience to the maker or the viewer. It is only when it embodies an interpretation of the subject, and when it is bound into a whole by formal qualities of design, that it begins to be art at all. If, in spite of emphasis on clay techniques, this naturalistic representation is becoming of too great concern, as it often does at adolescence, the children can be encouraged to substitute an allied craft for modelling. Either clay work can be directed into the channels of pottery, which gives less scope for illustrative content, or carving can be taken up. It is very difficult for a beginner to carve naturalistically in hard materials—so attention tends to be concentrated on the broad shapes of the whole rather than on insignificant detail. The simple planes and formal relation of the shapes which are obtained by the first cuts come to be of interest in themselves and focus attention on the aspects which are neglected by mere representation. So for the painstakingly naturalistic type of child, as well as the facile, carving is the craft indicated. Carving often gives, too, a peculiar satisfaction to the tough heavy boy who lacks any capacity for delicate imaginative work, because he finds that his strength and persistence can also serve to produce a piece of craft work.

There is another group who may with profit be introduced to carving. These are the children whose modelling tends to be flat, who work only in bas-relief. These are usually of the visual type, and some of them never acquire a feeling for form in three dimensions. If this is apparent after a few attempts it is better that they should stick to work in which their own special capacities for two-dimensional pattern can develop. But with some, the trouble is that they have never really grasped the possibilities of solid form, and a block which can be handled and turned all ways may suddenly bring it home to them. This is more likely to happen if they are presented first not with a characterless cube of plaster of Paris with flat sides but with a piece which already has some character of its own, a suggestive lump of alabaster or chalk which needs only a little working to clarify the object it suggests.

This is one introduction to carving proper, which demands a more considered approach than the direct attack possible with modelling. In modelling the final form is built up from additions (either separately or pulled from the lump), so the value of each addition can be assessed as it is added. In carving the final form is that which remains after cutting away, so each cut has to be assessed in relation to something which as yet only exists in the carver's mind and which must constantly be readapted to the material. Also, because clay is soft, any addition can be altered in relation to the whole. In carving each cut remains permanently and cannot be undone. To tackle a shapeless block with a fairly clear conception of the finished form needs considerable mental power. Can the contrast with clay modelling illuminate farther the nature of carving in hard materials? It was pointed out that progress in modelling would come probably in one of three ways—the translation of things seen, of emotions felt, of sensations experienced, into clay. Now progress in each of these three ways results in an increased particularity; the model becomes more individual. But sculpture (with the exception of portraiture, which is usually, in any case, modelled in clay and cast) tends towards the universal rather than the particular. Sculpture is concerned with the relations of forms to one another. Pottery, too, is concerned with pure form, but its shape is also dependent on the use of the vessel, so the problem is more complex. The changing vision of adolescence may lead to an intensified search for those individual, particular forms of which we spoke, in which case modelling will be the most appropriate craft, or to an increased awareness of abstract forms, in which case either pottery or sculpture will be more satisfying. While the usefulness of the products and the speed of the work may incline choice one way or another, the physical response to the materials is an important factor. The hard resistance to the tool increases the satisfaction for some temperaments and gives them what they could never get from clay. This positive pleasure in its hardness must be present, or the long, demanding work of carving would become a drudgery. Those easily discouraged and lacking in the confidence that their ideas will be worth such a prolonged undertaking will hardly benefit from it or enjoy it. So while all children should have the chance to try some carving not all will want to go on with it.

Sculpture is concerned primarily with form, and I am convinced that a sense of form, particularly three-dimensional form, usually matures later than we have allowed for in our teaching. Perhaps it would be more correct to say 'the visual appreciation of form', which is after all a highly intellectual thing. So what we do have to work with and provide for between ten and fourteen is the *kinæsthetic* appreciation of form. I have found that children of these ages can relate shapes to one another by touch far more than by sight. Since sculpture relies on just this relation of forms in a whole, it must be approached in this way if it is to give its full sensual as well as intellectual pleasure. This is true both of the sculptor and his public. Three senses come into play when we look at a piece of sculpture. First vision, because sculpture is seen. But to anyone who has worked with his hands in the round, his seeing is translated into terms of another sense, the kinæsthetic, that muscle sense which makes us aware of the shape of objects when we put our hands round them—literally embrace them. Since we came to know the world in this way as babies, we have become largely unconscious of this process and we have failed to develop it consciously. We have come increasingly to rely on our eyes. Besides the visual and kinæsthetic appreciation of form, the third sense involved is that of touch. This tells us the quality of the surface, whether rough or smooth, sandy or metallic, velvety or waxed. For the spectator in a gallery this threefold appreciation has usually to be limited to a visual enjoyment since we are unhappily not encouraged to go round stroking public works of art. We have come, by continually associating a certain appearance with a specific touch sensation, to know by looking at marble, granite or waxed wood, how it would feel. So we get a kind of second-hand sensation and some pleasure from that. But the further discrimination on which increasing appreciation must rest can only come through the experience of actual sensation, by handling real things.

In perceiving subtle relationships between forms, in apprehending their solid bulk, and in a fine discrimination of surface texture, the practice of carving will lead towards an appreciation of mature sculpture. But that of course is secondary to its real justification as a school craft, the joy and satisfaction of creating.

What materials are available for carving? We have spoken of wood carving, but what of the materials which lead up to stone carving? For the younger ones plaster of Paris and various proprietary cements are useful. These can be poured into cardboard boxes to make blocks of any size and shape. Plaster can be carved during the first hour when it is still slightly soft or made beforehand and used quite hard. Youngsters may want to paint the figures or animals they carve and should not be dissuaded. But since we want to direct their attention to *form* in especial, it is often better to tint the whole of the mixture with a pinch of ground-colour which avoids that dead whiteness without obscuring the shape. While plaster of Paris and others of its kin may be useful and easy to obtain, it does seem desirable, since carving involves so much actual handling, to use materials which have in themselves more tactile character. Natural lumps of chalk have a firm, almost silky texture, and are interesting in that the pieces are often of a strange and suggestive shape. Soft brick lacks this advantage of shape, but often has a pleasant colour. Housing brick will do, but the very soft insulating bricks (which one may find thrown out when a furnace is relined) are better. This brick has an open spongy feel which has its own attraction. Alabaster has been a great success with young children. It can be picked up loose in the districts where it occurs naturally, or a sack of broken pieces can be ordered from a quarry or a mason's yard. The variegated markings focus attention on the material itself, and inspire the worker to search for forms which will bring these out to the full. The children feel their work is given dignity by a fine material, which so obviously permits their products to rank as 'real sculpture', a permanent addition to their homes. We have tended to forget that up till the Reformation our English school of 'alabaster men' was famous all over the Continent, and that they perfected a type of portable, intimate and almost popular sculpture for the home which we sadly lack to-day. Such a thought-provoking link with our past may be an additional reason for choosing such a material.

In using any of these materials with young children it is important to start with pieces which can be held in the hand, though later a sandbox will be needed. In this way, the tendency to work from only one angle is mitigated, and the weight and balance and surface of the stone are being unconsciously apprehended all the time. This is equally true of sea-chalk carving, which is capable of such delicacy and intricacy of detail that it is specially suitable for older children. The school which produced the work in Plates V and XVII*b* has the advantage of a coastline where such lumps of chalk are found worn smooth by the sea into simple satisfying shapes. In the two carvings shown, the subject has obviously been adapted to the natural form. Only a section, cupped, as it were, within a larger curve, has been worked, and one part of the figure is formed of the almost untouched chalk, which shows a respect for the natural shape and surface of the boulders themselves. In some of their smaller carvings these schoolgirls have achieved at points an almost lace-like treatment. The way in which one can turn some of these carvings this way and that and then suddenly find a little piece of loving elaboration, as within the whorl of a shell, gives the shock of pleasure one gets from perfect placing.

There must be many possible materials for carving lying on our uplands or among the rocks of the moor or the shore. It is better to investigate the craft materials which are around rather than sending always to the store for the standardized and too often characterless substitute. The school which is tackling sculpture seriously will want to explore the recognized stones and then experiment with others. Plate XX is a carving of a tusk by a boy with considerable experience of stone carving. Much of what needs to be said and resaid about crafts is set forth in this carving. First, see the appreciation of the material. The whole form, beautiful in itself, has been preserved and here the subject seems to have been suggested in the first place by the given shape of the tusk. Then see how the mode of working the material has dictated the stylization used: the summary treatment of the features just indicated by planes and cuts in the intensely hard surface of the bone; the cowl used to bind head to body and avoid cutting in too far for the neck which would destroy the tusk shape; the direction of the

XVIII.—RABBIT AND BEAR

There is another group who may with profit be introduced to carving. These are the children whose modelling tends to be flat, who work only in bas-relief. Some of them never acquire a feeling for form in three dimensions. But with some the trouble is that they have never really grasped the possibilities of solid form, and a block which can be handled and turned all ways may suddenly bring it home to them.

This photograph of carvings in muffle brick by two Primary school-children illustrates two stages of that discovery. The rabbit, although it is carved, is still 'seen' only from the side, as though it were drawn on the longest side of the brick and cut through. The bear, on the other hand, although its compact mass is very suitable for the original brick shape, is really conceived in three dimensions and is interesting from every angle. These were the first efforts in this medium.

Boys of 12 to 13.

Cradley County Modern School,
Staffs.

XIX.—BULL AND DOG

While plaster of Paris may be useful, cheap, and easy to obtain, it does seem desirable—since carving involves so much handling—to use materials which have themselves more tactile character and interest of surface.

Alabaster is a lovely material, comparatively soft, and the texture and markings focus interest on the material itself. The children feel their work is given dignity by a fine material. Here is a young bull carved by a boy of 12 and an early attempt at an animal by a younger child. This shows how much the carver has enjoyed the smooth surface and varied markings of the material. One can see how the simple form had been constantly held in the hand, to which it fits so comfortably.

Boy and girl of 12 and 10.

Teacher: Nommie Durrell,
Burgess Hill School,
London.

This is an independent progressive school, which without having very special accommodation gives great encouragement to art and crafts.

XVIII

XIX

XX

XX.—MONK IN TUSK

Much of what needs to be said about crafts is set forth in this carving. See the appreciation of the material, how the mode of working it has dictated the stylization used, how the composition underlines instead of destroying the original form, the restraint which characterizes the whole. This happens to be an unusual medium, but it is surely a brilliant example of the result of sensitive teaching in the appreciation of the inherent qualities of the material.

Boy of 17.

Teacher: Donald Potter,
Bryanston.

arms and the way in which their thickening towards the base in their cowl-sleeves both preserves this same shape and echoes the whole; the concentration of the detail all on one facet in features, crucifix and hands so that one has the contrast of untouched tusk and the artist's elaboration of it, with the simple arm shapes leading gradually from one to the other; above all the restraint which characterizes the whole. This is an unusual medium, but it happens to be a brilliant example of the result of sensitive teaching in the appreciation of the inherent qualities of materials.

CARVING

Suggestions for minimum equipment and tools.

For chalk, plaster of Paris, unfired brick, etc.

Pocket knives, old kitchen knives. A potato knife is excellent.

For the animals in muffle brick an old chisel and pieces of scrap metal were used. Damping the brick makes cutting easier.

For alabaster and soft stones:

Stone-carving tools, the point, the claw and the chisel, and a hammer, one set for each child. Boxes or bags of sand to hold the work steady. Glass-paper to finish.

The little alabaster animals in Plate XVIII were done chiefly with old knives and glass-paper, as they were small enough to hold in the hand as they were being worked. But stone-carving tools are not expensive and well repay a small outlay.

The sand boxes or bags can be stacked under ordinary working tables or benches, in a multiple-purpose room. The greatest drawback is the dust, which makes it pleasanter to work out of doors, and chalk and plaster of Paris produce a white dust which is easily tramped around. A garden shed or room with a french window is ideal.

Materials:

Plaster of Paris varies greatly from the rough plaster type from a drysalter which is much cheaper, to the fine dental plaster from a chemist or decorator which carves best. The addition of a little size (a tea-spoonful to a gallon of water) makes it slower setting.

Chalk may be picked up from river beds or fields or sea-shore in a chalk district. Or it may be obtained from cement firms who throw out lumps of it.

Raw unfired bricks may be obtained from a local brickworks, and the best carvings may go back there to be fired, but the composition of bricks and patience of local firms must obviously be personally explored.

Alabaster may be obtained as bagfuls of chips or as 'spoiled pieces' from a monumental stone-mason, or in large pieces from the British Alabaster Industries, Ltd., Weston, near Stafford. They will cut pieces to a convenient size, say, 8″ × 8″ × 12″, but this is an expensive way to buy it.

Bath stone, which is one of the cheap and softer stones on which to start carving, may be obtained from the Bath and Portland Stone Firms, Ltd., Bath.

But there may well be suitable stone lying around in the neighbourhood. Try there first.

CHAPTER ELEVEN

BOOKMAKING

BOLTON WOODS AND THE STRID

AFTER we visited Bolton Abbey, we crossed the Wharfe by means of the bridge and on the other side of the river, we noticed a large stretch of sand and we rested here to eat our sandwiches. Before proceeding further, Mr. Wadsworth asked us to notice how the river

FIG. 25.—A chapter heading, showing lino cut used to record and convey information, from the booklet on Wharfedale referred to in this chapter.

MOST of the reasons given for teaching this subject in school are common to many crafts, but two are peculiar to bookcraft and deserve consideration. In the Primary School it provides a pleasant way of using the children's patterned papers to make more personal common objects of school use such as books and jotters. In the Secondary School, bookmaking can foster an interest in the making and care of books themselves, which are the repositories of so much of our culture and are, in some form, in everyone's hands. Both these reasons are extraneous to the craft itself. They are not concerned with the satisfaction to be got from the activity of cutting, gumming, stitching. Yet they are good enough reasons for including bookmaking as an occasional activity, if its limits are firmly kept in mind. The materials and the activities involved do set very stringent limits to its value as a craft subject. It does not foster the young child's development in any of the ways mentioned as the particular responsibility of the arts side of the curriculum. It does not give scope for the development of the senses, as does work with clay or the rhythmical activities of pattern-making or dance. It gives little opportunity of expressing emotions or for extending their range through entering into the feelings of others as in painting, modelling, drama. It gives less scope for imagination than almost any other type of handcraft. On the other hand, it can be used to pose certain problems and present certain concrete intellectual exercises. In one school [1] at least it was given a place in the time-table directly to that end, and in many others that is the aspect which is in fact uppermost. In many schools bookcraft is included frankly as a method of inculcating numerical accuracy and so belongs more properly to arithmetic. Too often a list of cryptic measurements is put up on the board: so many pieces of paper or card of such and such sizes; a strip of bookbinder's cloth so much by so much. The children are quite puzzled as to the precise part each item plays. But if they obediently do what they are told without asking why, the whole will be assembled at the end into a book. But if one measurement is wrong they can go on to the end without discovering why every piece is failing to fit. Since they do not even know what the finished article is to look like they have no power to mould it as they go along. Here the *choice* is limited until it hardly exists at all, perhaps only in the colour of binding they may use. They cannot determine the final size or shape, so they are having no opportunity to choose proportions and then to assess whether they approve of their own choice or not. This cannot be called a craft. At its best it is the merest technique.

Even where the teaching does not run counter to fundamental educational principles, as in this extreme example, bookcraft usually remains in Primary Schools the most deadly dull of occupations, resulting in the most stilted and dry of products. It is then palatable to the children only because nothing better is offered, and because their thirst for making will welcome even

[1] Larkhills, see John Duncan, *The Education of the Ordinary Child*, London, 1935.

this break from other lessons. At a later age, when an interest in technique is growing, they may be eager to learn the successive steps by which a book is constructed. In the upper ranges of the Secondary School bookcraft, incorporating typography, bookbinding and perhaps woodcut illustration, can become a craft in its own right at the highest level. But even so, it is one which, by resting largely on a mature appreciation of such abstract qualities as proportion and spacing, will appeal at school age only to a small number.

Having admitted its serious limitations, it now remains to see how bookcraft can best be taught so as to minimize these and to take advantage of the opportunities it does give for literally binding together other interests.

Why is junior bookcraft so depressingly dull? I believe it is quite simply because it is taught as though it were an exercise in arithmetic, as though there were one correct product to be turned out at the end of the lesson, identical for every pupil. This is far from seeing *every* work done in handwork as in art, as an expressive gesture by an individual child. And it is quite unnecessary, quite unprofessional to teach bookcraft in this way. I myself taught it by measurement for years. I became so depressed by the fact that as such it could have no relation at all to the rest of my art and craft teaching, that I went to learn with a professional bookbinder to see if this was all there was to it. To my surprise and shame, I only then discovered that the craftsman binder practically never uses a ruler, and certainly never thinks of his books as a product of that careful measurement stressed in school bookcraft. He uses a cutter which can be set to repeat lengths, but the sizes of the parts of a book are related directly *to one another* and the envisaged end, *not* to preset measurements. The difference between his method of building up the book as a solid thing in the hand, and assembling an assortment of unit parts as in the other method, has to be experienced to be fully understood. I found it an exciting and revealing experience.

This method is most appropriate for schools, too, because, while the steps in the method can be soundly taught so as to lead on to adult bookcraft, each individual product can be different, in size, shape and material. What are the materials for the simplest first book? Each child can use one of his sheets of printed or painted patterns for each double page, and make a colourful scrapbook, using the plain backs on to which to stick cut-outs. Or he can use plain coloured paper for all the pages and decorate the first and last as covers. Or he can make a scrapbook of the stronger type of newspaper, and fold round the outside one of his patterned sheets (before stitching) and cut it to size as a cover.

One explicit example of the very simplest sort of bookmaking in the hand for juniors may help. This can be done with a variety of papers, newspaper, odd sheets of brown wrapping, or pastel. Each child will end with a different book.

One large sheet of paper for each child will make the first book. It can be folded down the middle lengthwise or breadthwise as each chooses, and torn or cut.

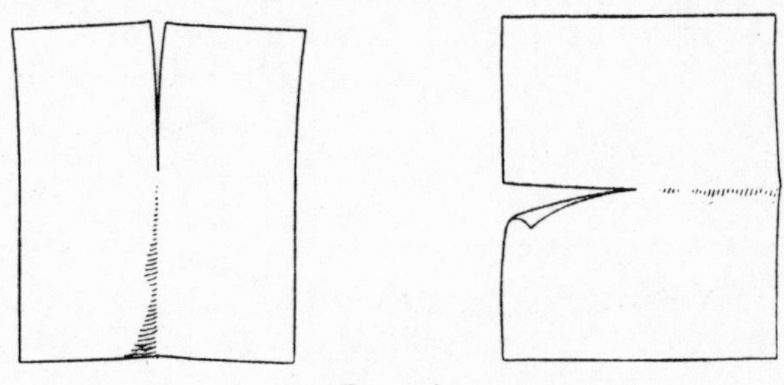

FIG. 26.

Then these two pieces laid on top of one another can be folded either way, giving two different shapes for a large book of four leaves.

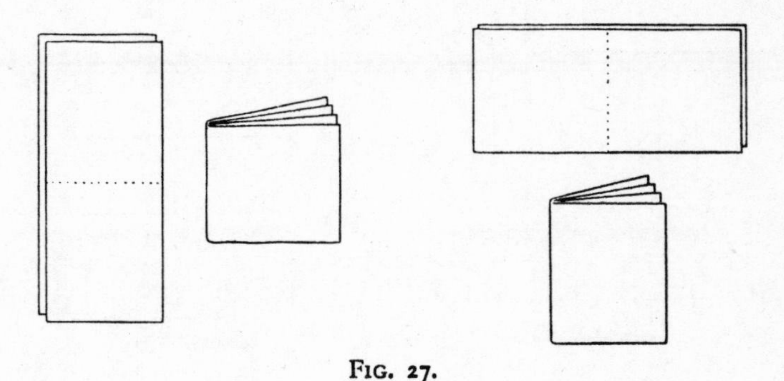

FIG. 27.

By quartering the paper two tall shapes of books with eight leaves can be made.

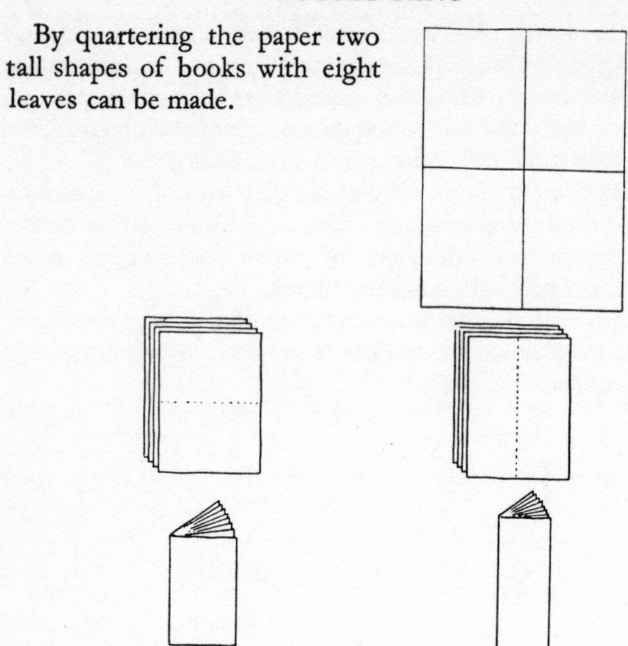

FIG. 28.

And by tearing or cutting it into four strips long narrow books of eight leaves are obtained.

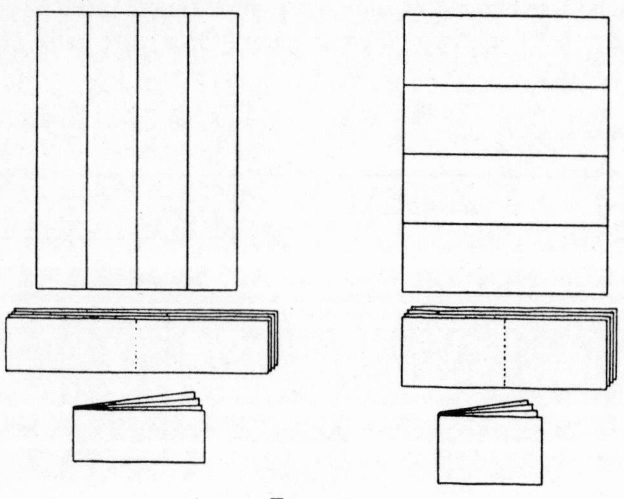

FIG. 29.

This gives four different shapes of book from any shape of paper used, making an infinite variety without any wastage in cutting—though admittedly two of these shapes will be more suitable for holding lists of words or writing long lines or patterns than more normal uses. Later the original sheet can be torn in three, giving a new range of shapes and sizes; and having this knowledge of the possibilities, the children can go on to trimming the sheets to any proportions they wish. With all the pages folded inside one another (and the cover, if separate, folded round the outside) the book is ready to sew. A strong needle and coloured thread is used and, with the pages knocked even, the book is laid open at the middle and the centre of the fold pricked through to the spine. Then a prick is made half-way to the head (top edge) and half-way to the tail (bottom edge) by eye, if we wish to train the eyes, rather than by measurement. Beginning in the centre inside and leaving a long loose end, the thread goes out the spine, in at the top hole, out again at the bottom hole, and in at the centre to be tied in a knot. If meanwhile some of the children have got so excited that they have stitched with some odd arrangement of their own it is not a great tragedy. They have made their first book, of which numberless variations can be made all up the Primary School. Books can be made with alternate white and coloured pages for writing and illustrating a story, or scrapbooks can be made from used brown paper ironed out. They can also use their painted and printed papers to cover jotters and thin school books or to put stronger covers on these little books they have made. Again no measurement is necessary. The open jotter is laid on the wrong side of a piece of patterned paper, rather bigger than itself, which has been pasted all over. It does not matter at this stage whether it is 1, 2 or 3 inches bigger all round. It matters much more that the children should choose a paper that they will like to see often. Now the corners are cut off the patterned sheet to very near the jotter corners but not quite touching them. The projecting patterned sheet is folded over the top and pressed down. Since jotters are seldom clipped or sewn right to the top the whole set of pages can be lifted a little at the head and the cover paper slipped under and pressed down right across the back. The tail end is done next, then the sides. To cover the awkward inside covers end papers are now needed. For the first few times the first and last pages of the jotter can be used for

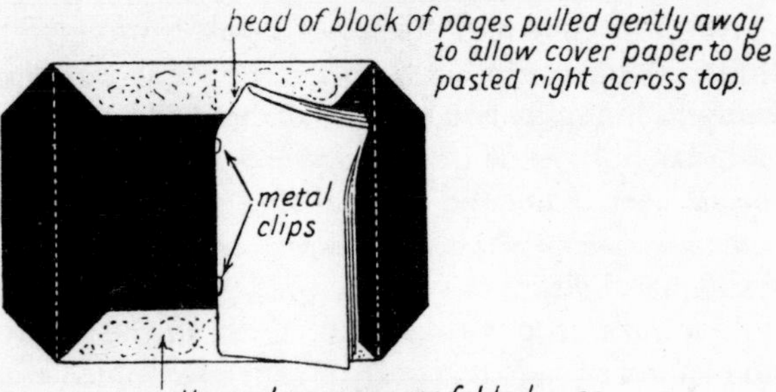

FIG. 30.

these, by pasting them on the side next the cover and putting the book closed under a weight (preferably with a sheet of blotting paper between these wet covers and the block of pages).

Later patterned or coloured end papers can be torn roughly to size and slipped in between the cover and the block of pages. If one half of this folded paper is then pasted to the first page and both halves trimmed to its size, the other fold serves to line the inside of the cover, following directly on the last method.

These processes are simple enough for Primary School children to understand thoroughly and be able to carry out on any shape or size of book. So once shown the children can go ahead on their own, covering books of all shapes and sizes, learning to shape and trim neat corners with practice. Several of the fundamentals of bookcraft are embodied here so that they can go on at an older age to stitching multisection books, to strengthening the spines, to half and quarter binding, without having to unlearn baby methods. But since the justification of bookcraft in the primary years is the end—the gay individual books—and not the activity itself, it is important to keep to a simple process which can be fairly quickly carried out. Only so will the children be able to go ahead—without being held up constantly for supervision—to try out combinations of many shapes and materials. All this time they should be making choices—of colours to go together, of a plain colour to go with a patterned paper, of size and shape of book for their purpose, later of the scale of the pattern for the whole. In addition to looking at proportions and suitability for the job, they are also living with their own patterns day by day. Occasional discussion will help them to make up their minds which patterns they continue to enjoy, and which they grow tired of in time.

INTRODUCTION

This year the Fourth Form scheme of work in Biology has linked up with the B.B.C. Broadcasts in the series "How Things Began", which is heard every Monday at 11.20. Mr. Wadsworth, the Geography teacher, has co-operated with Mr. Ashford in the scheme and is teaching the Geological side, which is the study of rocks.

The first broadcast we had was named "What is a fossil?" We were told that a fossil is either a print, cast or actual remains of skeletons embedded in the rocks, and also how a fossil is formed. We then heard about the life under the sea in Cambrian times long before there was any life on land. The following broadcasts told us about the past history of the earth in different periods, such as the Ordovician period 450 million years ago, the Silurian period 400 million years ago, and the Devonian period 350 million years ago. In the broadcasts, a man called Jim Smith tells two children, Alice and George, about the past when the only living things on earth were fish. Jim Smith pretends to be an observer from the past and takes us back millions of years. This is the most interesting part because tbe observer comes across different creatures, such as fish, amphibians, reptiles and mammals, making the whole thing very interesting and exciting.

Mr. Wadsworth and Mr. Ashford thought it a good idea to visit the area where, about 300 million years ago, these rocks were being laid down and where these strange creatures were living, so that we could see what the rocks are like and hunt for fossils which have been mentioned in broadcasts and lessons. The place chosen was Wharfe-

FIG. 31.—One complete page of a book written, printed, illustrated and bound by boys of Castleford Secondary Modern Boys' School, recording an excursion to Wharfedale, in the course of which geography, history, legend, nature study, English (in the subsequent writing up) and art were combined happily.

Bookmaking also serves to put into a handy and permanent form an individual or group piece of work. The children may make a book first and write into it the story of some project, or the separate pages with a wide margin on both sides may be made and assembled by the method shown here and stitched to their cover. Or each child might make a study in lino cut—perhaps a portrait of a classmate—and the whole be bound into a book of this simple type.

Used imaginatively the making of a book can, however, be a communal piece of work which embraces and holds a permanent record of work in what would formerly have been many separate subjects. Such a one is illustrated here by some fragments which can only give an indication of the fresh and delightful whole—a day's excursion to the country by some boys and masters of a school in a Yorkshire mining area. The teachers concerned say that they could not often undertake the labour of setting up the type and printing—as was done in this case—but undoubtedly the recording in some form, even writing into a specially made book, or the binding of separately written pages, is of great value.

Apart from this method of teaching the children to make quickly and easily books or covers for themselves, it is possible to teach bookcraft at about twelve or so, as a branch of general knowledge. Children of this age are interested in how things are made and why they should be the shape they are. To make even one multisectional book, to round the back, and strengthen the corners, will give them a new respect and care for books. But to turn a term's craft lessons over to hospital treatment for the whole school library, as I was once asked to do, is to mistake the purpose of craft teaching. Such work is monotonous and quite uncreative. If after their bookcraft lessons a few children care to take on this job as a piece of voluntary work, that is excellent. But if the care of the library becomes the responsibility of the craft department then a special period for those who enjoy such work must be set apart for it.

The few who want to carry on bookcraft to the craftsman stage will want to make several types of multisectioned books, perhaps to write their own in script or lay type for them, to work with different kinds of paper and cloth, to relate the illustration to the lettering as well as the contents, to bind in leather and tool and letter the backs. Here is a field in which that relation of the parts to the whole and of the whole to its purpose (which is the essence of design) can be studied indefinitely. But since the possibilities are limited by the accepted form of a book, the rectangular solid, and by the intractable material, the field for individual creation is narrow. Bookcraft proper will probably

FIG. 32.—A lino cut used in the text to illustrate the book on a day's excursion to Wharfedale. This illustration does not only give some factual information but does convey some of the atmosphere of the place and the glow of excitement associated with the whole day.

appeal chiefly to those literary adolescents who love the *matter* of books and come to care secondarily for the form, or the painstaking less daring ones who feel happier working within a strictly limiting framework.

But since this is not a book on techniques, only the preliminary approach is suggested. The exploration of the field itself must be left to the inspiration of the individual teacher.

BOOKCRAFT

The equipment for such simple bookcraft as is suggested here is that normally found in any art and craft room: scissors, glue and paste (cooked flour paste or Tapwata, which is simply mixed with cold water), needles and strong thread (linen is best). Bookbinder's cloth can be obtained from Dryads and other firms, and the patterned papers are made by the children. By collecting cardboard and stiff paper a saving can be made.

We have been perhaps a little unimaginative about the material for covering books. Many cloths are suitable, such as fine linens, cotton slubs, the children's own woven strips, provided these are not too bulky. Woven straw cloth has a pleasant texture and is specially suitable for some subjects, while scraps of rich silk can be used under a cover of strong cellophane or open-weave nylon. To cover their books with their own printed fabrics gives children great pleasure, and slip-on loose jackets of printed fabric or paper will protect books in day-to-day use.

The great bulk of books we have to consider in bookmaking will be those the children write themselves, individually or in groups. The handwriting built up on ease of movement now being taught in many schools provides a form as pleasant to look at on a formally planned page as it is natural and expressive in a letter or notebook, and needs no equipment except the special pen.

The teaching of such a form of writing in many schools bids fair to rescuing handwriting from the slovenly and illegible scrawl to which it has often deteriorated, and to bring some of the scribe's care of the planning of pages and the spacing of letters into ordinary writing. It is surely healthy, too, that children should learn handwriting in order to record what they have to say rather than as an 'art form' of script lettering divorced from common usage. Seeing pattern-making as one aspect of writing, these children break into occasional decoration with the pen to fill the vacant end of a line or add a tailpiece as unselfconsciously as did the mediæval scribes. Robin Tanner has done an incalculable amount in this country in the study and teaching of writing in schools and those interested will find inspiration in his books and his recent work in this field.

The equipment for the simple sort of bookmaking described here is that which is commonly found around the art or craft room, paper, paint, lino, and so on. A press is useful but not essential.

Small children will tear their pages along a fold, and later will cut with scissors. The older ages will find themselves involved in more and harder cutting. A card cutter is an expensive item, but one which saves much energy and patience. Sharp knives, metal rulers and metal plates to cut on will serve instead.

The expansion into bookbinding proper requires a much greater outlay, and except where the *whole* process is undertaken (typesetting, wood-engraving or other appropriate illustration), and where the teacher's passion for her subject makes it specially profitable, it is suggested that such an outlay might at the school level be better spent on a less rigid craft.

But even then he did not forget his Yorkshire dales, and it was said that he could always hear the ripple of the Wharfe in his mind. He never forgot what it was to be poor and when he had plenty of money, he gave thousands of pounds to hospitals and schools.

This is a composite article by:- P. Monks, .H Norton, J. Lamb K. Robinson, P. Withers, B. 'Appleyard, B. Godber.

FIG. 33.—A tailpiece showing a lino cut used imaginatively to record a scene from memory, adding to the atmosphere of the whole book.

Fig. 34.—A woodcut of a nearby village, by a boy from a Yorkshire coal-mining town. This was a Christmas card sent to friends of the school, a Secondary Modern one in Castleford.

CHAPTER TWELVE

LINO PICTURES AND FABRIC PRINTING

SINCE I am much more concerned to put the case for the three-dimensional crafts, I will speak about only two of those which are carried out on a flat surface. It seems profitable to choose for discussion two of the most common school handcrafts, cutting lino pictures and fabric printing.

It is possible to begin lino printing by choosing a picture already painted, and translating it into lino. This, the painter's, is one of several possible introductions, but I would suggest just the opposite approach as more fruitful. The basis of any craft is an understanding of the material and the tools. To transfer a work originally planned and carried out in paint into such a completely different material is to introduce an unnecessary complication in the process of understanding lino. Just as play with clay, the fondling, handling, squeezing, without trying to make anything, and the feeling for the possibilities of the material which results from this, underlies all later craftsmanship in pottery, so I believe that the foundation of lino printing is exploratory play with lino. If each small group has a set of tools and access to printing facilities, and each child is given odd scraps of lino, he can make cuts with different tools and print an impression every few minutes. So he will learn first the range of strokes possible and he will be saved a lot of time mistakenly spent trying to reproduce a pen or paint line. And secondly he will grasp the essential fact of the pictures being built up by the taking away of substance—not the adding as in painting or drawing. (An understanding of this may have come through potato cuts in earlier years.) The young artist cannot begin to convey an idea or a feeling in lino until he knows something of what effect a light thrust or a strong deep stroke with the tool will make on the lino. Then he has to learn what effect will be printed in reverse from such cutting. These experimental cuts will suggest groupings which convey an

FIG. 35.—Trying out lino tools. These are the first experimental cuts of a beginner getting to know the feel of her tools on an odd scrap of lino. But the first two prints placed together like this form a pleasing pattern.

idea, the spiked thorn, the petalled daisy. Gradually a language of different cuts is acquired, but each problem of representation will make the student search for forms in which to convey what he is trying to say. The first little motifs (which can be stuck on empty cotton reels for ease of handling) can be used for greeting cards, or programmes, or tail-pieces. The first picture subject tackled might well be one which gives opportunity for finding new uses of tools in surface pattern, perhaps a jug of flowers or leaves against a plain background, or an interesting animal or figure shape against a patterned background. The subjects which are most difficult to tackle at first are those which demand recession into the distance, e.g. landscapes, and those which need a three-dimensional treatment of light and shade—closely packed groups of figures and objects. To ask children to represent realistically, or to convey what they have observed closely, in early lino cuts is to court frustration and disaster. We should rather use those qualities which only lino can give us—the peculiar quality of a cut line, thin or wedge-shaped, the dramatic contrast of light and dark —and exploit these to the full.

The limitation to two colours, black and white, focuses attention on the arrangement of the masses, and leads to an appreciation of composition which can be related to the student's painting. Printing on tinted papers is often pleasant, and absorbent typing paper gives a surface texture unobtainable with normal drawing papers. Such papers can be dyed by pulling through an ink bath.

A lino-cut picture is so different from anything done in paint or pencil that we cannot expect that one attempt will give the boy or girl enough understanding of this new medium to design well in it. But cutting lino pictures, if it is to be pursued at all, is worth carrying on to the stage where such satisfaction is possible. Such suggestions as are offered are to emphasize the fact that here we are working with a flat surface, a new set of tools, a new technique with its own possibilities, which need a radically new approach. When the student is familiar with the language of cutting and engraving he will be able to translate through it the visual impression of things seen, or to convey feeling by massing lights and darks. To make a series of studies will hold the interest through successive attempts while such a technique is acquired. Such a collection might be of musical instruments, of buildings or architectural details, of shell forms, or of plants—any field in

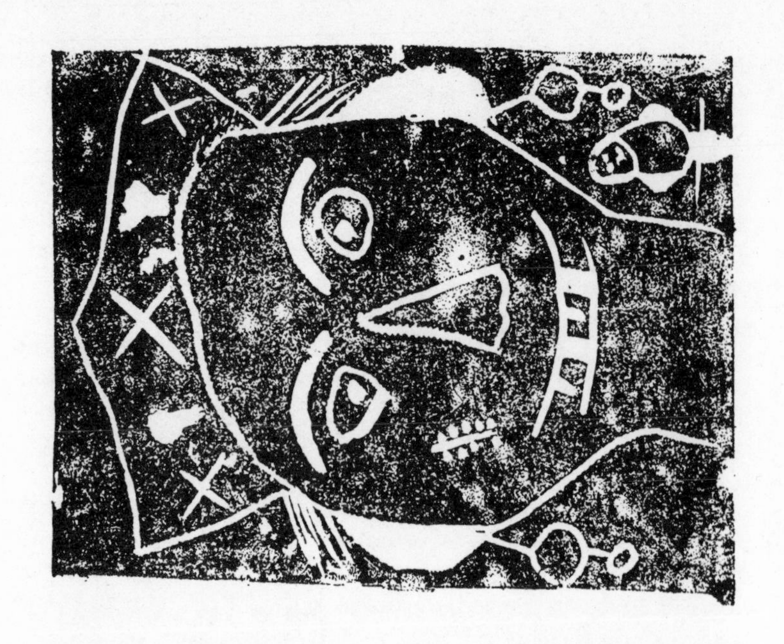

FIG. 36.—These prints of a king's head, a first lino cut by a boy of 11 from a West Riding mining village Secondary Modern School, show how the conception grows by printing as he goes along. After the first few bold cuts he goes on to add character and finally elaboration, deepening some of his tentative cuts and achieving a design well fitted to the space in which he works.

which individual interest is strong enough to inspire such prolonged study. Such a series might be mounted as a picture calendar or bound on the inspiration of the mediæval Book of the Hours, or might illustrate a booklet if typography is practised in the school. Simple lino cutting may lead on to two or three colour blocks, or to wood engraving for those who are temperamentally suited to such patient and meticulous work. But the

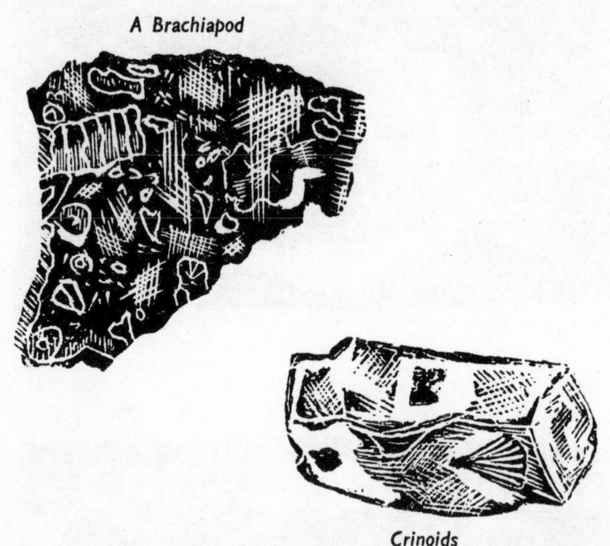

FIG. 37.—'Crinoids' and 'A brachiapod'. Lino illustrations in the text of the Wharfedale excursion booklet.

satisfaction of craftsmanship will only come in this particular material as in others, if its use is carried on and familiarity is gained over a number of years.

While lino is extensively used for fabric printing in schools it is much better to begin this craft with potato printing. But since most fabric printing is in the form of repeating patterns it is necessary to look at the whole problem of teaching pattern-making to children.

The profound desire of all human beings for order, for organization, and for some sort of significant grouping rather than chaos, emerges clearly in children's desire for pattern. Very early they tend to arrange objects in patterns, to repeat musical phrases and movements with slight variations, and to demand a 'pattern' in the daily order of events which gives their external lives coherence and security. The making of patterns in paint or materials, the fun of balancing repetition with just enough variety, is their elementary form of that satisfying arrangement of shapes and colours at which we all aim in decorating a room or planting a flower border.

I believe that the earliest pattern-making is done with objects, and the handling of pebbles, sticks, beads, flowers suggested in Chapter II will give endless opportunities. But making patterns by a rhythmical movement of the finger, in wet sand or mud, is a close second and this can be given colour and permanence in 'finger painting'. Flour or starch paste, or thin 'Tapwata', is brushed over a sheet (a large house-painter's brush is quickest) and the patterns are drawn direct with the finger dipped in dry powder colour. Here are all sorts of delightful sensations, the rhythm, the satisfaction of dipping one's own finger in the paint, getting straight to it, the joy of seeing the outward and visible *trace* of the delicious inward feeling of movement, the wonder of seeing the colours mix when they are scrubbed one into the other. Young children seem to need this scrubbing circular movement, *pushing* the colour into the page, and if they are too early given brushes *and* freedom the brushes are quickly ruined. The solution is not less freedom but no brushes until they have worked through this stage. Quite soon this particular satisfaction wanes in the face of the greater variety and flexibility which can be achieved even with the large hog-hair brushes which are the best introduction to painting proper. Pictures can also be made by finger painting, and often prove a good method of loosening up older children or adults who cannot free themselves from a tight and niggling style. If adolescents have no previous experience and have to be introduced to pattern-making, one possible way which avoids a suggestion of 'babyish work' and provides exciting surprises is to use candles. The first pattern is drawn free-hand with a candle on white paper and a wash of thin colour put over the sheet which leaves the pattern white against a tinted background. This brings to the notice of the student the way in which the result is a permanent trace on the paper of a rhythmical movement of the hand. Such a pattern can be elaborated with pen and ink, or additions in candle can be made and a different coloured wash put over which will give three colours in addition to the white, two

FIG. 38.—Direct lino cuts. After talking about the Good Friday story, these boys of 14 cut without any drawing, direct in the lino, their impressions of the head of Christ. The extraordinary pathos apparent through the diverse treatments shows what an expressive material lino used in this way can be.

Headmaster: Mr. Yates,
Saltire Road Secondary Modern School,
Shipley, Yorks.

washes and another colour where the two washes lie one above the other.

The type of pattern-making I have found much the most valuable with young children is the 'centre pattern' which grows outward from a centre dot or motif by the addition of new elements. Here the 'structure' of the pattern is the simplest possible, and is within the grasp of quite young children. The final effect does not depend on an intellectual grasp of the whole, or on any *exact* following of a repeat, or on meticulous execution, but on adding one new element at a time and relating it in colour and form to what is already there. Children see the similarity of this aggrandizement to the inflorescence of a plant or the ripples from a stone thrown in a pool, and they use it again in their arrangement of flowers' heads or shells on a plate. With younger children I let the pattern grow and grow until they come against the edges of the sheet or want to stop. But soon their attention can be directed to the shape of the sheet into which their pattern can fit if they relate the edges of it to the square corners. Just occasionally a diffident child will get on better if he is encouraged to start in one corner the first time and 'grow' from there. I have found that it is not helpful to tell the children to begin by putting *any* shape they choose in the centre—a triangle or square does not lend itself to rhythmical growth, and puts a stamp of angularity on the whole. A leaf shape, flower head or a moth shape gives opportunity to embroider inwards and outwards in sweeping curves.

While the centre pattern in varied forms can be enjoyed and extended for many years, by the middle years of the Primary School we should be helping children to discover and explore other kinds of patterns and especially those which repeat. There are three main ways of doing this.

FIG. 39.—Pen Patterns. While colour can be an important element in pattern-making, sheer lack of materials made us experiment with ordinary school pen and ink. We found that the children came to appreciate the possibilities of a pen through exploring a range of lines and textures with it.

Three centre patterns showing the variety of pattern and texture which can be achieved. The last one is interesting for the fact that this boy has incorporated his own name in the pattern, thus linking pattern-making with writing.

Centre patterns, boys of 11. Teacher: P. Clarkson, Student, Bretton Hall.

Kenneth Kenneth

(1) A piece of paper can be folded repeatedly and a shape cut or torn from the folded piece, so that many similar pieces are obtained which can then be arranged over the sheet. Using tissue, crinkled paper or even cloth in place of the torn paper all make the result more interesting. This is a quick method of giving the idea of repeating units, but the resulting pattern is apt to be disjointed since it is made up of quite separate pieces, and it is liable to be monotonous since it is made up of identical units. The first defect can be lessened by connecting the stuck-on papers by strokes of paint or ink scribbles. In this case the second defect often disappears because the additions have enough variety, being free-hand to make it lively. In this case, neither the tearing of the folded paper nor the licking (or sponging) and sticking on is in itself a rhythmical action, so the final effect of pattern will depend on outline form and spacing, involving more intellectual factors, rather than on the bodily activity itself.

(2) Secondly, a repeating pattern can be made from printing with a potato or some other unit over a page. This is not so likely to look monotonous as slight variations in pressure give variety in colour and texture which are pleasant. If the units are widely spaced at first, they can again be related by brush strokes or the flat surface of the potato can be cut into a new unit and printed over or between. The pattern can be varied in both these methods by altering the spacing of a single unit, putting alternate rows up and down or turning four ends to a centre as in the Maltese cross.

Here the cutting of the original block is a static activity—so with young children this part should not occupy too long—but the printing should be a rhythmical activity, and the weight and spacing of the prints can convey something of this.

(3) Thirdly, we can make a pattern by painting it direct, creating the repetition by rhythmical movements of the arm. This is the method of writing patterns, and it is extremely important because the resultant pattern is the imprint, as it were, of a rhythm of the body. It is delightful to a child—or to anyone—to see an activity which *feels* so pleasant issuing in a shape which mirrors it before one's eyes. But in addition it forms that permanent record of which we have spoken before, which can be considered and assessed. When the pattern

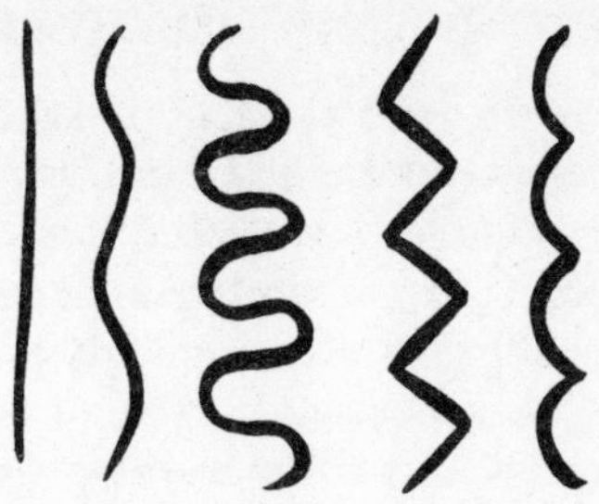

Fig. 40.—We can choose one of many different kinds of lines.

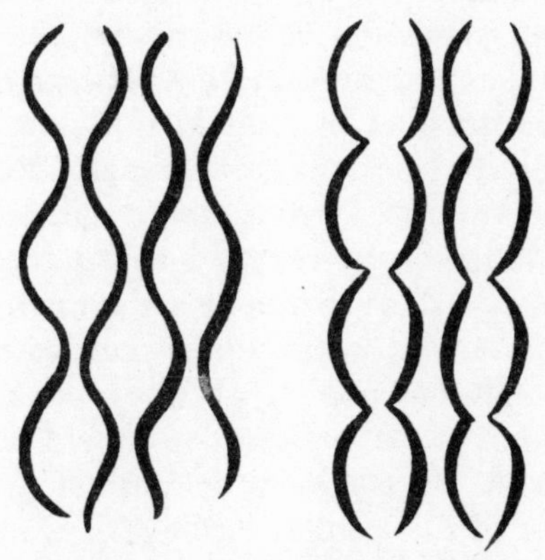

Fig. 41.—And by repeating it, or reversing it across the sheet, we can build a grid or structure of a pattern.

Fig. 42.—The elaboration may be a development of the lines themselves, or it may be a motif designed to fill the spaces left between.

emerges jerkily or irregularly, the child knows that his movement has had that character, and he can see where it has fallen short. Where a continuous line is used running either down or across the page, this forms a simple grid or structure, which can be elaborated by filling out into the spaces between. Once a child has grasped that a certain degree of regularity in fitting his lines together will give him an all-over grid, he tries to develop that control of the hand which will give him this.

Building a grid first will, in addition, emphasize the fact that the *whole*, not the single unit, is the pattern. The essential character of a pattern lies in the relationship between the parts, rather than in the units themselves (and in many satisfying all-over patterns it is difficult to pick out the unit at all!). Rather than work out one unit in detail first, I have found it more rewarding, both in the activity and the final result, to build up the whole loosely, and gradually to crystallize, elaborate and enrich with successive additions. Concentration on the single unit, with elaborate calculations with repeating units, half-drops, counterchanges and various contortions, is the *mechanics* of pattern-making, and has little to do with the development of sensibility. If we are clear about the *purpose* of this pattern-making, the forms it ought to take will follow.

Every child can achieve satisfaction and make individual objects through patterns. But it has its own virtue as a means of education and makes its contribution in three ways.

First, it provides an absolutely simple expression of the underlying feeling for rhythm, grouping, coherence, within the reach of very young children, but capable of the utmost complexity and elaboration in adults. The Celtic interlacing patterns, the Moorish pierced stonework, Brussels lace, in which one can spend hours following the intricate near-repetition, are examples of this.

Secondly, it provides a medium for isolating one aspect of art, and concentrating for a time on the exploration of that, unhampered by meaning or content. This can be directed deliberately but unobtrusively by the teacher, as a means of building up a sense of colour, or introducing a new medium or mixture of media (such as pen and ink on top of paint), or of pointing out the interest of using different shapes or different sizes to avoid monotony.

FIG. 43.—Two grid patterns on handkerchiefs done in pen and leather dye by boys of 13 who had become fascinated by pen work.

Teacher: Student of Bretton Hall.

Following on this, the new awareness of colour or texture will come into play next time a picture is tackled, and so by an alternation of pattern- and picture-making one element after another can be explored to enrich the final expression. Some artists in their own development have followed something of this oscillation, concentrating at one period on abstract pattern, or on line or on colour, and finally incorporating these experiences in a richer and more satisfying interpretation of experience.

Finally, pattern-making in mixed materials, in torn paper (which may be combined with ink or paint or pastel) and in scrap materials, string, cloth, buttons, steel wool and all such things, is a valuable training for such children as are ultimately more interested in pattern and texture than in content, those who will turn to the weaving crafts, jewellery or lettering as their mode of expression. Except for one of those specific purposes suggested, I question whether repeat patterns should be drawn or painted at all—whether it is not better to use some technique which involves repetition, such as potato printing.

But whereas with young children pattern-making and the decoration of surfaces is an end in itself, the time should come, from early adolescence on, I believe, where they increasingly see how most of the patterns around them spring from much more fundamental causes. A brick wall and a tile roof form a pattern not because someone thought that it would be fun to put some jolly markings on as a contrast to plain surfaces, but because the units (bricks or tiles) *must* be arranged in such a way if they are to do their job. The pattern springs from the materials and construction. The patterns made by shells and by leaves on a branch have their origin in the needs of the organism. The patterns made by ladders and stairs are seen to spring from the fact that human beings are roughly symmetrical and move their bodies in an alternation of the two sides—as indeed the pattern of footsteps in the snow brings home to us.

Thus, while the making of patterns begins as fun and the element of sheer decoration can remain an enhancement all through life, the study of pattern in nature and in man-made things does lead to a deeper understanding of the world in which we live.

So, with young children pattern-making can be undertaken without any specific purpose in view. Numbers of patterns on paper are turned out fairly quickly, and some can be used for covering books and jotters as suggested in the chapter on Bookmaking. But with juniors there are many other uses for those gay papers. Some can be cut to fit the window-sills and frequently changed so that they are always clean and bright. Some can be used in the frivolous decorations and for paper hats for Christmas and other festivities. A frieze can be maintained all round the room by joining strips of the same depth and adding new ones at one end while removing the old at the other. Or they may take their part in making the 'mixed material' phantasies. They can be contrasted with plain sticky paper in making torn paper pictures.

When books are to be covered with these printed papers one can begin at about nine or ten to discuss scale. 'Is this paper too big in its pattern for this small book?' From there it is an obvious step to thinking about the use for it *before* the pattern is started—but this must not be forced. It is much more important to make plenty of free rhythmic varied sheets of patterns first, and to develop a sense of spacing and balance.

Because of the importance of seeing the whole pattern rather than the isolated unit, I would give children a good deal of practice in the free type of painted pattern, centre patterns, grid patterns and so on, *before* they approached pattern-making from units at all. But this other approach provides variety and leads directly on to the serious craft of fabric printing.

I prefer to introduce fabric printing as vegetable rather than lino printing for three reasons. The vegetable, such as the potato, is much easier to cut and does away with the need for sharp tools. Its texture is very pleasant on the print. And being absorbent it does away with the need for flocking when dyes are used. Potatoes have practical advantages too. They can usually be brought from home. When cut they can be kept for some days if stored in water, and after printing, the surface with the dye can be cut off, leaving a clean surface to make a second unit. The natural shape is usually pleasant in itself, and a half potato is so much easier to hold in the hand than an unmounted lino block that a rhythm in printing can be obtained. This rhythm in the actual work of printing is important, both for the ease with which such monotonous work can be continued for a considerable time and because the eventual patterns will have a better quality. I say

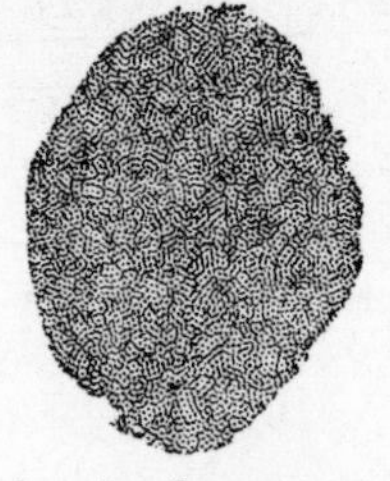
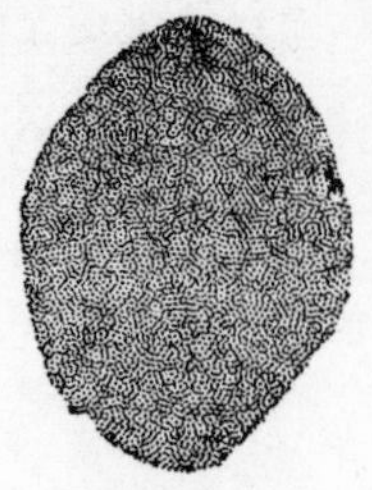

The potato shape used entire first to get the feeling of printing.

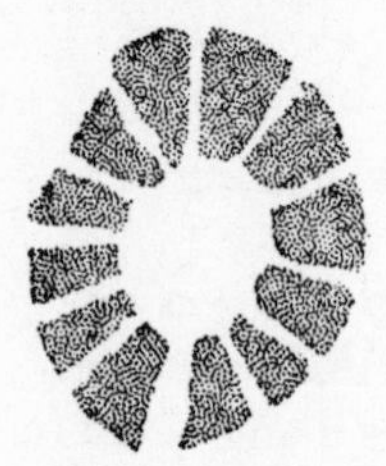
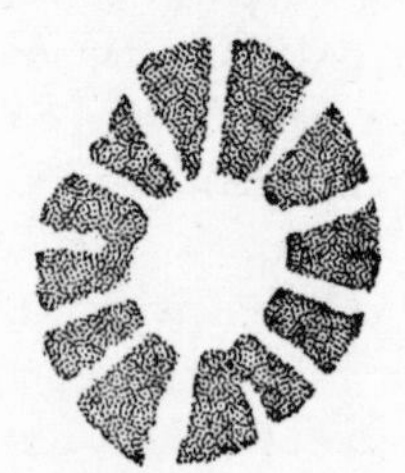
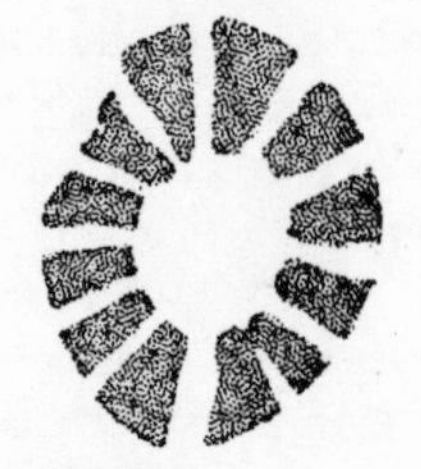

The same potato cut directly and printed to see the effect.

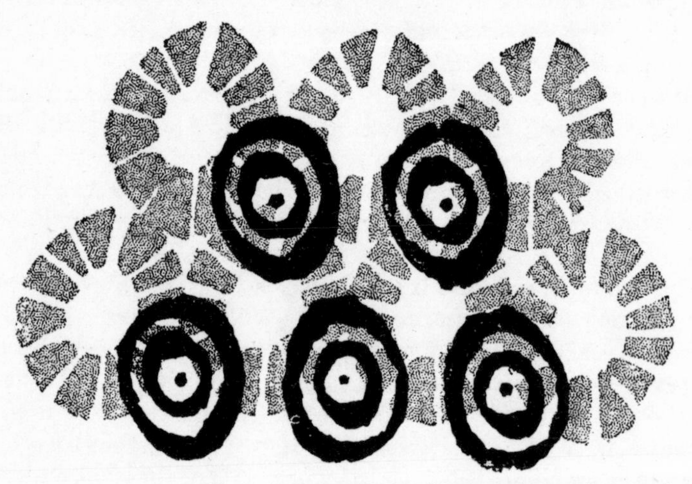

The same potato printed closer to get an all-over effect and overprinted with a differently cut potato in a darker colour.

FIG. 44.—Potato printing. These were first attempts by a child of 10.

eventual because in the early stages the important thing to encourage is *not* correctly placed, evenly pressed prints. If the child's attention is too concentrated on this effect his muscles will become rigid with the effort, and though the immediate result is more accurate he cannot progress to the final stage of ease *and* quality. The first thing to achieve is ease, to let him find a bodily rhythm which suits him without fatigue. For this reason it is better to begin with a simple form of repeat, keeping the potato or lino one way up always (in which case the spacing can be varied), until a swing has been achieved: press on the pad, lift, press on the paper, lift. For this reason a pad is preferable to a brush. After this, more complex arrangements can be tackled. I stress the rhythm, not, of course, in the preliminary testing of alternative spacings, which must be slow and thoughtful, but of printing a length of cloth once the work is in progress.

I have found fabric printing with different vegetables very successful if the cloth is not longer than a yard or two (with long repeated use, the potato surface gets soaked and breaks up). The texture produced is often more pleasant than that of a lino block, and the natural vegetable shape provides a pleasant starting point and avoids the preliminary sketching on paper which is apt to lead to such derivative results. It also avoids the difficulties and time lag of sticking the lino on plywood blocks and of flocking. Vegetables are easily available and cheap, and the simplest tools will do, such as a few old kitchen knives and some penknives or potato peelers. Potatoes are most useful, but turnip, if not too loose in texture, will give a larger print (most useful for printing drama costumes) and carrots are delightful to hold and give a close texture, permitting finer cutting. All this makes it quite feasible to do fabric printing in a Primary School, with the inks which need no fixing. The best of these that I have found are Lawrence's, and in order to get them to seep right through the cloth and prevent that heavy sticky surface which has been the drawback to fabric ink printing, it is necessary to thin them down very much with the special thinner provided. This means that thin material is more likely to be successful, and we have printed on the lighter shades of muslin, organdie, artificial silks, moss crêpes, cottons and fine wools. These inks are provided in a very large range of colours and I am sure it is important either to provide enough colours for the children to build up their individual

XXI.—SIMPLE PIECES OF FABRIC PRINTING WITH VEGETABLES

In the centre is a round tray cloth in organdie, printed in one colour; on the left is a length in dusky pink printed in two shades of olive green, and on the right a yellow stole printed in black and grey. The two left-hand prints are from potato, the right from two sizes of carrot, and all show an appreciation of the natural form used.

On the right is a boy of 12 wearing a tie potato printed in one colour, and he is holding another printed in three colours on a brown background.

XXI*a*

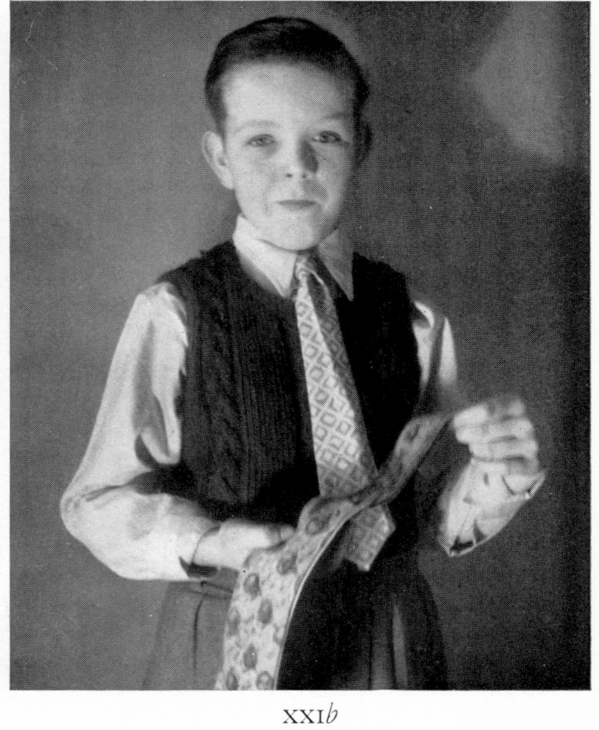

XXI*b*

XXII

XXII.—FABRIC PRINTING IN USE

Patterns in fabric printing should be designed in relation to the material to be printed and its use.

The little tray-cloth in organdie is almost a first attempt, and is printed with potato in two colours on organdie. The pattern is well placed round the edge. The hanging is a combination of a screen and a block in two colours, and the skirt a three-colour screen print all-over pattern.

The tray-cloth and hanging were made by students of Bretton Hall and the skirt by the wearer.

Girl of 17.

Teacher: Miss Birchall,
Levenshulme Girls' High School,
Manchester.

colour schemes on their background material, or enough of the primaries and black and white for them to mix to their choice. The thinner is worked into the paste with a palette or old kitchen knife on a glass slab or tile, and spread on to a pad. This pad is just a block of wood wrapped round with soft rag, but a better one can be made by padding the block and covering with American cloth. Over this a temporary cover of flannelette or soft wool cloth is pinned to spread the dye on, and only this outer cover is changed for each colour. If the children are not familiar with vegetable printing, I usually begin fabric printing by doing a potato print in paint on paper, aiming at ease and good spacing. Then they cut away parts of the potato and do an overprint in another colour which links the whole together. Next, they may wish to cut up the pieces and print small motifs between, or to begin again and shape the potato the first time.

At this point one may move on to fabric and fabric ink without any new technique to learn, except mixing the ink. A clean washed hankie or a short length for a scarf can provide a practice piece and soon the children will be making head-scarves, aprons, cushions and so on (Plate XXI*a*). It is sometimes more difficult to find appropriate things for boys to make. One or two two-yard lengths of fabric—fine wool, poplin, linen—can be bought communally and cut into *diagonal* strips about 3½ inches wide which will make many ties (Plate XXI*b*). The strips must be at 45 degrees to the selvedge to make up well, and the two triangles left over at the corners will make head-scarves.

So far, in this description of a fabric-printing course, the natural shape of the vegetable has been used as the basis of the design. In fact these are large 'spot patterns' possibly linked with a lighter overprint to give an all-over effect. This simple method of beginning offers countless variations. But exploring the full range of fabric printing must include making patterns which are really continuous and join at top and sides. An easy transition to this needs considerable thought and skill on the part of the teacher, and is perhaps best made along with the change to lino. Large potatoes or turnips *can* be cut to squares or rectangles by the children to form the basis of a continuous pattern, but pieces of lino are almost always rectangular already and if they are to be stuck on plywood blocks these are most economical if cut to that shape. So I would suggest that, as we accepted the natural shape of the potato, we accept the square or rectangle of the lino as a self-contained shape, and concentrate on cutting this new material without the complication of a design which runs across and entails careful 'joining up' in printing. Without any previous drawing, the children can cut straight on the lino and build up an abstract motif within the rectangular shape. This exploring of the tools and the material first without the hampering effect of trying to follow a pencil-drawn line will avoid niggling shallow cuts which fill up with dye, and will lead to a more imaginative use of tools. It is also so much quicker that the children can print a few repeats on a handkerchief the very first lesson and gain more immediate satisfaction and understanding of their medium. The next lesson another block of the same size can be cut, and the two used in combination to form a larger repeat, suitable for a head-scarf, cushion, or even skirt length. A small linear motif can be used to tie a diaper pattern together and get yet another variation from the original blocks.

So far, I have presumed that we were working in one colour of dye, though alternate blocks could be printed in different colours. The subtle effects to be gained by printing one colour over the top of another (these dyes are *not* opaque) can easily be introduced by printing rather plain bands or stripes of a light colour and more intricate and definite shapes above—running along or across them—in a darker colour. Such overprinting can be charming on a striped or checked material if the block is really planned to fit that material. When the cutting and the process of printing and the placing of these rectangular motifs have been learned on several pieces of 'real fabric printing' then the more intricate process of planning a continuous design (where the blocks must match exactly) can be better tackled.

Potatoes can be cut with an old knife or a nib inverted in its holder, but lino needs some tools. There are tool sets on the market with a wooden handle and interchangeable blades which are cheap and conveniently packed, but as the blades are not

---

In the following pages *one* method of covering the early stages of lino printing is suggested. There are, of course, many others, but the essentials are that printing should not be delayed until elaborate cutting has been done, that the possibilities of simple things should be explored, and that the steps should be thought out to follow one another easily.

FIG. 45.—After the first experimental cuts, see p. 172, a small block of stripes or textures has been cut, using rather than ignoring the rectangular outline. This is printed in various ways, perhaps first with alternate spaces (which avoids the difficulty of 'matching' the edges till the method of printing is familiar).

FIG. 46.—Or this same block might be used as a diaper pattern, or to print a handkerchief, as below.

FIG. 47.—Or it can form a border pattern when printed close, or a basket-work all-over, suitable perhaps for a cushion cover.

Fig. 48.—Now a different motif can be cut and printed in various combinations.

FIG. 49.—Or it can be combined with the first, offering alternation of motif and visual texture.

FIG. 50.—Or it can be overprinted on the textured block in a darker colour.

very sharp and break off rather easily I have always found it convenient to have at least a few proper gouges.

It will be seen that even with the small blocks easy to handle and store, the possibilities are infinite. It is the imaginative use of the material and the tools themselves (rather than the attempt to imitate—or to be more original than—textiles previously seen) which is of value to the growing person, and which incidentally produces the most charming results.

Lino blocks are usually mounted with glue on three- or five-

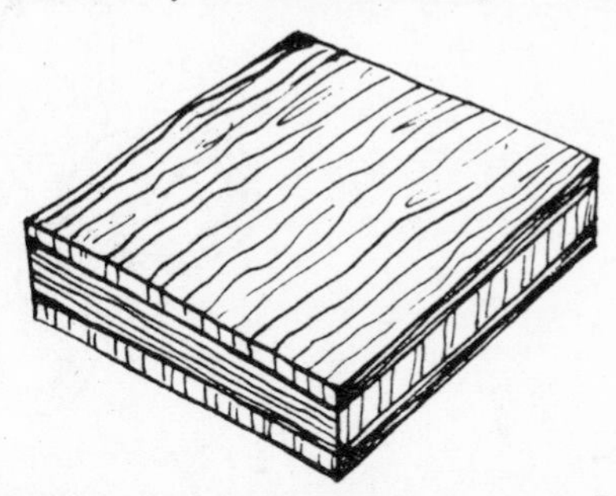

FIG. 51.—A wood block (on which to mount the lino) of three to five thicknesses of graining set alternately will not warp as a simple block would.

ply wood blocks for easier handling. But small blocks can be printed without this by rolling on the back with a rubber roller. The lino surface can be pressed straight on the dye pad for very thin materials, but it is better to flock it—that is, give it a felt surface to absorb enough dye to go right through the cloth. This is done by rolling a little flocking mordant out on a tile and coating the lino surface thinly. Flock powder is sprinkled on to

FIGS. 52 and 53.—Using the natural shape and texture of the potato to print from leads on to the idea of using other natural objects. Small children will print with excitement any flat surface they can hold, a cotton reel, a veined leaf or piece of bark. This is exploring and discovering rather than creating, but by selecting and arranging interesting textures found, new patterns can be created. The illustrations show patterns built up on the surface of wood blocks by pressing string patterns on to the freshly gummed wood. This 'building up' of the surface to be printed opens much wider and more varied possibilities for fabric printing.

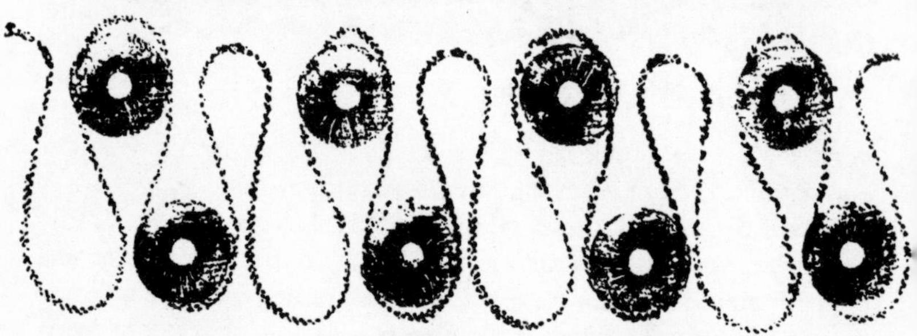

(*a*) A piece of string was laid in loops on the gummed surface of a board, and a tiny cotton reel printed in the loops to give weight.

(*b*) A piece of string coiled on itself.

(*c*) Spot formed by combining four of the previous unit.

FIG. 52.—First attempts at 'built-up surface' units.

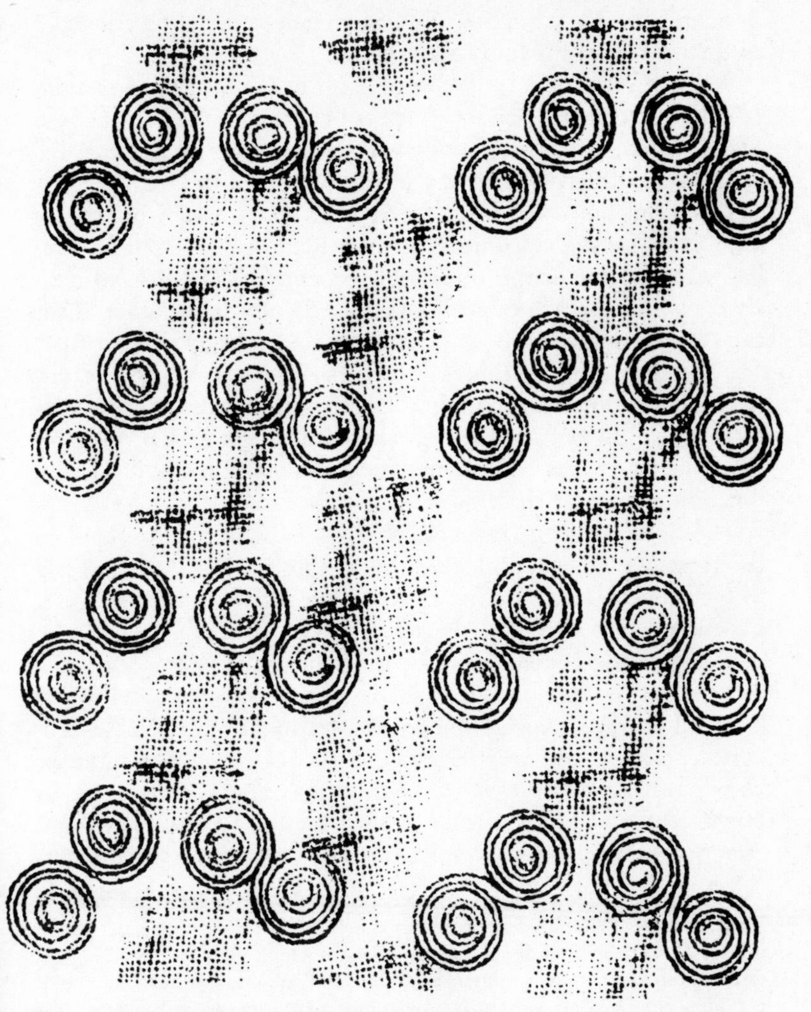

Fig. 53.—Double string coil printed over hessian textured background for a dress print.

this and after drying for a few hours the whole process is repeated two or three times. White flocking powder is better than brown as it contrasts with the lino.

Making the printing unit by building upon the surface with pieces of string, cork or nails (as the old paisley-pattern blocks were sometimes made) is also worth trying. In this way a pattern of delicacy and rhythm can be quickly made, and a different series of textures from the lino cuts obtained (Figs. 52, 53[1]).

While a great deal can be done with fabric inks used imaginatively, a Secondary School which adopts this as one of its chosen crafts will want to give dignity and complete permanence to the work of practised students by using proper fabric dyes.

When this book was first prepared the problem of firm dyes for schools was a difficult one. The introduction of Helizarine dyes has widened the scope of fabrics in schools. These have clear bright colours which can easily be mixed with one another. They can be used thick or thin and can be painted directly with a brush, opening up new possibilities in textiles. With wax resist or direct painting, costumes and hangings can have the vitality of spontaneous work. In the same bath, scraps of fabric and threads for embroidery can be dipped and the different fibres will take on different shades of the colour.

The Solodon dyes (manufactured by I.C.I. and now supplied by Reeves) give beautiful strong clear colours, but they are fixed in a mild acid bath. We have used them successfully in schools. Instructions for their use are supplied with them.

The other equipment required for pursuing fabric printing to a more advanced level is a strong table suitably covered, and an old dumbell or mallet to hit the block. A triple-purpose table converted from an old wooden table is shown here. The ordinary wooden or zinc or plastic top is used for general craft work. A box at one end holds a roller from which is unwound felt and American cloth which provides the soft waterproof surface suit-

[1] This can provide a valuable introduction to the use of the word 'texture' in art. Texture is literally what is felt by touch. But, as was mentioned earlier, it is often used to describe a flat visual effect which *suggests* something interesting to the touch. Children who are familiar with the real texture of carving or modelling are sometimes puzzled by the use of the word for marks on a piece of paper. I have found it helpful with young adolescents whose painting lacks this quality because they have never thought about it, to stroke with eyes shut a piece of sandpaper, perforated zinc or bark, and then to make a print from it and say to them, 'This was what you felt, this is what you see, the visual impression corresponding to what your fingers touched.' Many painters, of course, do not use texture to imitate a real surface, or as a representation of what they depict, but create a surface to be enjoyed for its own sake, as we may find in paintings by Vlaminck or Piper.

able for fabric printing, and this can be stretched by its wooden cross piece being slipped over hooks at the other end. Or alternatively, an ironing blanket and sheet can be unwound from the other end.

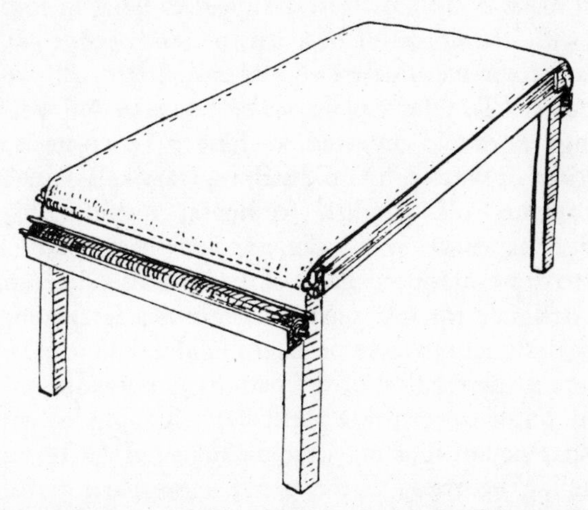

Fig. 54.—A triple-purpose table, showing the ironing felt drawn out from its box and stretched slightly by slipping the rod attached to the free end into slots in pieces of wood screwed to the table corners. The American cloth which can be drawn over it for fabric printing is shown rolled in its box.

Screen printing has certain advantages but the methods used in most Schools of Art are not suitable for general school practice. Old picture frames can be used to avoid the cost of screens, and fine muslin substituted for the more expensive organdie. Instead of the complicated process of treating the screen first and developing it photographically the pattern can be painted direct on to the muslin, so that an effect of brush strokes can be gained rather than the harder outlines of a lino print. In this as in other methods, the peculiar effects of this medium should be used to the full rather than pencil-drawn pattern adapted. Small accents of other colours can be made to a screen print by well-placed additions with a block.

So, with comparatively little equipment, fabric printing in several forms can be practised as a serious craft. Instead of ending with depressing scraps of useless cloth, it can be approached as an opportunity to make simple but individual clothes or furnishings of appropriately patterned material, to be used in conjunction with needlework or woodwork.

Even the first piece of printing can be designed for a purpose, an organdie tray cloth, a tie, a washable cosy-cover, a set of luncheon mats. Soon a pattern designed to hang in folds can be tackled, with its interest of how this pattern needs to differ from that on a flat surface. But we should ask, first of all, why do we decorate cloth? To relieve plain walls? To make dull weaves more interesting? To avoid repeated washings? To create a mood in the onlooker or wearer, by bold stripes, jazzy splashes? To evoke an atmosphere—old English freshness, restful sobriety? To camouflage shapes we do not like, or to emphasize those to which we wish to draw attention? Each of these needs a different pattern skilfully designed for that purpose. Here is a fascinating field in which the designer can to some extent influence human behaviour. Then there is the relation of the pattern to the cloth on which it is printed. Some patterns are particularly suitable for voile or for the transparency of muslin; some make use of the texture of the cloth coming up through the print; some need a plain heavy fabric—or should we rather say the fabric needs them? Into this the whole question of scale enters, and developing a discerning sense of the relation of scale to the fabric and the use needs practice. There is the question of the wittily appropriate motif, and of the serious combination of any particular pattern with the other units of the whole design, whether a room or an outfit. There is the possibility of using pattern, not all over, but to give emphasis to edge or neckline. We can hardly begin to explore these possibilities in one term or one year. Yet the fundamental criteria can be applied to the first job, perhaps something as simple as a head-scarf. This entails looking at the purpose of the finished article, and choosing materials, colours, motifs which are appropriate in a head-scarf for this particular person. There would be no point in having the pattern printed chiefly in the centre, because, if the scarf is to be folded in two diagonally, borders and one corner will show most. From such beginnings in relating pattern to purpose, it is possible to progress. If dressmaking material is being printed it is obviously better to have a pattern which will look well upside-down. If a child's frock is envisaged the scale of motif and type of material will lie within a narrow range of possibilities. However much or little printing is actually achieved, this craft can make the student alive to the uses and abuses of pattern in daily life, and vividly aware of its possibilities in the enrichment of his immediate environment.

LINO PICTURES

Suggestions for equipment and materials.

Offset pieces from floor *lino* may be used if the lino is thick and soft. A local firm may well salvage this once you have established with them the type which is suitable. Such firms as Dryads also supply lino, and the boxes of *tools* referred to with interchangeable blades. Proper *gouges*, **V** and **U** shaped of various sizes, are more expensive in the initial outlay but last much longer. A set of, perhaps, three of these and a knife can be shared between two or three children.

A rubber *roller* and a *flat slab* (an old tile or piece of plate glass) should be shared between four children, so that blocks can be printed frequently as they cut.

The type of *printing ink* which can be washed off with water makes cleaning up infinitely quicker than one which needs turps or meth.

Lino pictures can be printed on many kinds of paper, wet or dry, but just occasionally it is pleasant to have a sheet of good jap paper (can be obtained from Lawrence, Bleeding Heart Yard, Hatton Garden, London, E.C.1), to make a good print from the most successful. This shows the children what an important part the background texture can play, and leads on to consideration of fabrics in fabric printing.

FABRIC PRINTING

Suggestions for equipment.

The simplest equipment is *potatoes*, pocket knives and printing inks, used with thinning medium as described (inks from Lawrence, Bleeding Heart Yard, Hatton Garden, London, E.C.1.

Printing from flocked blocks:

Lino and tools (see above); wood bases, as described, from a local firm; flocking mordant (2 large tubes should serve the class for a term), from Dryads; white flocking powder (1 lb. goes a very long way), from Dryads.

Flocked blocks can be used with printing inks on certain materials. The most versatile dyes are Helizarine (Skilbeck Bros., Bagnall Ho., 55 Glengall Rd., London, S.E.15) which can be used for printing, dipping or painting. Their great advantage is that the wet colours show approximately their final colour, permitting mixing and colour decisions at each stage.

While pieces for handkerchiefs or head-scarves can be pinned to a drawing-board on the desk, longer lengths require a steady table. A lino or strong rubber top makes an excellent printing table, but a double blanket covered by American cloth can be used over an ordinary strong table.

Printing from screens:

Wooden screens or old picture frames with flat backs.

Organdies or fine muslin to stretch over.

Screen shellac (from the I.C.I.) or thick copal varnish to block in pattern.

CHAPTER THIRTEEN

NEEDLEWORK AND EMBROIDERY

By one of those strange accidents in the history of education, embroidery—which is decorative needlework—has become separated from that needlework which is its basis. Very often the domestic science teacher—in the Secondary School at least—teaches 'plain needlework' and the art or craft teacher teaches 'embroidery'. Sometimes, even where they are taught by different members of staff, there is real co-operation and the two are brought into the close relationship they ought to have. But too often they are considered quite separate subjects, and never applied to the same piece of work. This is as strange as if pottery making and pottery decoration were taught by different people and in different lessons and never integrated in the same pot.

Yet this state of things is understandable when we consider how it arose. In the last century, when 'fine needlework' was much more general, the making of garments included their decoration by a delicate and painstaking type of embroidery, such as drawn thread work, broderie Anglaise, or lace insertion and pin-tucks. Now this, if quite unsuitable for the greater part of school needlework, was in itself sound. The fine white underwear and baby clothes were appropriately decorated by this type of stitchery and the work formed an artistic whole. But this type of embroidery tended to become very stereotyped and to lack any originality. The same combinations of form and stitch were used over and over again, the same designs for broderie Anglaise and lace insertion were copied from one garment to another. It ceased to be really creative. Embroidery for furnishing was usually canvas cross-stitch or coarse flowers writhing on plush or wool to valance the bed, or petticoat the overmantel. After centuries in which each generation of women adapted old and evolved new patterns in the idiom of the day—whether it was Elizabethan diaper work, Jacobean stump work or the delicate floral sprigging of the eighteenth century—after centuries of this alive tradition, by the first quarter of this century, embroidery in Britain was rigid, painstaking, unimaginative and almost dead. Then a group of needlewomen, of whom Rebecca Crompton was the best known, showed us that embroidery should and could be alive, free and exuberant. But to emphasize this, its freedom, it seemed to them they had to separate it from the garment making and furnishing to which it had been tied and to give themselves complete freedom, with no conditions to fulfil except those inherent in the materials themselves. These embroideries might later be made up into a picture or cushion but were not tied down to purpose in their inception. In much of Miss Crompton's own work we see a new type of embroidery. The basic material is used only as a background to superimposed layers of materials, buttons, French knots. The lines of stitchery wander all over the surface, often not outlining but providing a descant to the main theme. They are alive and exhilarating—a gust of fresh air through the narrow channels of the drawn thread and the inserted band. If this style of embroidery has since been adopted by others as a mannerism, that does not detract from the service done to us all by the originator. This, like all revolutions, emphasized the elements which were being neglected—freedom, spontaneity, striking combination of materials. This very free and direct type of embroidery will always have some place in our scheme because it does something essential for us—it stimulates the imagination, it dwells on the tactile delight of materials, it expresses a feeling or a mood. It is, in fact, a sort of painting in thread and stuffs. In the right hands it becomes a true work of art. It inspires the embroidery practised in most of our more lively art departments. But we cannot afford to lose sight of another aspect which was usually present in the old dead 'pin-tucks and drawn thread' type. Embroidery, like any other decoration, is rooted in the basic craft of needlework of which it is the flowering. Just as the nature of clay—its plastic impressionable texture—determines the nature of clay decoration (slip trailing, impressed edges, incised hollows, etc.), and the form and purpose of the finished pot determines the type and position of the decoration, so should the nature of cloth determine the decoration and the purpose of the constructed whole, determine where and how needlework shall blossom into embroidery.

Now what is the nature of cloth? It is a soft pliable fabric *woven*, that is, formed of threads crossing one another usually at right angles. This *structure* of the cloth, the fact that it is formed of crossing threads, determines all that we do with it whether in the way of structural needlework or embroidery. By structural needlework I mean the making of three-dimensional coverings, whether these be clothes, or toys to be stuffed, or furnishings in the way of cushions or chair-covers. The problem is to cut out and join together two-dimensional pieces of cloth so that they will form a hollow three-dimensional shape. In this it has certain similarities with constructional wood and metal work. The problem of covering a rounded form with pieces cut flat has to be met by cutting a great number of pieces and joining them—as a child's soft ball is made of many lozenge-shaped pieces or a skirt of many gored pieces; or by taking darts in the material; or by gathering it. Now in all those ways the substance of the material itself, the fact that it is formed of threads of a certain type crossing at right angles, is supremely important because it determines the hang. Heavy threads in the warp and fine in the weft will hang one way but not the other. Some materials will hang better cut on the cross. This concentration on the structure of the material is obviously an essential of constructional needlework and it can be brought home to students by a short course in weaving, *not* with the aim of turning out weavers or even of turning out cloths, but simply to make and study the extreme cases of structural effect and to develop a sense of texture. But it is also necessary for schoolgirls to handle larger lengths of varied cloths to appreciate their feel and hang, their pattern and texture. The beginnings of this study will lie in the use of these lengths I suggest for dramatic work. But it is inspiring to have attractive pieces kept for practice in folding and draping as an introduction to the dressmaking course. A striped material or a corduroy which has been looked at only in the flat presents new and exciting possibilities when seen on the curve, and the angle at which the stripes shall be brought to meet one another in shaping a skirt or covering an armchair is a problem of design which requires an understanding of the structure.

So we have two extremes in the use of both constructive and decorative needlework. Materials and threads can be used as a palette, as elements to be combined, contrasted, composed freely and spontaneously. Or, on the other hand, the rectangular structure of the material can be kept firmly to the fore, shaping fullness by parallel tucks or smocking, limiting decoration to that built on the basis of the thread in lines of stitchery, drawn thread, blackwork and so on. With these two extremes in mind we are in a position to consider the needlework suitable for the growing child from the first handling of cloth and needle to the fully adult craft. If we agree that the chief function of the art and craft of the Primary School is to develop the senses, the emotions and imagination, then our needlework as well as other craft activities must do this. This means that we cannot early insist on any kind of fine, meticulous work because instead of developing sight, the sense chiefly concerned, that destroys it. But this is now fairly generally accepted, though it is hard still for teachers not to encourage eye-strain and inhibit imagination by the indirect means of praising out of proportion the extra careful and laboured work when it does appear. But by now it is generally admitted that younger children should work with large needles on strong stuff with coloured threads. This is good, but what has been the result? Too often harsh yellow calico is laboriously stitched with one type of crudely coloured thread in a series of running, hemming, over-sewing and cross stitches, a set of exercises which is almost as meaningless to the child as writing a senseless string of words in order to learn to write. Usually the first exercise is a small mat or a feeder. What child of eight or nine really wants passionately to make and possess a mat or a feeder, especially of harsh calico which is unpleasant to the touch? In a world where we are daily surrounded with innumerable ugly things, lamp-posts, nineteenth-century school buildings, poster-plastered hoardings, the additional harm done to the æsthetic sensibilities of a child by making him handle, look at and pour his valuable human effort into such deplorably ugly handwork cannot be measured. Anything which the child makes he associates intimately with himself. In this case, feeling of quite another kind may well be involved in that he is excited by making something to take home to mother. When the power and opportunities for making are so limited, anything, however deplorable in taste, can give this pleasure. But the close association of this laudable satisfaction with the lack of interest in or even positive dislike of the materials and the work itself creates an emotional situation too complex for a child of this age. The result is too often a hatred of the whole subject, with the result that the boys drop it with alacrity and the girls never develop in adolescence that interest and gratification in making some at least of their own clothes which can be one of the greatest satisfactions of this period. Furthermore, it is useless for the teacher to say to a class of eights, nines, or tens, 'Imagine you want to join two pieces of cloth together, then this is how you would do it, this is the stitch you would use.' The imagination of the young child is so closely linked to his feelings that if there is no feeling roused, it is a very great effort to *imagine* the situation. The child has to *want* with his feelings to give him the impetus to learn, not just be told he ought to imagine he wants. And here, of course, is the key to all we can say about needlework in the primary years. Needlework regarded as a useful skill should be learned in the closest possible relation to its use. We must wait until the child sees its use and himself wants to join two pieces of material together. Then only will it have any reality. So the *introduction* to the use of the needle can never be to set a whole class down with identical pieces of material and teach them a series of stitches—that stage may come later, though the material need never be all the same colour and the same size. The sort of Hiawatha project described provides just the right opportunity for beginning needlework. The children want Red Indian trousers. Here is sacking which is heavy, strong stuff with the 'grain' of the material pronounced. Here are very large needles and thick brightly coloured threads. The children can be shown how to hold the needle, but at the beginning, any sort of strong firm stitches which will do the job are suitable. If their game is held up for too long while some particular skill is demonstrated the interest in the project will flag and all will be lost. In that less exuberant time towards the end of the day or towards the end of the activity, it may be easier to settle down quietly to making headbands of feathers, or belts or reins of pleasantly coloured braid, and to learn in groups stitches with which to decorate these.

Another approach for boys and girls to needlework may come through making dolls or toys. In one slum school in a large city the small children all made themselves toys out of scraps of cloth, raffia, felt and wooden clothes pegs. These toys were sublimely different from the expensive and delicate playthings given to more favoured children. But they served their purpose better. They were symbols of the roughest construction. A bundle of raffia or straw was tied round the waist and clothed with bright scraps which were tacked on with large obvious stitches. But they were glorified by the most lovely combination of colour and decorated with numerous bows and gaudily painted hair of cotton wool or darning wool. The boys had dolls or animals of a wildly fantastic nature of wood, fur and rag. They could not have been more dearly loved. Their clothes could be quickly ripped off (without parental scolding for destructiveness) and replaced with others newly made for the present game or phantasy. In fact, these children put in a great deal of time in a rough sort of sewing without any urging, and consequently came to look on needlework as a useful and desirable skill. Surely it is supremely important to encourage, and do nothing to discourage, this attitude in the first place. In dressing-up clothes and in toys the emphasis is also on *construction* of however simple a kind. This same type of work at ten and eleven will be more thoughtful and more careful in cutting and sewing. The problems of how to construct a conical witch's hat for a play, of how to make a skirt which is wide at the bottom but not gathered at the top, of how to 'take in' a jacket from the old-clothes bag will all provide experience in shaping. A good deal of work in paper for little plays or school celebrations will give confidence in cutting. The witch's hat, for instance, might be made by quite small children in paper, and decorated collars of stiff paper, simple body armour, and the sort of paper or card masks suggested in the chapter on dramatic work, all provide the disguise suitable for a hastily planned piece of acting, and yet involve real problems in shaping.

In all this the stress has been on construction. The actual needlework involved has not given weight, though in making such things the children will ask for and take the trouble to learn those stitches which they need for their project in hand. All those activities discussed are rather ephemeral so we need not demand any standard of workmanship other than—will it hold together? But before the end of the primary years the children will want to make things of a more permanent nature and these make rather different demands. They must last, therefore they will have to be soundly stitched. They may have to be worn, so the inside must be comfortable. There is no reason why the process of joining together should be invisible, but if it is to be seen constantly it must be pleasant to look at and therefore the stitchery must have a certain regularity and design. This is the time to learn attractive joining and edging stitches which serve both in the construction and the decoration of the first serious pieces of needlework. Then there are certain practical necessary skills such as sewing on buttons and darning a sock which boys as well as girls should have before they leave school. These frankly pedestrian tasks can be made more palatable by the appeal to the growing independence of this age. By the time they enter the Secondary School girls should be ready to make garments and handle a machine. But at present there is apt to be an unfortunate gap between primary and secondary needlework. How is continuity to be achieved?

There are three elements in needlework and embroidery to be given due weight: the construction, the stitchery and the feeling for materials, which includes suitability, texture, combination or contrast of cloths and threads. Almost invariably, stitchery is emphasized during the primary years, construction from block or pattern introduced rather suddenly on entering the secondary, and the feeling for materials is seldom provided for at all. I believe that the sense of needlework as a constructional craft should be developed first and used in play activities as I have been suggesting. This interest in construction can be maintained while the new technique of competent stitchery (which is necessary for garment making) is acquired on simple garments such as mittens, slippers, caps, aprons, or homely furnishings ranging from a tea-cosy to a hot-water-bottle cover. But if this is truly to be a link between the former spontaneous play and the thoughtful designing of the 'teen years, the children must solve the problems of covering a certain size and shape for themselves. If the teacher gives out cut pieces ready to sew, it is, true, a class in sewing, but not in needlework in that broader threefold sense. But children used to making capes, trousers, hats for play, and to forming dolls or toys, will quickly learn to cut and try paper patterns for such simple objects as a coal glove, a pixie hood or cushion cover, and can progress from there. It is still important, as it is at every stage, that each child should *want* to make this particular thing, and so there must be a considerable choice. But as well as the stimulation of the desire for the finished object, we have a very powerful stimulant in the pleasure of the materials themselves. We have to balance up here two factors. The children must have freedom to cut for themselves and freedom to make mistakes. If they are terrified by the threat of wasting material all the time they will be nervous and not only lose all the pleasure of it, but probably cut wrongly out of sheer fright! Yet they must have materials which give positive pleasure in the handling. To achieve both is not impossible. Felt can be obtained in pleasant subtle shades as well as crude and harsh ones, but it is too expensive to be wildly experimental with. But old jerseys and scraps of faced cloth of pleasant colours can be collected and used instead. These warm materials have a great advantage in that the first shape of mitt or slipper can be made from them for practice and then turned inside-out for a warm lining to the real thing which can then be tackled with more confidence. Any pretty scraps of plain or patterned artificial silk or gingham which are not strong enough for the actual structure can be used in the same way for lining a bonnet or bag. All this, too, provides experience in combining materials.

I am convinced that the stimulation of beautiful and interesting materials is our strongest ally. Obviously it would be wasteful and ridiculous to let beginners practise cutting out on lengths of expensive material even though it were financially possible. But the range of materials provided through the normal school channels is deplorably uninspiring. However, the alert teacher just going about her normal life is constantly coming across 'remnants' and odd pieces of pleasing and varied stuff which can be bought inexpensively. The range of available materials *must* be widened in some such way as this. It is not entirely a solution to let the children buy their own because they need a great deal of practice and discussion before they are capable of really appropriate choice, and because if she is paying for it they are dependent on their mother's idea of what is suitable. It is often said that the schools should be training the taste of future consumers. While I think that this is much too narrow a way of looking at the question, it is true that such taste should be a by-product of our craft education. But such a standard of taste, if it is to be other than completely superficial and therefore at the mercy of whims of fashion or mood, can only be built up over years by free choice from a wide range of alternatives. What possibility of choice is there if the whole class is provided with identical material differing only in colour? However many lectures are given on taste or appreciation they cannot develop this *internal* conviction of good taste except by (1) choosing, (2) handling and working on, (3) living over a period with what they have chosen to reassess it.[1]

The feelings for combining materials, the third element in the craft, will be encouraged through making dolls and puppets, but the teacher can stimulate it directly by the provision of exciting materials for use in the needlework lesson. It was suggested that a child's activity might be stimulated by something inside himself pressing for expression, or by something outside himself which holds his attention and gives such physical pleasure that he wants to continue playing with it. Beautiful, varied and unusual materials of all sorts, cloth, cord, tassels, buttons, nets, lace, feathers, spangles, beads, scraps of fur and leather, are all fascinating new experiences to the young child. He wants to look at and handle them, to press them to his cheek, to stroke them. He may be content just to delight in them in this way for a long time, thoroughly absorbing them. But, given time, he will soon begin to group and combine them together. With a large needle the toddler will spend an hour stringing beads of different colours and will learn a great deal of muscular control in the process. A little later the youngster will sew large beads or buttons on to a piece of cloth in a pattern or just haphazardly. This is one of the introductions to embroidery and this combination of the hardness of wood or glass with the softness of cloth is a fundamental experience for later work. But provided with an assortment of all those things and also with paper and paint the primary school child may use gum as well as stitches to combine his elements into a picture, and some delightful pieces have been produced in this way. Since the freeing of the imagination is our chief aim at this age, and since in this quick spontaneous way the child can throw together many

[1] This is not to say that the child should necessarily be given an infinite variety from which to choose in the first place, that, for example, she should be offered velvet, linen, silk, tweed, cotton, muslin, when starting a summer frock. It might be quite a good idea for the teacher to have pieces of all those on the spot and discuss why some are quite unsuitable, and finally narrow down the range to those which are washable, lightweight, opaque, and inexpensive. But while it is necessary to provide a range of suitable stuffs and there should still be a limited area in which the student is allowed to make mistakes of taste—to use inappropriate decoration, to make mistakes in scale of belt, collars, in combination of colours and so on. It is often possible to keep the 'area of freedom', and therefore of possible mistakes, to parts which can later be altered on a garment.

different pictures and so try out and learn about many different combinations, this is to be encouraged.

But it also provides at every age an excellent method of designing. The sense of pattern can be developed along with the sensuous appreciation of the materials of needlework, by building up centre patterns like those discussed in Chapter XII in rick-rack or Russian braid, narrow ribbon, thread, lace, beads. Such a pattern can be planned for a cushion cover, a tea-cosy, a beach bag, and related as it grows to the shape it is to fill. On hessian it might begin with a cut-out shape in felt, and grow outwards and inwards from that. Or such a pattern might be built up entirely of stitches, the design and colour scheme growing with the work.

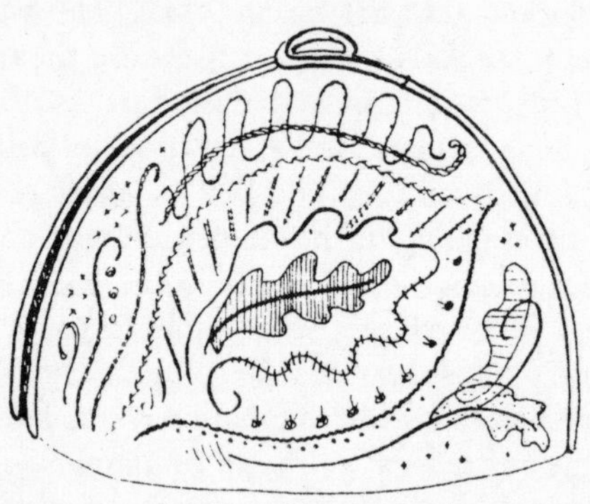

FIG. 55.—A centre pattern developed in embroidery by a girl of 13. Three shapes suggested by leaves were cut in material, the rest was built up from them as she worked in rick-rack braid, cord, thread, buttons, etc.

By the use of loose ribbons, string, buttons, rings and so on, an infinite number of designs can be produced in a few moments, simply by moving them around. Moreover, the scale of the units in relation to one another, which is such an important element of design in any material, can be much more fully understood. Perhaps the buttons chosen are too heavy to be looped with such narrow ribbon? Perhaps the whole of the movable ingredients are too light in scale for hessian and ought to be put on cotton instead? Obviously, spangles are not usually appropriate on crash or common string on silk. Yet this is much more obvious when one is handling the actual material. With slightly older children very lovely effects can be obtained by overlapping layers of net and material or by sewing coloured materials behind transparent ones. Experience in cut paper work will have given practice in combining forms, but it is possible to create original and fascinating designs by combining in groups or patterns the outline shapes of such common things as leaves or shells.

With the younger ones their 'mixed material' pictures or abstracts can be made for the pure fun of doing it—and there is no reason why this same fun should not figure occasionally at older ages. We discussed how scraps of attractive materials can be used in the primary years for making small useful articles such as bonnets, slippers, tea-cosies. Rich scraps from the remnant counter or rag bag can make sewing much more attractive to the adolescent. To see a group of girls poring over a handful of brilliant silks, velvets, corded ribbons, gold and silver braid, picking them up with little screams of delight, or pausing in rapt absorption, is to realize how much they hunger for such pretty things. Small pieces of similar weight will make a stool or cushion cover of formal patchwork, but probably their interest will dictate more personal articles. House slippers can be constructed of many tiny velvet scraps, and evening bags for the more sophisticated, of useless remnants, silks and ribbons. Then there is a whole realm of work in white materials, especially organdie and voiles, which prove a particular delight to girls of this age. It may be questioned whether white organdie is a material suitable for the vicissitudes of school needlework, but in fact the very contrast of its delicacy to the usual school surroundings is such a delightful shock to many girls, and answers such a strong need in themselves to express their growing femininity, that they take particular pains to keep it well. The tea-cosies or tray-cloths or dressing-table sets or collars which they can make from it launder so very well that it is not at all impracticable.

From the time they enter the Secondary School the girls will be using sewing-machines, and organdie provides a delightful alternative to linen or cotton for machine practice. A design can be drawn on paper, and by putting the organdie over and pencilling through, the lines are quickly transferred to the stuff. Then with a coloured thread in the machine the necessary practice in machining is put in, in the pleasantest possible way, and the sampler can be made up into a tray-cloth or toilet-bag. Once facility with the machine has been gained delightful decorative embroideries can be built up in appliqué and fastened down with different coloured threads in an ordinary machine. Whipping or looping the machine stitching with embroidery thread gives richness, or a heavy silk thread can be put in the shuttle, and the work stitched on the wrong side. This type of embroidery is playing about, as it were, with textures on the surface. But it must eventually be related to the structure of the material about which we spoke earlier. This structure is emphasized by materials which are striped or checked in the weave (not those in which the pattern is printed on afterwards). So those materials prove a useful way of keeping the structure in front of the young student. In the primary and early secondary stages, it is interesting and helpful to take, say, striped shirting, or checked gingham, and build patterns on the structure of the material by laying bands of braid or binding along the thread as in the checked apron, or by emphasizing the stripe by adding stitching or braid to it. Plain material can be divided into bands or squares in this way (like a 'grid'), which gives smaller units to work and so holds the interest. Whereas the free type of built-up design emphasizes texture, but may be weak in composition, this structural design always has a sound, firm basis and grows out of the weave of the material. At a later stage designs may be built up on the thread of plain material, using one of the filling stitches, such as laid work, or drawn thread work, or the familiar cross stitch. But since this involves much repetitive work it is not so appropriate for the school years when we want to encourage the creative imagination and open many possibilities which may be explored in later life. I have, however, found that a modified type of this work could be very useful for college students who had only two ideas of embroidery, the flaccid, characterless type of thing indefinitely multiplied in lazy daisy stitch, and the 'embroidery picture' which their drawing was too weak to design adequately. For these, the emphasis on the essential structure of the material, and the discipline of working to the thread and building up on that, had a healthy astringent effect. This type of designing *in* the stitch in regular bands or blocks encouraged those who could not draw by showing them that an original design could be evolved from the materials themselves with a minimum of draughtsmanship.

Embroidery at its height is like a language finely spoken, in which the stitch—like the word—emotionally and intellectually appropriate is chosen and placed to perfection, and the whole conveys an idea worthy of consideration. But this can come only after years of practice in using the vocabulary of stitchery.

Since a relatively small amount of thread and material is used in embroidery it is often possible to use a fine quality. One enterprising teacher [1] spun and vegetable-dyed to a wonderful range of shades enough embroidery wool for her classes. This enhanced their pleasure in the work very much, and gave those girls without the advantage of spinning for themselves opportunity to work with wools of fine quality. Since such small quantities are needed, those who cannot spin might consider buying handspun worsted wool—which has a vitality and variety within the thread not found in the lifelessly regular machine-spun—and dyeing as part of the needlework course. Nothing develops a sensitive response to colours as quickly as experience of dyeing.

It is not my intention to consider here fully the crafts of spinning, dyeing and weaving, since I hope that that is even now being done by those much more fitted than I am to do so. I can only speak of my own pleasure in, and understanding of, wool and cloth, which have grown with a brief experience of them. In its simplest form this is a craft which can be practised with a minimum of equipment. With a piece of bamboo, and a wooden wheel from Woolworths or a clay whorl, children can in half an hour make a spindle costing about sixpence, and a beginning can be made with wool from the hedges and fences till a fleece can be obtained. The substances for vegetable dyes are all around us, but the knowledge and experience of a skilled teacher can enormously reduce the wastage and heartbreak of learning only by experiment. Even the earliest spinning of the children can be knitted up into mittens, caps, and so on. Weaving, although it is comparatively widely practised in schools, needs a radically different approach if it is to provide sensuous, emotional and imaginative experience comparable with the other crafts discussed. Its invigoration would seem to lie in the imaginative use of some of the more delightful machine-spun threads—perhaps artificial silks, fine cottons, or worsted embroidery threads—as warp, along with the children's first spinning as weft. It is in the creation of texture and the excitement of producing new colours by the juxtaposition of coloured threads in the process of weaving, that this craft intrigues. The infinite number of possi-

[1] Miss Broom, of a school near Redhill, Surrey.

bilities to be obtained by simple variations of the check and stripe are a more genuine form of pattern-making than the laborious counting of over and under threads, or the mechanical manipulation of learned 'threadings up' which belong to a much more advanced stage of the craft. This elaboration of technique—as in every other craft—should not be introduced till the student is so at home in his material that he can create *through* the technique. The simplest tabby loom is just a sandpapered box with a good heddle, round which the warp is tied thread by thread so that its pattern is before the eyes all the time. This is more likely to develop sensibility in the early stages, by offering a simple field in which to adventure widely, than are tablets or multi-heddles which stress the technique and in which the pattern is ruined by one mistake.

While limitations of space, and the difficulty of the loom being out of action for others while one warp is on it, make the wide adoption of foot looms in schools impossible, the rhythm of weaving can only be fully appreciated in this way. And the spinner's perfection of co-ordination inducing an almost ecstatic sense of well-being can only be experienced on a wheel. But any experience of wool in the fleece, as of other raw materials, will result in an increased sensibility to all its forms and so to discrimination and pleasure in cloths and their varied uses.

The reprinting of this book makes possible two comments. Forms of weaving intended not for wear but for decorative purposes have been developed (chiefly, so far, in America) on lines originated by Ethel Mairet. Into these are woven not only synthetic fibres, strips of cellophane, etc. but natural and manufactured objects. The conception of a constant width to the weaving is often abandoned in favour of a shaped or many-tailed piece which is a evocation of ancient methods.

The meaning of the term 'embroidery' has been enlarged by contemporary embroiderers (notably my colleague at Goldsmiths' College, Constance Howard), especially through huge collages often on tie-dyed backgrounds. These techniques have been carried by our students into schools, freeing and deepening the whole field.

CHAPTER FOURTEEN

THE ADOLESCENT GIRL AND HER CLOTHES

While some girls will find their greatest satisfaction in purely decorative embroidery, the greater part of school needlework will be the making of useful garments and furnishings. But an enthusiasm for stitches and materials will rightly overflow into a desire to decorate these. Since dressmaking is such an important part of school needlework, I want next to consider the whole question of the girl and her clothes.

While I think it is an excellent thing that boys in the primary years should learn simple stitchery, needlework is a traditional feminine craft in this country and continues to be practised mostly by the women. We must admit that the average housewife uses her needle chiefly on the family mending, but most women, from reasons of economy if nothing else, make or remake some of their own or their children's clothes. Since a considerable time is perforce spent in needlework, it is surely a very great pity that needlework should not be seen as an art and yield its own fund of inspiration and satisfaction. Needlework is usually taught in schools as a useful skill. That is but one half or less of its contribution to our lives. Making clothes and furnishings can be tremendously satisfying to the whole woman, not just necessary to the busy housewife. Women are inevitably (though there is a healthy sharing of this responsibility in these days) the chief homemakers, and the satisfaction of gathering together and keeping in condition the furniture of the home is enhanced out of all recognition if this is seen as *creating*. The young couple setting up house, or the bachelor man or woman settling into a home, must take an area of space enclosed by four walls, fill it with isolated pieces of furniture and textiles mostly mass-produced, or picked up from many different sources, must adapt and arrange them and bind the whole together into a unity of a peculiarly personal nature.

Now if they see this as an opportunity for creating, both in their *selection* and in their *adaptation* (distempering walls, covering furniture, etc.), and in their own additions (cushions, curtains or rugs they have made, carpentry, garden furniture and so on), it will take on the nature of an exciting adventure in expressing their individual and chosen way of life.

The whole of our art and craft education should be a training in an honest and thoughtful search for such a mode of individual expression. More perhaps than we allow can be done to encourage such an attitude in the adolescent at school. An account of one such experiment will be given in the chapter on environment. But the parallel self-expression through dress is more completely within the power of the individual and therefore gives greater scope. But the opportunities to make use of this in the needlework lesson are lamentably thrown away. In our civilization, for reasons explained in that fascinating book *The Psychology of Clothes*,[1] manifest interest in their dress is largely confined to women. And with an expression of regret for the lack of convenience, pleasing form and interesting colour in the vast majority of men's clothes, I shall confine myself to a discussion of the importance of women's dress in craft education.

How often do we hear teachers—too often women—deplore the fact that their adolescent girls spend so much time in thinking of their clothes and their hair styles! Instead we should be profoundly thankful that those girls have a real enthusiasm for something, not only harmless, not only natural, but so completely right for their age. Let us turn back and see again what are the transitions the adolescent has to make in growing up, what are the problems which those young people are consciously or unconsciously concerned with. They must (1) adjust to their own physical growth and development, (2) achieve emancipation from the family and attain emotional independence, (3) accent their own sex rôle and adjust wholesomely to the opposite sex, (4) find economic independence and a suitable vocation, and (5) develop their own philosophy. When we reflect, it becomes apparent that this overpowering interest in clothes and in her personal appearance is an exaggerated concentration on the first and the third of these because of the frustrations encountered in other ways. It is a very rare thing for the adolescent at school to develop a coherent

[1] F. J. Flugel, *The Psychology of Clothes.*

philosophy, the most mature and demanding of these adjustments. It is impossible for him or her to attain economic independence and enter a vocation while supported by parents or the State. And this economic dependence reverberates on the problem of clothes and appearance. It is very difficult to achieve emotional independence from parents while still supported by them, but it must be striven after. It seems to be human nature for parents to wish to keep their children as children for as long as possible.

Now, for an adolescent girl, clothes become a kind of symbol for the adulthood she strives towards. For the parent they are one department of a daughter's life in which independence *can* be encouraged without the natural concern felt about its other manifestations—the wish to stay out late, to drive a motor-bike or car, to go independent holidays. Since in so many departments of our complex life the parent, along with other authorities like the school, must curb the desire for real independence, why not welcome this one, the matter of independence in clothes, which cannot do harm? What the adolescent needs most is to feel that he or she is achieving some real independence, is getting some compensation (the truly adult compensations seem so far away at fourteen!) for leaving the comparative irresponsibility of childhood. Since, for reasons into which we must go deeper, the adolescent girl's emotions are closely bound up with her clothes, here is the opportunity to give her a sense of becoming grown up, of showing that we give her the right of all adults to make her own choices and to live with her own mistakes.

But of course clothes are most closely associated with the other two adjustments, to physical development, and towards acceptance of the appropriate sex rôle. The disturbing bodily changes cannot be ignored. But very often we *do* try to ignore them, not simply by not talking about them, but by continuing to dress girls in clothes and particularly uniforms appropriate to the unformed pre-adolescent figure. It would make acceptance of these bodily changes easier if we greeted puberty with some dignified ceremony or new costume, such as has been the custom in primitive and peasant communities, and has been adopted into modern education in such schools as Miss Shaw's in Uganda.[1] But the very least we can do is to recognize outwardly these changes by encouraging the girl to dress according to her forming figure and

[1] Described in *God's Candlelights*, by Mabel Shaw.

so give her the satisfaction of her growing adulthood being recognized and accepted.

But clothing is primarily a form of decoration, as Professor Flugel has shown. (If this proves difficult to believe, I can only recommend his opening chapters as showing that warmth and modesty are less important factors.) It is a form of decoration which, during the sexually virile years at least, if not all our life, has strong associations with sex. We must recognize this as an important (but not the only important) factor if we are to help the adolescent girl. Very often it is at first an unconscious drive, and the interest in dress and appearance develops before a conscious wish to interest boys has appeared. Now since, to the schoolgirl, direct sexual stimulation and satisfaction are far ahead, there are years during which sexual energy must find other channels if intense frustration is not to be experienced. Part of this will be spent in flirtation, which is the normal prelude and preparatory period to choosing a mate, and much of it is most suitably directed into one of its own normal channels, that is, self-decoration. The more other channels are blocked, the more likely is a greater amount of sexual energy to be used here—out of all proportion, we may be tempted to feel. But if we appreciate the strains and the unnatural conditions which our civilization imposes on the adolescent, we shall be sympathetic and welcome this interest which can be such a source of delight to us with whom she lives, and such a satisfaction to the girl herself.

With the infant and the primary school child we have by now accepted the educational tenet that we should start from the *child's* interest. But strangely enough we have too often neglected this at the adolescent stage. Perhaps this is because the more intellectual children come, at that age, to share the interests of us adults and so we can genuinely give our own enthusiasms free rein and count on them to follow and derive real benefit from the study of history or languages or mathematics or whatever we want to teach. But what of the children who don't want to learn a language, who have to be driven to history or mathematics? Surely we are neglecting the greatest ally we have—their own interests. If their interests are in relationships with the opposite sex, or in clothes or in babies, we cannot *blame* them, any more than we can blame ourselves for not being more interested in higher mathematics or the more abstruse philosophies. We can only start from their interests, and lead them outwards. And an extraordinary amount of education can spring from the subjects of clothes or of babies! Why should arithmetic, history and biology, geography and social studies not stem out from that as well as from any other point?

But I am particularly concerned with art and craft. If we accept that this interest in clothes and in personal appearance is of absorbing interest to adolescent girls, and that that is not merely quite natural but fundamentally *right*, then we can consider its place in our scheme of things. Obviously the first essential is to imply in all our teaching, in ordinary conversation, and in the provision of subjects in craft, that such an interest is *good*. I am sure that the disproportionate interest and attention, the adulation of American magazines and the imitation of film star styles, springs largely from the frustration of this perfectly natural aspect of the sexual instinct. That an enlightened encouragement of discussion and experiment does, *in time*, do away with the wilder extravagances I am convinced by experience. It does take time and it does mean leaving that 'area of freedom' to go wrong. Since it is much more a question of the prevailing attitude or atmosphere, the whole staff, but especially those who teach art and needlework, must co-operate if it is to be successful.

School uniform is defended on the grounds that it effaces the social distinctions. Even though this were true, which is doubtful, I am not sure that it would compensate for the harm done in other ways. During the 'gang age', which may last till fourteen or so, the overwhelming need is to be like others, and then uniform may serve a useful purpose, and may in fact be adopted by children who are left free. But when the individual becomes more conscious of himself as a unique person—and surely this is a process we wish to encourage in a democratic country—he or she must have personal freedom to express that feeling. To keep girls in identical uniform when they have fortunately outgrown the need for it is to insult them and retard their development. And to insist that fully developed young women of seventeen or eighteen wear gym frocks above their knees may be to make them self-conscious and embarrassed about their physical appearance for years. We simply must admit to ourselves that there is no colour, and far less any shape of garment, which will suit *all* girls from eleven to eighteen.

And uniform can penalize unfairly the poorer children (whom it is supposedly designed to protect) because they may, like myself in adolescence, be unable to afford to buy another set of clothes, since they grow out of them so fast, and therefore be condemned to spend week-ends and holidays in the hated uniform. The result may well be a period of wild unbalanced experimentation with unsuitable clothes, once economic independence is finally reached.

But all the justifications of uniform on the grounds of levelling can be met just as well by a form of dress which, while *equal*, is not entirely *uniform*. As an intermediate step, why, for instance, not adopt a style of blouse to be worn with a gym slip or skirt of a chosen material but of any shape, which can then be adapted to the many varieties of changing figure? Or why not have a range of chosen materials in several colours from which dresses or blouses can be made to a shape appropriate to the wearer? It will certainly be uphill work for the craft teacher trying to encourage a dress sense in girls who are compelled to wear an ugly and inappropriate costume all day, but even in those circumstances something can be done. A personal example from Milltown may be the best explanation, because though all this happened twelve years ago, it still occurs to-day. My form of thirteen- to fourteen-year-olds had suddenly taken to fantastic hair styles, which frequently tumbled down and necessitated lengthy withdrawals to the cloakroom. Often an American fashion magazine would be handed to me with a strong word by another mistress who had confiscated it in mathematics or French. Lipsticks were found lurking in desks. A secret magazine was handed round which, when shamefacedly produced, turned out to be nothing worse than '3 B's Beauty Club Magazine' with sketches of elongated females parading in exotic clothes. Here was an open field for the art teacher—not an opportunity to say 'These figures are not very good, we shall do figure drawing for the next few lessons', but to sponsor a real 'fashion club', to bring all this subterranean energy and activity above board. We decided together that instead of lurking hidden in desks the club magazine should take the form of sheets on the form notice-board. Those could be offered by anyone who wanted to air her ideas on personal appearance or clothes, and could take the form of writing or sketches. Tables of morning exercises, new hair washes, and a lively correspondence column also figured there. The lipsticks were brought out to air and compared for colour and perfume. In quick sketches we tried out the effect of different shades with red, fair and dark hair, and in relation to different eyes and different clothes. It is not to be supposed that weeks of school-time were spent in discussing lipsticks. Some twenty minutes or so with a class established the fact that when an interest in make-up was already there, it would be welcomed but promptly subjected to the friendly criticism which went on in all art lessons. Since these were very sensible northern children they soon suggested that hair styles, extravagant bows and fancy clasps were perhaps getting rather out of hand. So someone suggested that anyone in the form who came with a new hair style must be prepared to parade it for the frank criticism of her classmates. The exhibitionists had to be curbed and the shy ones encouraged, but when all this became an established thing I had to do very little about it. Given direction it had its own impetus to go on. But it did give a new force and emphasis to a scheme of fourth form art and craft which I had introduced. By the fourth form (that is, the fourteen- to fifteen-year-olds), almost every girl was interested in clothes and houses, so this could be undertaken as a form activity. The first term was devoted entirely to painting from imagination or observation subjects related to those interests, and any girl who preferred to carry on with that for the rest of the year could do so, but most elected to join in the 'homes and clothes' course. One term was spent entirely on dress, one on houses, and from then on this interest found outlets in many other types of work, needlework, fabric printing, studies of architecture and so on.

First every girl made a 'model' of herself cut out in plywood, or constructed in the form of a stockinette doll, roughly to her own proportions—or a little nearer the ideal. This was then provided with hair (painted, or sewn on with wool, artificial hair or silk) and complexion and eyes to match her prototype. Then we discussed underwear. It may seem astonishing but it had not come within the experience of some of these girls that this may be all to match or that it may have any relation in shape, type and colour to what goes on top. Then we planned—in sketches—a winter or a summer wardrobe within a certain cost. One garment from this was chosen to be constructed on the doll, and our school rag bag was reinforced by all the scraps which could be collected from home. Girls who were usually apathetic in school and those who were apt to be the most difficult threw themselves into this along with the others with considerable abandon. These dolls or models accompanied their owners round in school cases and were affectionately addressed by their names. No time was lost. The morning after I had explained how we would dress them the next week, I was met with a crowd of models that had been completely dressed overnight, to the detriment of set homework, I suspect. As anyone who knows adolescent girls may imagine, they turned out, almost without exception, in glamorous evening dresses, usually backless, sometimes strapless, tight-waisted and very low. Since this was an expression of a personal ideal which was denied expression in reality, through economy, through parental and school control, it obviously served a therapeutic purpose and so it was encouraged. For the next item in the wardrobe a few chose to make a new model, but more often the same one was undressed and dressed again. My mild suggestion that since she was now well set up for the evening it might be a good idea to have some day wear was ignored. Next week a new crop of glamorous dresses appeared—complete with sequins, ostrich feathers, evening cloaks. All these dresses showed the haunting self-ideal which we all need to hold before us, and which is adapted gradually in the process of growing up. These gawky girls, whose regular wear, day in day out, was navy gym slips and black wool stockings, who often fell noisily over one another up and down stairs, who did not know what to do with their hands and were probably tongue-tied as yet in the presence of their boy friends, saw themselves as suave, sophisticated worldly women, always in command of the situation. As teachers, our job is to close the gap, to give reality to the ideal by bringing it within their power and their limitations, and to help them towards poise, dignity and ease in the world by giving them self-confidence, courage and powers of expression.

It must be made clear that these models were not dressed with small replicas of garments which would take off and on. That would have been much more difficult and the technique of constructing miniature fastenings and setting-in sleeves would have been so difficult as to inhibit their flow of ideas and feelings. The purpose was quite different. It was primarily to make them *think* about clothes, not just moon over them, to help them to appreciate textures and colours, to make them feel that here was a realm of creation in which they could, in fact must, all operate. Even the most ridiculous evening frocks were accorded the respect of our serious attention and discussion. (The models used to be slipped into a groove in the window-sills, and stand there all day inviting comment and criticism, and many a girl would keep glancing over at her model, pondering on whether she really *did* suit that vivid colour after all?) The most interesting thing to me was, that having made two or three evening frocks, almost every girl then started on more practical wear, perhaps an afternoon frock or a frivolous summer frock first, and then a tweed suit or coat more appropriate to our northern climate.

Not all the garments in the outfits were worked out on the model. Some were sketched in paint and a piece of the material gummed by one edge to the sheet (to encourage handling it). Draping lengths of fabric as described later is more valuable and more realistic, and now I keep various lengths of several fabrics for this purpose, these can be pinned into place. After a discussion of style and suitability of accessories, and the study of many examples in advertisements, shoes and gloves were selected, with scarf, handbag and so on. Scraps of the actual leather, suède or stuff were attached. This is of far greater value than painting or describing, since the textures were handled and appreciated in actuality. Then the whole sheet was grouped pleasantly with some sketches and a description of the way in which the garment was to be constructed. At first I insisted on this text being in script lettering, but I gave that up and preferred their own best handwriting arranged in blocks or bands to connect up the various items visually, and present a unified sheet. These notes were often in the first person and might begin 'My winter coat will be green . . .' or 'I shall have a summer dress of flame and pale blue striped rayon, and I shall make it by gathering a full skirt into a darted bodice . . .' When one or two of these sheets had been prepared, with intermittent discussions of cost, washability, wearing qualities, we were beginning to think on really practical terms. That is not to say that these girls would never choose a silly or inappropriate garment when they did buy or make clothes. But a beginning had been made. Some of the garments they did actually work out in the needlework class, and obviously this is the most satisfying thing to do. But I am sure that we need to encourage the making of more interesting, more personal and more daringly individual clothes in needlework. And we need to help girls to see their physical appearance, both the permanent, unalterable structure and the alterable details such as hair, as an outward and visible expression of *them*, as unique and valuable human individuals.

Because of its biological significance, fashion will always, I suppose, play a part in women's clothes in any free society, but we need to help girls to develop a *criterion* by which to choose clothes, which has more permanence and more validity than fashion or novelty alone. It is amazing how so many of those who paint beautiful pictures do not see that clothes rely to a great extent on the same basis of pleasing proportions, combination of colours and contrast of textures. For instance the length of the skirt determines very largely whether we can have a contrasting blouse or not, since equal areas of contrasting colours tend to be disturbing. The type of sleeves must be closely related to the neckline, which is the connecting link between the two arms. But apart from those permanent and fundamental factors, clothes must be a personal expression and so the suit bought along with all its accessories, however expensive, will not serve because it is so impersonal. Even if many of our girls prefer, in these days of reasonably priced manufactured garments, to spend their energy in other ways than sewing they can be helped to select the ready-made which is both appropriate to the use they envisage and suited to their own personality. (In fact the selection may help to build up and reinforce the rather shaky conception of that personality.) Then they can be encouraged to find the hat, the blouse, the gloves, the ornaments which seem just right to them and so, even out of mass-produced units, make an individual whole.

CHAPTER FIFTEEN

CRAFT AND DRAMA

THERE are certain school activities in which art and craft may function as part of a larger whole, such as producing a play, holding a pageant, or decorating the school for a party or festival. It is perhaps a pity that we do not make more use of festivals in education, since they produce more sense of community than uniforms and badges, and since we, the common people of this country, lack nowadays dignified and seemly forms in which to express our sense of community. Festivals are the most powerful way of handing on to children those traditions we cherish because ritual and ceremony make an appeal at the subconscious level and can make a lasting impression before reason has developed sufficiently to grasp that complex of ingredients which make up our culture. The feasts of the Church and the pagan festivals, such as May Day, Hallowe'en and Hogmanay, used to serve this purpose of gathering the people together from time to time to participate jointly in a ceremony embodying their tradition. Nativity plays and Christmas trees we still have, but schools might well celebrate May Day as an occasion to greet summer by specially decorating the school with flowers, Hallowe'en as a time to remember the pagan customs of our forbears and Harvest Festival as a ceremony to present fruit and flowers for orphanage or hospital.

All the arts could play their part at such times, just as when we produce a play art and craft find a new function within the complex whole. But in all these, we are concerned not so much with the individual expression as with the interpretation of an idea already existing, and all must conspire towards one unified effect. Such co-operation may reach a pitch where it is a creative fusion of every art involved, acting, speaking, movement, costumes and staging all contributing to the whole experience. The production of a play in such a spirit—whether it be the spontaneous eruption in thrown-on garments of the primary years or the carefully conceived and rehearsed production of adults—does provide a unified form of education.

With infants and young juniors this may take the form of playing out an experience or a story, or of improvising on a suggested incident. Another approach is that of starting from characters chosen by the children themselves, perhaps by suggesting that they become 'the person you would like to be if you were not yourself'. Then they can be left to meet and talk as those characters and let the little scene grow out of the natural reaction of one child's masquerade to that of another. All this may grow out of movement study as it is now practised in many schools, and may well be related to mime or dance, but the main point to make is that it is the spontaneity and unselfconsciousness of these childish concerns that are their justification and their joy. Therefore no elaborate preparation in the way of words or setting is necessary or desirable. Small children act as naturally as they move or paint, and they must not be encouraged early to be conscious of an audience. All those present should be willing to take part in the ceremony, the Nativity drama or whatever it may be. Children's playing is for themselves or one another, and so the orientation of it should be inwards towards the centre of a group, not artificially in one direction towards an audience. Therefore they should never play on a stage, but preferably in a large room where the centre and the corners serve as little worlds, individual children withdrawing into a corner to play some quieter drama or to rest, and coming out again to join in the main events when those interest them.[1]

These little children are not acting consciously in our sense of the word. They are *living* the part as they understand it, and criticism has no meaning for them. When they begin consciously to portray feelings without being completely absorbed in them, then they begin to act. From that time on they can be helped, through acting, as in clay work and painting, to develop that sensitive imagination which feels for and with others. They can be encouraged to describe by the tone of voice, the stance and gait the feelings assumed, just as the painted or clay figure takes on

[1] Since writing this I find it all much better and more thoughtfully described in A. R. Stone's *Story of a School*, Ministry of Education Pamphlet.

at this age more individuality and becomes a particular person in a particular mood, sad, or tired, or jumping with joy.

Towards the end of the primary years and the early secondary, a little play performed to friends can be a real group effort. By that time most of the children will be capable not only of the spontaneous acting and speech, but of closer co-operation and of a more sustained interest which will last through lengthier preparations. It is wisest to let each child build up his own idea of the character he is playing, making up his own words and costume. (The words need never be written down and will probably come out a little differently each time.) At this age, each child will take more interest in making a costume to reflect the character which he himself is acting, so this method is preferable to setting some of the group to be the actors and others to do the costumes for them. There is an infinite choice of subjects. Some are as near at hand as the familiar characters who live in a street, the policeman, an old woman with her cat, the quarrelling neighbours, the young man with a motor-bike, the girls who powder their noses. The amount of careful observation and candid comment evinced can be amazing. Or the subject may be more remote, a historical event or a fantastic scene. Once in a while, a variant of the old morality play with allegorical characters will provoke thought, and place the qualities impersonated—Pride, Jealousy, Anger, Fear—at an objective distance. It will also provide an opportunity for discussing the relation of colours and emotions, and of rhythms and movements which are expressive.

At a later stage the adolescent is prepared to accept his contribution as only a facet of the whole, and to submit to the producer as to the conductor of an orchestra. Now we can have more specialization, and while it is good for everyone to act, some will prefer to be responsible for lights or scenery or costumes or make-up, and make their contribution in that way. A few children of literary bent will find their art and craft centring round this interest in theatre. They may well embark on a sustained course involving puppets and model theatres of various kinds from the little concertina paper theatre which folds up in a folio, to the card or wood structure with wings and drops. But I would plead for this to be approached in the spirit of learning about the living theatre and its possibilities. To use a model theatre as an end in itself is to enjoy a pleasant toy. But to use it as a means to gain knowledge about effects which repeatedly contribute to the class or school production is to be involved in something much more rewarding. 'Designing for the theatre' only on paper or with models is too unreal and too limited. The adolescent is ready for something more responsible and finally satisfying. I am not envisaging this as a vocational course, a preliminary to stage designing —though an occasional student may be inspired to make it a life's work—but rather the practice of a craft in the sphere where the interest of the student is already aroused.

After such a training, all stage productions seen for the rest of one's life will be enjoyed with a sharpened and heightened appreciation. But in such a complex art as this, standards and values will not come with one or two lessons. Few schools will be able to see enough good productions to set up a criterion. If we are concerned in the Secondary School with the enjoyment of the visual arts in later life, we might do well to turn our attention to the film. Those schools which have time to do both, or where the enthusiasm of the teacher inclines him strongly to the stage, will be fortunate exceptions. We must admit that for most of our scholars the ubiquitous film will be the form of entertainment at which they spend most of their leisure time. It will also be for many of them their only form of continuing contact with any art. On the average each will probably see a dozen films for one book read, and six dozen for one visit to a picture gallery or a concert. Many of the better films eventually reach even the smaller towns, and the number and standard of these will only rise, under the present economic conditions of production, as there is a demand for them. Under these circumstances, it is extraordinary that we have almost completely neglected film criticism in schools, where literary, musical and art criticism are accepted without question. We do not have to urge our pupils to this employment. We do not even have to ask for that most precious commodity, school time, to see the films which will form the material for our discussion, since the children will probably be seeing them as part of their normal life outside school. But this fact has a much more important side than that of mere time-table planning. It means that the 'appreciation' which is encouraged is appreciation of something which the children regard as a normal facet of adult life and not a school 'subject'. I hope the whole tenor of this book will make it clear that I do not advocate adding odd bits and pieces of subjects to the already overloaded time-table. I endorse most heartily the opinion put forward by Newsome [1] that it is better to teach a few subjects well. But here is a 'subject' which, by virtue of the fact that it is already attended regularly out of school, is in a peculiar position. Less than one hour a week at the upper end of the Secondary School devoted to a study of films will not interfere with their enjoyment out of school and will give, at the very least, an awareness of film as something more than mere passive entertainment. Whether this is tackled by the English department or the art department or anyone on the staff with a particular interest in film does not matter. Tackled it should be. Where a projector is available, films can be given several showings and the successive impressions considered. Does it perhaps hold more than could be grasped on a first seeing? Or films can be stopped anywhere on the run and analysed part by part. When one shot is obviously intended to recall a former one as a comment on the unfolding story, the two can be frozen and compared to discover their visual affinity. Even when a projector is not available a great deal can be done by discussing the comments of reliable critics and comparing them with the group's own reactions to the film. A notice-board entitled 'What's on' for which the children write their own criticisms can be a great source of interest. A discussion group will at least stimulate a positive critical attitude rather than an unthinking acceptance of what the local cinema chooses to present.

To return to the contribution of crafts to the school play, we may say that this will most frequently consist of costumes and accessories. Every school, indeed every form, should have a dressing-up box, added to by contributions from the children's homes and begged from friends and neighbours. Such costumes will suggest to the children certain characters for their spontaneous dramas because the associations with clothes are very strong. But as well as dresses and cloaks and hats which have already some clearly defined suggestion of their own, it is a good idea to have a number of lengths of material of various colours which can be turned to many uses. When we adopted this idea during the war the only stuff obtainable was dyed hessian, of which we had a dozen squares and a dozen three-yard lengths. The material was stiff enough to stand repeated use without crumpling, and the subtle colours went with one another in almost any combination

[1] J. Newsome, *Education of Girls*, London, 1947.

because of the underlying bond of the natural hessian. These were folded in a box after use and served the whole school from babies to seniors. When a Roman scene was to be played in a Latin lesson two short pieces hung from the shoulders made a soldier's tunic or one long piece a toga. The squares were turned into head-scarves for peasants or mediæval serfs, into shawls for old ladies or cummerbunds for brigands. They proved very convenient in that they were donned and doffed so quickly, and were a real contribution to the art of the school in that their simplicity in colour and draping were a constant lesson in combining simple units into pleasing wholes. They also served as an introduction to the symbolic use of stage costume. These pieces were of course never cut or sewn together but simply folded, plaited, or gathered into an elastic round the waist, or draped with a large clasp. We could only obtain hessian at that time, but a softer material would be more suitable for most uses. Small children will find these and the

Fig. 56.—The use of squares and lengths of unhemmed hessian, quickly put on and off, for impromptu class-room drama.

box of assorted costumes, along with the class-room and garden furniture, flowers and branches, all that is necessary. For special occasions such as a nativity drama or a May Day or harvest ceremony, a little more preparation may be called for, and they may want to make wings for angels, or shields and axes for battle scenes, but since spontaneity is the keynote of their playing, they must not be allowed to grow tired of the preparations before they get to the real thing. If the making of rough costumes, such as the Hiawatha trousers, has been tackled from time to time in the course of activity lessons, the beginnings of needlework will be closely linked with garment-making as I suggest in the needlework chapter. Through the making and wearing of such hastily constructed costumes the children are acquiring much useful knowledge about the evocative qualities of colour, about the behaviour of different materials, and about decorative effects (as for instance how the use of patterned materials together gives an exciting and disturbing effect, but too many will cancel one another out and result in confusion). Potato or lino printing may be called in to decorate the costumes. Patterns in house-painter's paint on hessian or sacking will give a rich texture, or cut-outs of velvet or plush may be stuck or boldly stitched on.

Gradually it emerges that there are three levels on which the costumes have to interpret a drama. Each has to express the individual character—in conjunction with visage and make-up. We must know something about him before he opens his mouth. Then it may evoke his mood (which, while the character remains constant, may change in different acts). In addition it must bear a visual relationship which we can easily grasp, to the others of his class or type in the play. The class to be indicated may be social class, as where all noblemen wear cloaks, all peasants jerkins. Or the characters may fall into another grouping to be accented by dress, such as men and immortals. And since such groups will probably stand and move together on the stage, the colours, too, must blend together and express the distinction between such groups—in this case an obvious suggestion would be lustrous colours for the noblemen, and natural earthly colours for the peasants. But thirdly, individuals and groups are essentially components within the whole play, which must have a unity of conception, that is, the whole—costumes, furniture, scenery—must be all realistic, or all fantastic, or all reduced to a mere suggestion as in the Chinese plays, where imagination supplies the substance.

In schools, we are usually working with whatever costumes and scraps we can lay our hands on, but with this ideal in mind there is a good deal we can do. We learn from watching young children at their own little dramas that to them costume is a symbol, not a realistic representation. A crown and a cloak will serve to indicate a king as well as a complete garb. A peaked cap and sack announce the postman and a black face and brush the sweep. It is usually the adult who strives for a degree of realism in costume which the children who grasp essentials would never demand. But if about twelve to fifteen they become infected with a desire for professionally complete costumes which are outside their scope, the choice of a different type of play, and materials which suggest a more formal treatment (such as stiff paper costumes), will direct their energies into channels where there is more hope of achievement.

Fig. 57.—A brass door-knocker and a carved wooden bench-end of a bearded man, both sketched in the local church, suggest a decorative treatment for masks.

Since we are chiefly concerned with the visual aspects of the production we have to consider another property—the decorative mask. The fantastic has a peculiar fascination for humanity of all times and all ages. It is an absolutely necessary relaxation from the serious business of life for a while—hence those old ceremonies of the jester's reign and saturnalia when everything goes topsy-turvy and folly is supreme. But as well as this general attraction of the fantastic, the mocking of adults and adult practices has a special attraction for those who, while no longer children in their own eyes, are still denied the status of adults. The normal child of ten who is constantly under the thumb of his elders, claims a power over adults by mocking them. While much of the play of this age is a serious imitation of adult activities, when a mask is put on there seems to be a freeing from social inhibitions (this is true even of the change of atmosphere with the donning of paper hats at an adult party), and so we often get mockery of the funnier and

FIG. 58.—Simple masks made from two pieces of pliant card, fastened together at the tip, and with cut eye-holes. They fit to the sides of the face and tie behind. They were inspired by native carvings.

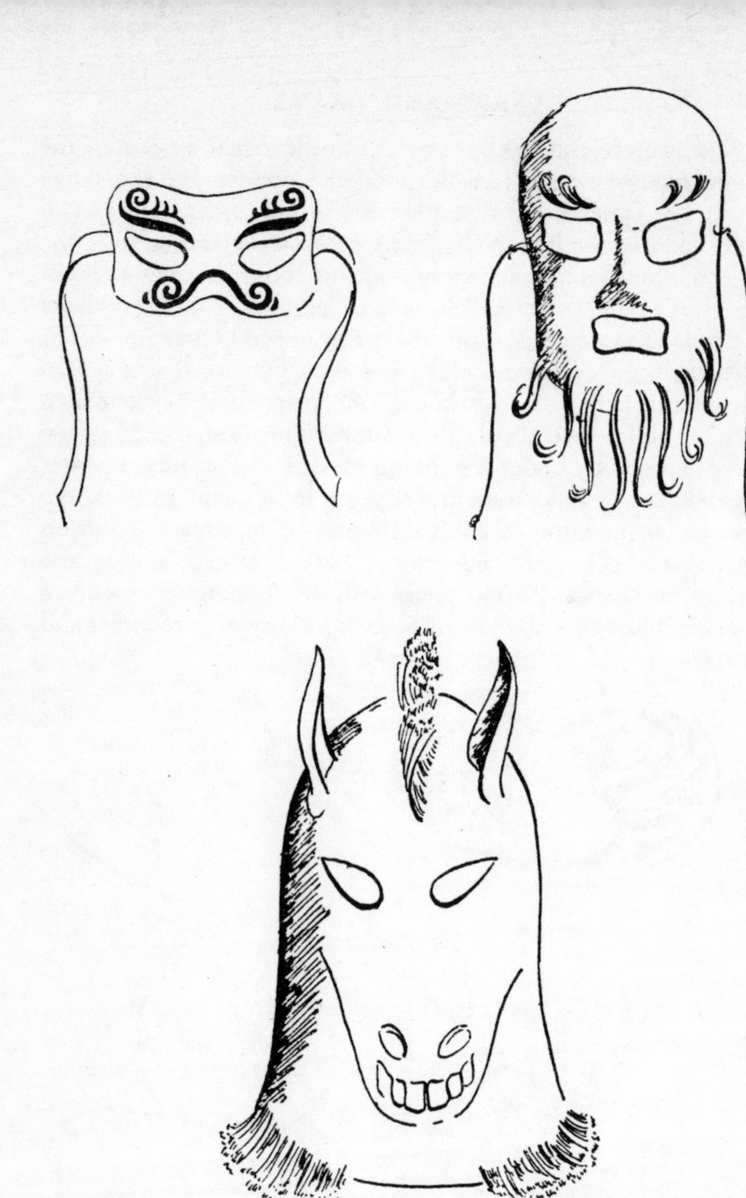

Fig. 59.—(I) Mask for eyes only, leaving lower face free for singing. (II) Whole face mask with untwined rope for beard. (III) Whole head mask, shaped over bowl and basket.

sillier aspects of the envied state. In this relieving of tension, and in giving the personality an alibi to hide behind, masks serve a useful function. If one wants to be wild and shriek and do war dances in a way one is never allowed to do at home, the adoption of a Zulu or Dyak war mask will make it right and logical to do so. It is as though the child felt safe because he cannot be blamed for the behaviour of the mask which has taken possession. But the Zulu shrieks, the unrestrained behaviour of Gluttony or Envy in the morality play, would not emerge if a desire for it were not present already in the child. The subconscious selves, which are suppressed and hidden away in the process of adopting civilized behaviour and becoming social beings, take such an opportunity to poke their heads up. We all have to become social civilized beings in time, but it is quite salutary to relieve the strain of the process occasionally with a burst of such freedom.

The making of such masks provides a complete release from representational work. They can be made simply as individual masks, or better still, to play their part in either an impromptu drama or in a full-scale production. The face is usually modelled flat on a board out of plasticine or clay. After smearing on a thin coating of Vaseline, strips of tissue paper soaked in flour paste are laid all over about six layers thick. This method gives the best detail but is laborious. A stronger substance can be obtained in less time by soaking strips of cloth in Alabastine and pressing those on to the shaped face. Helmet masks to go over the whole head (such as those for the donkey in *Midsummer Night's Dream*) can be formed over a waste-paper basket turned upside-down with a basin on top. Witty and ingenious masks of paper sculpture can be made by older children for a more sophisticated production. Very small children are often frightened by masks. Hats, turbans, crowns, witches' hats, which suggest a character without obscuring the well-known face beneath, are more suitable for them.

One craft which embodies drama is puppetry. This craft has an intermittent courtly history from Greek times to the Commedia dell'Arte, and survived periods of partial eclipse in humbler forms such as 'Punch and Judy'. It has proved very popular in schools, and there are so many excellent books on the technique of different types of puppets that I need not speak of that here, but will confine myself to considering the educational value of this activity.

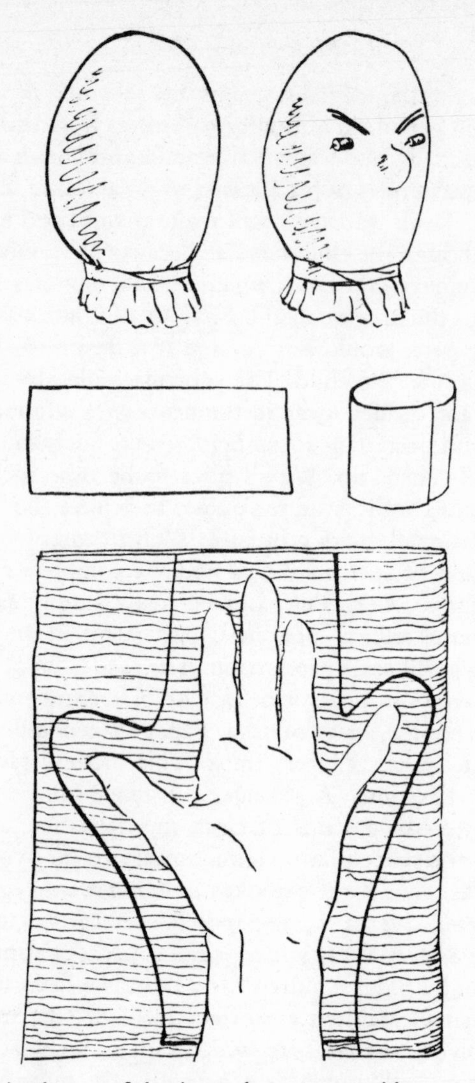

Fig. 60.—A simple way of shaping a glove puppet with young children. The head is a stuffed stocking toe, with a bead inside for a nose and stitched or painted eyes. This is tucked inside a stiff neck made of a strip of post-card bent to encircle the three middle fingers and stitched roughly to resemble a napkin ring. The foundation glove (to which many different clothes can later be attached) is made by drawing round nearly one inch away from the outstretched hand, on a double piece of material. This is stitched up and on to the card circle, outside it and near the top. Or it may be stitched to the base of the head where that protrudes over the neck-piece.

FIG. 61.—Two Javanese puppets which are representative of the long and important tradition of such rod puppets.

We have to decide which of the three aspects of puppetry we shall stress—the drama, including acting and speaking; the production, that is, the whole conception of the play to be put over and the scenery, lighting, costumes used to present that; or the actual making and dressing of the puppets. I am convinced that the greatest educational value of puppets is in their dramatic possibilities, and that if we stress the technique of making them, or tackle a type of puppet which is difficult for the children to construct, we are missing a great opportunity. A puppet which looks in the hand beautifully and carefully constructed may not be nearly so effective on the stage as a simpler one, and will not perform its rôle for the child any better. That rôle is to supply a personification with which he can identify himself in different moods and through whom he can play out his feelings. We have to be clear that this *educational* function is different in intention from that of the professional puppet shows which sometimes visit schools. Their pride is often in the marvellous skill with which the dolls are constructed and manipulated. But this skill is only of value when it is directed to the presentation of something supremely worth while as entertainment or serious drama. At the upper end of the Secondary School we may reach this stage where the production is regarded as a work of art itself and every facet of it, making, manipulation, lighting, *décor*, claims good workmanship for this higher purpose. But even here realism in the puppets themselves is the last thing required. These are not tiny replicas of men, but items in a whole drama played in the artificial conditions of the stage. One of the best professional companies has deliberately discarded elaborate heads for uncarved wooden eggs, but these are animated by the expressive movements of the body, by the lighting, and by the atmosphere which is gradually built up by the progress of the play. Such simple undifferentiated forms are capable of taking on an infinite number of expressions, supplied from the context, which the fully detailed face never would be. This is just what a bundle of straw stuffed in an old glove, or a roughly painted stocking toe, does for the child better than the doll of permanent set expression. It allows him to infuse it with the emotion of the moment through movement and voice, which may both change from second to second with the changes of feeling. All sorts of amusing men and animal puppets can be made from cones, nuts, vegetables which serve for a momentary game. One of the best ways of beginning glove puppets is with a strong paper bag over the hand and a face painted on it. Clothes are just odd pieces of cloth tied or pinned on for each occasion.

Because of this identification with his puppet, it is important that each child should be allowed to choose the character he will represent and that the same child who makes it should manipulate and speak for his own puppet. Only in this way will he be able fully to identify himself with it. At a much later stage—the upper

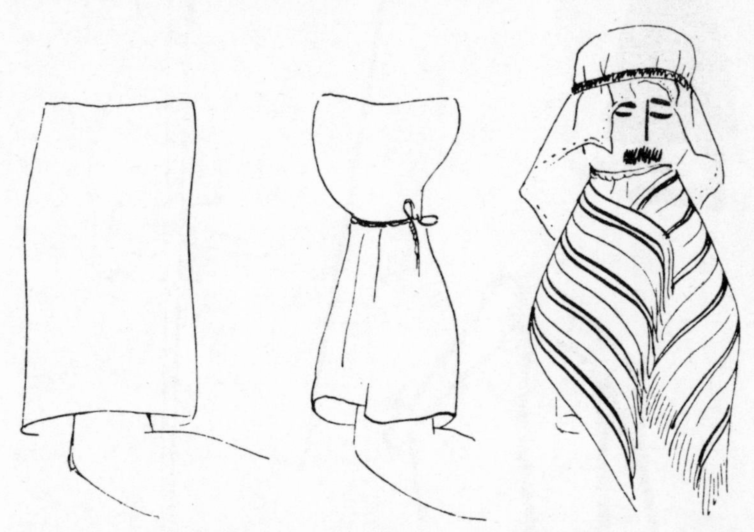

FIG. 62.—Paper bag puppet. A brown paper bag makes the basis of a fine gipsy or Old Testament character, with the addition of a painted face and a few handkerchiefs or scarves.

reaches of the Secondary School perhaps—there may be a division of labour and one worker manipulate while another presents the voice. But usually it is more satisfactory to children of every age to manage the whole character themselves.

The second aspect, that of production, is the one in which puppets have some definite advantages over live dramatics. There is the practical advantage that a performance requires little room. A completely gratifying performance can be given on the classroom table or between two coats hung on chairs. Then there is the educational advantage that the whole is more within the children's control, less liable to practical frustrations. If a stage is used—but this I would suggest only with older adolescents—there is more

Fig. 63.—Children's rod puppets. (1) The witch as her silhouette appears. (2) The witch from the back of the puppet, with the handle extended to act as a long support. The knitting needle was affixed with cellotape; the handle was glued on. The echo of the Javanese is more than accidental as it is a striking and exaggerated profile that is needed in silhouette. (3) A giraffe with a moveable neck so that it can be made to reach stage trees. (4) A dachshund with a moveable tail.

opportunity for designing sets and furniture for it than there is in a human scale production. Many different arrangements of the stage and costume can be tried. The whole can be given an artistic unity which is often not possible with makeshift materials. The new world that puppets open out for us is the world of magic and phantasy, which is just that which is difficult to convey on the school platform with its associations of school assemblies and Bible. The remote and other-worldly are the subjects which use puppets to the best advantage. The naturalistic and mundane, which can better be conveyed by real people in real surroundings, are not.

But, having discussed these positive advantages, I still think the educational value of manipulating puppets is greatly overestimated. It is very much better for the children to act themselves. They are then learning poise and expressive gesture in using their whole bodies as well as their voices, and puppets should certainly never become a general substitute for drama and mime. But there are some children who come to us already too shy to act, and some who go through agonies of embarrassment about their bodies during a clumsy adolescence. For both of these the gradual building up of confidence and the control of their limbs through movement training are the essential therapy, but at the same time they may be drawn into group efforts and enjoy great fun in puppetry. For all children the puppet provides, like the mask, a figure behind which to hide. The small child, who is desperately conscious of his lack of power and of his reliance on grown-ups for the essentials of survival, can become the strong, the bold, the powerful character through his puppet. Nor need we always pick the toughest in the class either in the play or the puppet show for the bully or the giant. Probably there is some quiet little mite who is longing to take the big lead. If he finds he can do it as a puppet he may be encouraged to do a little more of it in his own life. Or there may be an overplump girl who can realize her ambition as a fairy or a princess through her puppet. Eventually we must all come to terms with our real selves, but the relief of playing for a little while the part of our own ideal may make this acceptance easier in the end.

Another relief children may find in puppets is a frank indulgence in the grotesque. Their limited skill, and the nature of the materials of which puppets are generally made—papier mâché, stocking feet, wire and bandages—are likely to result in grotesque rather than fair representations. Instead of striving after either realism or beauty in such materials I think it better to accept this fact and use it for what it suggests. One of our most penetrating child psychologists [1] says, 'Children live in a world of magic, and the forced transition from the magical world of phantasy to the routine-ridden world of adult life presses hardly upon them. The sudden occurrence, therefore, of absurdity, the irruption of the irrational into the rational, is to them a constant source of delight.' So we may expect to find funny men with red noses, clowns with blue faces, or monstrous old women, buffoonery and nonsensical farce, turning up frequently in the primary years. That is quite healthy so long as there are other outlets, such as painting, for that fresh childlike vision which also seeks expression. In early adolescence with its sense of entering at last that world which has been both resented and desired, the grotesque has also a part to play, but with girls at this time, the increased facility in making sometimes serves to express a more delicate type of phantasy.

Shadow and rod puppets are two forms which could be more fully exploited. Shadow acting (against a stretched sheet between the audience and a source of light, window or artificial) is a great release for those who are petrified in facing an audience. Shadow puppets are a less satisfactory medium where space is limited, but as well as exploring the dramatic possibilities of a limited framework, they may be used as a means of concentrating attention on silhouette and related to painting or film studies.

Rod puppets are easier to construct than many other forms and they form a transition between the identification of a part of the player's body and the puppet, found with glove puppets, and the more remote control of strings. The silhouette of a rod puppet is cut out from a flat material, card, plywood, or constructed of wire or scrap materials, and has one or more articulated parts moved independently by a rod, while the puppet is held below view level by a handle. They move horizontally worked from behind a table top, or as silhouettes behind a screen. The articulated joint can be fastened with a round paper clip or a twist of wire. Their extremely simple construction means that they can be quickly made and quickly adapted to new creative ideas which arise in playing with them.

[1] Margaret Lowenfeld, *Play in Childhood*, Chapter IX, London, 1935.

Just because, at the present time, we have a wider general interest in puppetry, and more opportunity for seeing professional performances than in the other crafts, it is open to two dangers. I mentioned their dual history of court and market-place, because the teacher may—since puppets lend themselves to a high degree of sophistication—be tempted to aim at a more sophisticated performance than the children are ready for. It is precisely this quality which often makes them so attractive to educated adults, while children are happy to remain at the knock-about stage for a surprisingly long time. The qualities which made them the highly exquisite and artificial entertainment of courts are *not* the qualities which appeal to children, and to encourage these is to deny their real office for the young, which was performed in the crudities and grotesqueries of the booths.

In the second place, marionettes and their staging offer opportunities for so many clever devices and mechanical inventions, that it is all too easy in the upper forms to allow attention to be concentrated on these, and to lose sight of the fact that we are primarily concerned with the drama. There is a place for the inventive child to make his contribution to the group, in puppets as in stage production, but it must be subservient to the artistic purpose of the whole. In order to make his fullest contribution, each who takes part in a planned dramatic production, whether with puppets or live actors, must first comprehend that dominating artistic purpose. This effort, first to understand the group's conception which is greater than his own individual contribution to it, and then to serve by interpreting it in his own department, whether lighting, painting scenery, acting or dancing, makes the participation in a play one of the most maturing experiences in education.

XXIII*a*.—CRAFT IN DRAMA—THE USE OF COSTUME AND LIGHTING

The Insect Play, dressed and performed by students of Bedford Training College.

This shows how a discerning use of very simple materials and shapes can be made enormously effective by dramatic use of lighting.

Teacher: Peggy Denty.

XXIII*b*.—CRAFT IN DRAMA—SETS AND MASKS FOR A SHAKESPEARE PLAY

The masks are of papier mâché with a witty use of wire and raffia.

Girls of 16.

Teacher: Dorothy Brooks,
Pinner County Girls' School.

XXIII*a*

XXIII*b*

XXIV

XXIV.—RURAL CRAFTS

We have a fine tradition and a source of inspiration for our work in schools in our rural crafts. Here the results obtained by simple tools or equipment, the maker's unselfconscious attitude, the fact that these are local and living things, make them a better source of inspiration for children than museums or factory goods. This photograph shows a slip-lined pickle jar typical of several of our rural potteries, a Welsh broth ladle and sycamore grain scoop, an oak spale seed hopper, a fine Shetland shawl and fisherman's jersey from the Yorkshire coast, and a Welsh quilt, all on a background of Welsh tweeds.

CHAPTER SIXTEEN

OUR ENVIRONMENT

THIS book has been concerned with the practice of the crafts in education. But we live in an age in which almost all the things we use are mass-produced by industry. What relation then has craft teaching to the appreciation of the objects with which we are surrounded?

When we consider the long ages in which man has had to make each thing individually, with tools shaped by his own hands, and set against those the hundred years or so in which we have evolved mass-production, it is not surprising that we have not yet learned to use this great multiple tool, the machine, with the same certainty. We have for the first time seen the possibility of limitless production, of satisfying the material wants of all men, but the products of the machine, with their virtues of precision, clarity and economy, are yet a little cold and impersonal. Few of us would choose to live surrounded by nothing but mass-produced ware. In a kitchen sink, a radio, a telephone we accept standardization without question. But in the clean uncluttered atmosphere we have managed to achieve, we suddenly crave for a picture, a cushion, a jug which is not only distinctively our own but speaks to us of another human personality and bears the stamp of him who made it. So long as we feel the need for those personal and individual objects to delight and interest us and serve as focal points in our environment, so long we shall need the craftsman. To cherish only the antique and refuse to recognize the need of modern craftsmen to create within the contemporary forms is to confess sterility. In a machine age we need the craftsman as much as we ever needed him—not to produce in numbers but to preserve quality and provide individuality. Most of us want our clothes and our gardens and some elements of our environment to be uniquely our own, and here everyone can be a creator. Those who have found in school the satisfaction of producing such pieces of craftsmanship as are illustrated in this book may continue to create in this mode all their lives. Even when these productions do not reach a standard which continues to satisfy the adult—but the average person is perhaps more likely with sound training to achieve an acceptable standard in craft than in painting—the practice of a craft affords the knowledge and discrimination to appreciate the great craftsmen of our own age. And there *are* craftsmen working in our country to-day whose work can offer to the senses and the mind a contentment deep and lasting. A piece of well-wrought metal work, whether it be garden furnishing or jewellery, an individual and distinctive piece of wood, from a nut bowl to a sideboard, a hand-thrown supper set or a piece of blown glass can serve for constant interest and delight as much as a piece of sculpture or a picture. Into it the craftsman may have put just as much of himself and his feeling about life. In addition, not only the sight, but the constant using and handling of such things will make us more sensitive to all the objects we use, to their form and their functioning. We are constantly kept in touch with a live standard, a criterion.

But of course to say that because the products of industry are rather cold and impersonal and that therefore we must also have the work of craftsmen or be craftsmen ourselves, is to ignore the bigger question of whether the products of mass-production might not be more satisfactory to us than they are? Almost daily greater power is being harnessed to produce more objects, which will leave us more energy and give us the *possibility* of freedom to be more fully human beings. But we need not only more power, greater numbers, but immeasurably better designs. I speak especially of the common household articles with which we spend so much of our time. In them, material is shaped to form some object which should not only function well but should give constant pleasure in texture, form and handling. I stress this last apart from 'function' because there needs to be an awareness of the human being who is to use this product, of his size, structure, movement, rhythms. Too much industrial design is conceived ab stractly. A jug, for instance, can be of simple shape, appropriate to the material, can be designed to hold liquid and to direct a neat flow to the lip, and yet *feel* as though it was made to operate on a mechanical tip-up rather than to fit the human hand. The difference between a jug which has this awareness and one which has not cannot be described, but it can be *felt* physically if our senses and organs are not too perverted or dulled by constant assault. The shape of a scythe or a plough is conceived as an extension of the human body closely related to it and in use it *feels* undeniably right. To lift and ladle from one of those deep old wooden spoons, or to hold a seventeenth-century Lambeth pottery bowl in the hands, is to experience a sudden shock of pleasure. The weight is so exactly distributed for the size. The balance is adjusted as delicately as one's body's. The outer curve of the dish was formed to be embraced by human hands—see how the rim rests on the thumb balls—and the hollow naturally formed by cupped hands has been extended by the potter in this great bowl. So the experience of containing and offering is widened in turn by this contact with a material thing. So intimately is the object related to the body that it is felt not as separate but as an extension of it.

Why do almost none of our industrial products, however intellectually satisfying, give this physical satisfaction in use? I believe it is because the designers have never had or have lost touch with the material in its relation to the human body. I do not speak of designing in those new synthetic materials which, themselves lacking *vitality*, may need a totally different approach, but so far as the natural materials, wood, wool and so on, are concerned, the designers whose work is finally most satisfactory are those who have had a craftsman's training in their material. And the greatest sensitiveness both in designer and user is developed in the formative school years.

But we are concerned not with the training of designers so much as the education of that ordinary citizen who is to look at, select and live with those industrial products. How is he to develop that discrimination in choice which we call taste, for his own pleasure and deeper satisfaction? Firstly, as we said, the basis of any art is a physical one, it lies in refined and discriminating senses. This discrimination is to be acquired in familiarity with materials, in the physical knowledge of the subtle differences of texture, smell and appearance. So, as we said, children of all ages must in play have opportunities for such familiarity. Next, it depends on a knowledge, through experience, of what materials will do, of *character* and *behaviour*. This they will gain through the practice of a craft. The appreciation of the senses and the mental judgment of fitness are equally important. Such fitness is only judged in actual use over a period. And discrimination can only be developed in relation to those things whose use we understand. So a young child's judgment can only be exercised where he can both use and understand. We cannot expect him to understand the *material* and *manufacture* of industrially produced objects, nor the *use* of many purely adult ones, so judgment of fitness cannot be developed through studying these. We can only allow him to make what he needs or wants and then he will be interested in how far he has succeeded. So the construction of a toy wheelbarrow *may* in fact teach him more than the construction of an adult utensil, say a wooden knife-box for his mother. It is possible to press the need for making only real grown-up things too early. As soon as the child himself wants, say, a box to keep his tools in, any lack of efficiency in his joints and hinges can be left to impress his own lesson. In addition to all these, the form must bear a relationship to the human being who is to use the object. To give small children only things for use which are altogether out of scale with their own size and physical potentialities may tend to destroy this delicate sense. We do not know.

But even when the nature of the material is not violated and when the purpose is adequately met, there may still remain a choice of forms, and it is here that the æsthetic sensibility can be isolated from other considerations. Why should one form then be more pleasing than another? It is certainly not entirely an intellectual matter. If we say that it is physical and intuitive we shall be feeling in the right direction. We do not yet know of any method by which the selection of the intuitively satisfying form can be taught. But we can provide opportunities for practising these crafts which have been shown to develop bodily sensitivity, and we can provide the environment in which these two qualities are likely to be nurtured. Only in an atmosphere free from other pressures, where time is given to contemplation—meaning here a certain 'still regard'—only there is intuitive judgment fostered and confidence in it sustained. It is certain that we shall not have a high standard of industrial design until we have a discriminating public opinion, and moreover a vocal one. I believe that at the moment the standard of public taste in many directions is far in advance of what the manufacturers give us. This cannot altogether be laid to the door of the designers, who are in some cases frustrated by the firm's policy. A commercial timidity, the much greater financial risks involved in a new line of mass-production, the post-war avidity for any sort of non-austerity article, the bottle-neck of conservative and often insensitive buyers for retailers, all these combine to deprive us of the best that our industry could produce. If we are pessimistic about the standards possible in machine production we only need to look at Swedish textiles and rugs, Danish table silver and pottery. It is significant that the industry in those countries started in a small way alongside flourishing craftsmanship, and that the handcraftsman has continued to be closely associated with the industry. In our country the industry too quickly grew into a mammoth and stifled the handcraftsman before it was realized how much he was needed by industry. Up till the present time, at least in those natural materials I speak of, the handcraftsman is still the experimenter, the originator, and it is in 'playing about' with his materials that he lights on new combinations, on subtle differences of effect, which, adapted by industry, enable it to produce a new line in mass-production. A much closer relationship between studio and factory, for which the potter Bernard Leach, for instance, is always pleading, has been shown in several European countries to be of inestimable benefit to both.

How is our education to contribute towards the building up of the informed, discriminating and vocal public? In order to make their needs and wishes felt the individuals who make up the public must have a certain degree of *certainty* about what they want. They must be willing to demand and to strive for those things which they believe with conviction will give them lasting pleasure. To reach conviction more is necessary than a few lessons in appreciation. While I conceive the chief responsibility of us teachers of craft to the upper age groups in school to be the introduction of those satisfying modes of creation in material which I call craftsmanship, we have also a wider responsibility. It is true that we cannot expect that all our students will go on practising a craft after they have left school, though I cannot doubt that a more fitting course in art and craft would give that satisfaction to a greater number, as would a more thoughtful approach to needlework and knitting for instance. But even though they never lifted a tool again I would still consider the introduction to craftsmanship well worth while because of the experience it can give. I tried to describe this experience as an increased awareness and growing sensitivity which comes through handling the material direct; a synthesis, sensory, emotional and mental, achieved through a continuous but ever changing, almost rhythmical relationship with the material itself. This consists of a sinking of oneself in it, taking on its nature, and absorbing from it, alternating with a giving out, the expressing of an idea through it. It is a finding of oneself through finding a relationship with the physical materials of this world, and it illuminates all the rest of experience. It is obviously no use trying to describe this. It must be *experienced*, physically and emotionally, and I believe that helping children to experience it is more important than anything else craft teachers can do.

But while this is peculiarly a responsibility of craft teaching, seldom stressed, it is true that the wider field of art and craft teaching has a task which is more generally recognized, in the field of 'appreciation'. Lessons in appreciation usually take the form of learning *about* pictures, architecture, domestic equipment and so on. But unless this appreciation is to be an intellectual exercise—and æsthetics has too often been treated as such—it must be an active, not a passive experience and it must be linked up with the senses and the emotions. Æsthetic appreciation in the intellectual sense does not develop until about fifteen or sixteen when most of the school population is leaving. With the less intellectual types it is hardly to be expected even then. But there is a much more active and vital approach which is possible with much younger ages and is much more related to the ways in which such appreciation will enrich their adult life. Whereas not all of these children will practise a craft and few will paint pictures, they all, every one of them, will be concerned with arranging a small part of our whole environment, that is, that part connected with their own clothes, homes and furnishings. This is the aspect in which their emotions are already involved, in which the interest is there without the necessity of our trying to stir it up. This is the natural place to begin 'appreciation'. But while this is realized to the extent that it is now possible to take a School Certificate examination in the history of everyday things, and lectures with illustrations are given in many schools, I still do not think we are yet getting anywhere near the heart of the matter. I would hope to develop appreciation through doing and making, in especial through making the immediate environment of their class-rooms and schools. While it is immensely cheering to see how many authorities are trying to provide light, colourful and well-arranged rooms, I would not want us to have rooms which are so complete that there is no room for the sort of participation I mean. I would almost prefer the conditions of one school I know which moved into old and inappropriate buildings, and all the children set to work, and, with some professional help, learned how to knock out windows, to set in window-frames, to whitewash and paint, to build a new stair. If it had been nothing else this was at least extremely useful experience for every future householder! But even where this degree of construction is not called for or is not possible—as with younger children—there is still a great deal which can be done. Perhaps if I describe our experiment at Milltown it will provide a suggestion on which others will go further.

The school building was a long two-storied one in the shape of three sides of a rectangle, and apart from hall, library, laboratories and domestic science rooms, the fourteen class-rooms were identical. When first I knew it the school was painted grey and cream throughout—a very pleasant and restrained colour scheme. But the forms who 'lived' in these rooms—each form had a form-room—had nothing to distinguish their room from all the others except a number. Each had one door into the corridor, three windows opposite, and similar rows of stiff desks facing the door end of the room. With identical colour schemes and arrangements, the rooms were quite characterless and for the forms served merely as somewhere to have their register taken and keep their books. The library and laboratories had some variety in their aspect and outlook and in the furniture related to their specific uses, but still the same colour scheme. This was unpromising material enough, but if we were to talk of planning the environment, it seemed sensible to begin with what we had at hand.

The school was to be painted during the summer holiday, so here was the opportunity. I obtained books of the distemper and paint colours available and consulted with each form in turn. We looked at the aspect of their room, talked about its use and about the effect of colours on the moods. One, two or three colours could be used in each room, either keeping paint and walls the same, or walls one colour and two colours for the paint. This was ten years ago and I had not seen at that time the delightful effect obtained by washing the walls of one room in different colours, or different shades of one colour. I wished to experiment with coloured ceilings, but this was not feasible. However, after much discussion, each form produced a colour scheme. Some were quite unusual—peach walls and deep blue paint for a sunny room, pastel pink walls and plum and yellow paint for a cold north room, scarlet, turquoise and off-white for a laboratory. When they came back after the holidays the rooms were transformed. Whereas each had been identical now each was different, but as yet had no individuality. That can only be created as the imprint of personality, and to achieve this with thirty or forty personalities is much more difficult than with one. But we discussed together what they conceived the room to be, within the necessary limits. Was it strictly a scientific work room (as the laboratories had to be), or could it be more personal and more homely? Did they want a strictly formal effect or would an informal arrangement of furniture help lessons? Was it desirable to have a clear space for dramatic work, or did the room need to be converted at times into a picture gallery as did the art room? Having decided among themselves on the general line to take, each form in turn spent one art and craft lesson on considering how this was to be achieved. The stiff rows of desks, the teacher's desk and chair, which had previously held their rigid formation, now became mobile, and an amazing variety of arrangements appeared. Forms which liked discussion lessons grouped their desks in a double semicircle. One which wanted room for acting backed them all against the walls round three sides. Some rooms were oriented towards a corner, with desks in diagonal rows. While the old arrangement had certain practical advantages, the unfamiliarity of the new and the interest of trying to find a pleasing and practical spacing proved worth any inconvenience. We all sat together in the new room and discussed its further furnishing. Would block-printed curtains be an improvement? Should the cupboard doors have a painted motif in the panels, or be lined inside with a bright contrasting paint? Would the shelves for notebooks and jotters look better with a curtain in front? Would a cushion on the teacher's chair look better with a new cover specially woven to emphasize some note in the scheme? Some forms decided to embroider their curtains and a cover for the staff table. A piece of carving or a modelled group by one of the form might be used as a resting place for the eye, or a corner kept as a place of honour for each chosen piece to take its place in turn. Two or three forms embroidered hangings as a group project and hung them instead of pictures. Next we considered what type of picture would suit the conception of their room now taking shape. These could be chosen from a good collection of prints and from a few originals. The room with pastel pink walls and pale green paint asked clearly for the delicacy of Botticelli's 'Venus Rising from the Waves'. A bolder still life by Matisse had actually suggested a colour scheme to one form so they claimed this as their right. Others hung one picture, then another, now on this wall, now on that. We argued whether the picture should focus attention on itself or fit quietly into the whole. Sometimes, for a time, the children's own framed paintings were used. Some forms discarded pictures temporarily for other forms of decoration. One group used tiles they had made in pottery on window-sills and walls. One group, with an overmastering interest in live things, filled the window-sills with tanks of fish and had a bowl of gold-fish suspended from the ceiling! After the general appearance of the room had been achieved the next few weeks were spent in great excitement over decorations. The little bowls and plates of moss and stones described in the chapter on the Primary School were arranged with extraordinary skill and loving care. Some days there might be groups of varied toadstools, on others bowls of pebbles or cunningly grouped shells in water. All sorts of uses of foliage were tried out, great branches bunched in corners of the room or long window troughs of ferns or delicate garden flowers. We discussed the kind of flowers needed for each room, the type of bowl or jug suitable to the flowers and to the room. At first some horrors in 'art vases' were produced in good faith, but they had to stand up among a chosen group specially borrowed for a few weeks, which ranged from wedgwood moonstone ware and Swedish glass to local brown pottery, and gradually simplicity and good taste asserted themselves. Their own pottery came into use wherever it was possible. This enthusiastic interest in flowers was one of the great joys of school that year. I never knew what lovely sight would be waiting any morning. As autumn changed to winter we discovered the amazing colours of bare birch branches and the lace-like pattern which withered umbels made against a plain wall. After a brief interval in which special decorations embroidered the school for Christmas, the catkins began to appear and then the first few tiny buds of aconite and scilla in plates of moss. The flowers in the class-rooms were so enthusiastically provided and cared for that we suggested that any form who wished should 'adopt' some unclaimed part of the school, a corridor, the library, the entrance hall. Soon every corner of the school offered some arrangement to pause and enjoy. The corridors lost their rather bare cold look, and strangest of all, they stayed miraculously tidy—no scraps of paper, no oddments pushed into corners—without any of the persistent reminders which used to be necessary.

While the unpromising class-rooms were being transformed and acquiring distinctive personalities in this way to the pride and delight of their owners, those parts of the school which offered a little more scope were taken further. The prefects' room, with comfortable lounge chairs and small tables, demanded the treatment of a quiet sitting-room. The colour of the fireplace was fixed, so the scheme had to revolve round that, but cushion covers and deep bands for the foot of the window curtains were block printed. The gaudy fireside rug came in for harsh criticism, so as everyone was too busy at this age to weave a rug as we would have wished, it was turned upside-down so that the natural fawn underside showed and a new coloured fringe put on. The pictures here changed very often since many of the senior girls were now painting pictures which their contemporaries were glad to have on the walls. In the library, which again offered scope for trying furniture in different positions, we painted a mural on the wall. This was done in ordinary powder colour on a washable wall so that it could be washed off soon and a new one done. In all those additions and decorations there was no insistence on permanence. Next year everybody would have a new room, and (though they would have to accept the colours there instead of choosing them) they would have an opportunity to do this all over again if they wished to leave their movable objects behind. To introduce some elements not feasible in a class-room, a small alcove near the art room was adopted as a 'house corner' to try out a wider range of furnishing. At first I furnished this with things borrowed from the staff—a cool brocade hanging behind, a small coffee table, a rich rug, a piece of eighteenth-century English china. Next week it might be a Finnish bentwood stool, a modern printed fabric, a Leach pot. To these we added, in a period given over to that purpose, such flowers and illumination as seemed appropriate.

Perhaps a bronze kettle would be filled with yellow and rust daisies, or a tall glass jar would hold one tiger lily, one iris, one trumpet flower begged from such sources as could be expected to spare just one, with a glass paper-weight to echo the rich effect. When garden flowers failed there were black alder catkins or shiny evergreens from the woods. A flex from the nearest light was used to try out different kinds of lighting, low and shaded, or high and thrown upwards on the ceiling. A coloured light glinting close to dark laurel was one of the marked successes. After a week or two, during which each form who came to the art room in turn was encouraged to discuss it, the current arrangement of the 'house corner' was left to the older girls interested. They might be seen of a morning toiling up the school hill with a pet piece of small furniture from home, an old mahogany workbox or a stool made by a brother and covered with a block-printed or embroidered top. Combined with their sound training in domestic science we hoped that all this laid the beginnings of creating the immediate environment. But admittedly only the beginnings. Since it is a girls' school of which I write I have stressed the feminine angle, but for boys and men, too, I feel convinced that appreciation of everyday things comes from actually handling and arranging them, not as an abstract exercise, but as the making of the environment in which we are to live. I believe house-painting and decorating could be developed as a craft for boys with no pictorial leanings. The selection of the fabric which provides a texture pleasant in itself and enhances the texture of the rugs and flooring of wood, which is in keeping with the style of the furniture and yet makes its distinctive contribution as an element in the whole room, this sort of selection reflects and conveys the personality behind it.

If the children in our care grow up with, at every stage, materials which they can mould and arrange, with tools which they can use to construct, and if they are encouraged to believe that it is their birthright to be adapting the environment around them for use and for pleasure, they will not be content with the lethal ugliness of so much of our industrial landscape. Having found the joy and satisfaction of creating they will want to create still, and to bring a sensitive imagination to bear not only on their own choice of clothes and furnishings, but on the selection of public monuments, or new plans for new buildings or new towns, they will be concerned with the preservation of the best traditions, and concerned about the destruction of the countryside by industry or suburban selfishness, and so they may make a world more fitting for themselves and their children to enjoy.

CONCLUSION

Obviously it has not been possible to discuss all the crafts which might with profit be taught in schools. Metal-work has only been mentioned in passing, and the possibilities of spinning, knitting and weaving hinted at. I would not be capable of talking about every craft even were there space, so the chapters vary greatly in their approach. The techniques of woodwork and needlework are already in good hands, but because I believe craftsmanship can develop certain valuable parts of the personality which simply acquiring techniques can not, I try to suggest a wider view of these subjects. On the other hand, the techniques of pottery usually taught seem to me quite inappropriate for schools. So I have there concentrated on some simple methods to enable a start to be made. The teacher who decides to extend his pottery will have to go and learn from a master and he may find a local potter more suitable than an art school. In carving we have perhaps been unimaginative about materials, so it is a pleasure to record those experiments with varied materials which the photographs show. Indeed, my deep thanks are due to all who allowed their work to be photographed, and the inspiration of those whose carvings and pots, dresses and wooden utensils, embody much better than words what I am trying to say.

For each of us the horizon is limited by our experience. Perhaps even now some school is working out a way with plastics or with synthetic fibres which opens up possibilities of such development of the senses, the emotions and imagination as puts it on a level with the traditional crafts. Since I have not found it, I leave these materials alone. The two disadvantages of synthetic materials are that they lack vitality and they lack tradition. Just as the adolescent enters into the culture to which he was born by reading the literature and studying the paintings of his country, so we can save crafts in schools from triviality and eccentricity by an appreciation of the sanity and simplicity of such craftsmanship as now exists. There is the flowering of woodworking, stonemasonry, wrought iron of past times still to be found in our villages. There are the quilting, knitting of fishermen's jerseys, and rural country pottery still made (Plate XXIV). Then there is the work of contemporary craftsmen in modelling, carving, needlework and other crafts which can serve as an inspiration to older children. When they have absorbed the best of the past and the present, they will be ready not to go back, but to go on.

While there are many amusing and enjoyable activities which can be pursued as craft, it does appear that working in these basic materials which man, from sheer necessity to survive, has explored and learned to know intimately, concentrating one's whole being to produce a satisfying thing, is a special sort of experience. So I see crafts as making their chief contribution to education, not as a way of acquiring knowledge (though knowledge comes), nor as a perfection of bodily skill (though that is acquired and then made the means to a further end), but as a form of art, the expression of the human spirit on and through its environment. This may seem to be true of sculpture and embroidery, but hardly of a chair or a milk jug. But these, as every sort of thoughtful making does, express in their consideration of the materials, in the conception of the human body which is to use them, and the human needs which they are designed to fill, an attitude to life. To make things, and to be surrounded with tools, furniture and utensils, is a human, a utilitarian necessity. But to make things which embody our attitude to life in this special way is a spiritual necessity. If we can give children this experience, give them the certainty that the making of their environment is in the hands of men, we shall be educating indeed.

APPENDIX ONE

Chapter I A

VICTOR LÖWENFELD'S WORK ON MODES OF CREATION

THE kinæsthetic sense and the sense of touch are so closely bound up with the enjoyment of objects and with creation in materials, that it is useful to study the distinction made between two ways of creating by Löwenfeld in *The Nature of Creative Activity*. He says: 'We can clearly distinguish between two types both by the end products of their artistic creation and by their attitude to their own experiences.' He calls them visual and haptic types. The visual type—which is regarded as normal in our Western European civilization—starts from the environment, and is concerned with visual appearances. The haptic type, on the other hand, is concerned primarily with his own bodily sensations and the tactual space around him. Everything springs from his immediate bodily experiences. The haptic pupil, like the blind, models what he himself feels with his muscle sense, rather than what he sees of the appearance of other people and things. In modelling a head, for instance, he will make cavities for the eye sockets, and build a protruding eyeball in these. He will build the lips and perhaps the teeth into the structure instead of drawing them on the surface as a 'visual' child would. Any sensation which belongs to one side of the body only, such as pain or awkwardness or a deformed limb, will be differentiated in all or most of his drawings of people by a difference of colour or shape. Such people are often able to convey directly the physical or emotional feelings of others—as sadness, tiredness, gaiety—at an earlier age than they could *visualize the appearance which conveys* such feelings. Both are equally creative types, and both express their world of experience in terms of their fundamental mode.

For a full account of their work through which Löwenfeld arrived at these conclusions, it is necessary to read his fascinating book. I shall confine myself to one general quotation (p. 147):

'We may divide art forms into two large groups—the impressionistic and the expressionistic. Every work of art can be classified somehow in one or other of these groups. If we assign to the impressionistic group all those forms of art whose starting point lies in what is perceived by the external senses, then the expressionistic forms have as their basis subjective attitudes and bodily experiences. The impressionistic world is the world of appearances—the world of our senses. The world of expressionistic art is the world of expression, of feelings, of subjective processes. If therefore these haptic artistic experiences are to be sought anywhere they can be sought only where the inner states gave the impulse to creative activity and not where external perception was the integrating factor in artistic experiences and processes. Impressionistic art in painting and in sculpture has always been regarded as visual art whilst expressive art, originating from within, places the self in a value relation to its environment. We shall, therefore, find more and more haptic symbols of form and expression, the more creative activity is bound up with the self and the more immediately the self becomes the centre of artistic experience.'

The significance of all this for us teachers is, firstly, that the haptic, *non*-visual mode of creating is just as normal, just as much to be encouraged as the visual. And since we are all brought up in this country to a type of art almost exclusively of the visual category, and to an overemphasis on the *visual* appearance of objects, we must be on guard lest our limitations blind us to other forms of expression. In the Nativity Group (Plate XI*b*) these two types can be distinguished by the way in which they treat the face. The visual children treat the head as a shape on which to *draw* the features, the haptics building up the form with nose and eyeballs truly projecting. This means that we cannot make suggestions to children about the method of modelling, e.g. a face, which will be helpful to the whole group. We must try to study each child's way of working, and help him in his own method.

The second conclusion we can make from Löwenfeld's work is that in our civilization the more natural development of the haptic type may be towards three-dimensional crafts rather than towards the two-dimensional arts of drawing, painting, printing. There have been great civilizations in the past in which something of the haptic attitude has been expressed in painting, and individual painters like Cezanne have at times worked in this way.[1] But the tradition of our painting is visual

[1] Collingwood wrote of Cezanne: 'Everyone had supposed that painting was a visual art. . . . Then came Cezanne and began to paint like a blind man. His still life studies which enshrined the essence of his genius are like groups of things which have been groped over with the hands; he uses colour not to reproduce what he sees in looking at them but to express almost in a kind of algebraic notation what this groping has felt. So with his interiors; the spectator finds himself bumping about these rooms, circumnavigating with caution those menacingly angular tables, coming up to the persons that so massively occupy those chairs and fending them off with his hands. . . . We find ourselves feeling our way as one can imagine an infant feels its way, when it has barely begun to crawl, among the nursery furniture.'

and it needs great courage and conviction for a young painter to seek persistently for a means of expression so different from that with which he is surrounded. So the majority of haptics may well find a vehicle of expression in the crafts which depend least on visual and most on kinæsthetic forms, that is, in spinning, weaving, carving, pottery. These depend less on vision and more on the education of tactile and muscle senses and on rhythms which are closely akin to rhythms of dance.

Chapter I B

Rudolf Laban, who has been responsible for movement study in this country—and for significant work in industrial research and with the Ballet Joos—says some things which lead us to think more deeply about this aspect of craft training. He speaks [1] of the analysis of effort (used in his own peculiar wide sense) into 'dabbing, gliding, flicking, slashing, punching, pressing, wringing' and shows that most movements are compounds of these. He speaks of three 'effort characters'—time-effort, weight-effort, and flow—'and a fourth attitude towards the elements of movement which, if prevailing in an effort, gives it the character of either a struggle against or an indulgence in the flow effort'. 'As a worker—and one should include here all the people in any activities from, say, labouring to dancing—a person indulging in all motion factors will be able to deal with all tasks demanding free flow of motion, fine touch, flexibility and sustainment, such as delicate repair work or assembly work. Such a worker will find difficulty in dealing with tasks of the opposite kind. The person habitually fighting against all the four motion factors will best deal with work exacting controlled or 'bound' flow of motion, great strength, use of the shortest and most direct way in all his movements and an ability to function with quick impulses, such as lumbering, hand forging, and heavy repetitive work.' The examples given are chiefly from industry but this has an obvious bearing on those types of crafts which are acceptable and satisfying to different people.

(p. 65): 'It is true that the tremendous motion which is shown in the flow of material in modern industry is a part of this investigation, but its main ideal value lies in the recognition that behind this terrific flow there is always the bodily-mental effort of individual man. No mechanization can eliminate human effort; the handling of the terrifying powers of nature is entrusted to man's tiny and feeble hands. The responsibility involved in this fact must be fully recognized and the education of children and workmen—and who is not a workman if his life is not idle?—must take into consideration this responsibility very carefully.

[1] *Effort*, R. Laban.

'Effort study is a very valuable means for the most important practical issues. But there is something deeper behind it. Movement in itself is a language in which man's highest and most fundamental inspirations are expressed. We have forgotten not only how to speak this language but also how to listen to it. Movement fills our whole working time, no matter in what kind of work we are engaged. It seems a quite unimportant servant if our work consists mainly of thinking, writing, speaking, or any other so-called mental activity. But dealing with servants is quite a tricky business. They are apt to revolt if their drive towards what may be called the flow inherent in nature is frustrated.

'The inhibition of the freedom of movement and its degradation to the rôle of a means of production only is a grave error which results in ill health, mental and bodily discord and misery, and thus also in a disturbance of work.

'Movement has a quality, and this is not its utilitarian or visible aspect, but its feel. One most DO movements in order to be able to appreciate their full power and their full meaning, but this is carried out in our civilization in a very scanty, very casual and insufficient way.'

And again (p. 66 f.): 'Efforts can be transmitted more easily than thoughts. The lazy or diligent atmosphere of a workshop or class is an observable reality and something to which a newcomer often succumbs in spite of his personal qualities which might be quite opposite to the working mood prevailing in the place. Moods of a crowd, whether cheerful or sad, seem to originate frequently from the transmission of effort-tendencies and their uncontrolled growth.'

As teachers of crafts, especially at the secondary level, our ideal must be to find not only materials which are satisfying to the sense of touch but rhythms of work which give the fullest satisfaction to our children. The Ministry's Handbook on Art Education, 1946 (the little book with a yellow cover and stars), points out that the qualifications and enthusiasms of the teacher must largely dictate the subjects taught. This must be true, and love of and enthusiasm for her own craft, and opportunity to practise it, will be a very large factor in the education of her pupils. But it is apparent how far off the ideal we are in the present state of understaffed and ill-equipped craft departments, when we consider how inadequately we can offer the appropriate choice to the many varieties of student.

We need at the secondary level more and better qualified teachers who are enthusiasts for craft, half classes for crafts, and more equipment, so that students are not held waiting their turn. Until this is achieved craft teaching will not be able to do one quarter of what it could for the fuller development of adolescents.

APPENDIX ONE

Chapter I C

PLAY AND IMAGINATION

Margaret Lowenfeld speaks of play as 'the expression of the child's whole attitude to life'. She lists four purposes of play which are helpful to clarify the nature of play for us because she sees play not just as an activity of childhood, but related to the whole of later life. She distinguishes: [1]

(1) 'Contacting the environment', which she relates to *work*,
(2) 'Pondering', which leads to *philosophy and religion*.
(3) The external expression of the creative life, which we call *art*.
(4) Relaxation.

'Contacting the environment' means here not only moving through it and handling it in the physical sense but realizing it, getting into some relationship with the things and the way of life round about. Now, since craftsmanship is practised on and with the physical materials which surround us, the way in which the infant comes to know his environment has a special interest for us. At first, set down among sticks, blocks, sand, lumps of clay or bundles of straw, he will *explore* these materials without attempting to modify their shape or construct anything with them.

This is the essential preliminary to any work in a new material, and is in fact the first stage in making any piece of craftsmanship.

The second of Margaret Lowenfeld's purposes is 'pondering', which often finds that 'external expression' of which she speaks and so has at least the possibility of becoming art. It is necessary for our purpose to look more closely at the relationship between this pondering or day-dreaming and art itself. Let me repeat that there are two levels of thought, 'controlled thought' and 'pondering'. Controlled thought is conscious and objective, brings the thinker into touch with his environment, keeps the object to be attained or the goal to be reached clearly before it, and is exemplified as that type of concentrated attention which attacks a problem directly. It uses a great deal of mental energy. The other type of thought is subjective, not concerned with the present environment; it often uses a large degree of symbolism and it is exemplified by day-dreaming. When we come to consider the facts, we find that all creative thinkers are dreamers at times. 'Let poets dream, let artists dream, let philosophers dream: let all thinkers be dreamers,' says Victor Hugo. We all know of the trance in which Coleridge wrote *Kubla Khan* and of the rapt visions of Blake. Tchaikovsky refers to his somnambulistic state during which his ideas assumed a definite form, and Yeats speaks of being 'both asleep and awake',

[1] *Play in Childhood.*

when composing. Mozart has left us a description in a letter which throws light on his state of inspiration. 'When I am, as it were, completely myself, entirely alone and of good cheer—say travelling in a carriage, or walking after a good meal or during the night when I cannot sleep: it is on such occasions that my ideas flow best and most abundantly. . . . Those ideas that please me I retain in memory, and I am accustomed, as I have been told, to hum them to myself. If I continue in this way it soon occurs to me how I may turn this or that morsel to account so as to make a good dish of it. . . . All this fires my soul and provided I am not disturbed, my subject enlarges itself, becomes methodized and defined. What a delight this is I cannot tell! All this inventing, this producing, takes place in a pleasing lively dream.'

These are the artists, the musicians, who might be expected to dream, but is it generally realized that this dream-like state is also an important constituent of the scientific imagination? Dr. W. H. Rivers, the psychologist, stated that many of the scientific ideas he valued most as well as the language in which they were expressed came to him in the 'half sleeping, half waking state directly continuous with definite sleep'. Darwin saw the links between the salient facts of his revolutionary theory of evolution, not in a period of intense concentration, but in one of mind wandering, and day-dreaming. All this is not to minimize the tremendous amount of hard work these artists and scientists put in to their material either before or after this period of which I speak, but it is necessary first to recognize the place of day-dreaming as one component of creative thought. Nor should we regard the extreme cases of the artist or the creative scientist or politician or town planner as different in kind from the creative thought which is required of all of us in the situations of ordinary life. Surely life is narrower, has less potentialities—just as we do *not* see that to furnish a room, to serve as a hostess to a difficult company, consciously to extend our sympathies from our own race and class to those quite alien, is an act of creative thought. And it is just this type of creation with the ordinary materials and situations of life, that my students in Milltown, that the citizens of our country and our world, seem to lack. Therefore one of the most pressing needs of our education is to develop this quality through the school years.

We *do* try to educate the controlled and directed thought of our pupils in science, mathematics, history, languages, but it is the other type, the autistic thought, that they are not encouraged to use to the full.

It is necessary now to look a little more closely at this 'pondering'. It is a wandering of the mind, not uncontrolled, but controlled by inner necessities and urges. It is the state in which we are open to suggestions

—as we are not when we are concentrating—which may seem far-fetched, remote. It enlarges our horizons, not narrows them as does intense concentration. In it we are not tied down to necessity, or reality, but are exploring a much wider field. Thought is dispersed and the mind plays with ideas, combining them in new ways. It occurs at all ages but it is in fact the typical thought of the young child. Now this is tremendously important because autistic thought takes less mental energy. The young child is incapable of what we call concentrating for more than a few minutes at a time. So by far the greater part of his time is spent in this wandering sort of thought. But within that, he is playing with the ideas presented, by the outside world and by adults, becoming familiar with them, feeling round them so to speak, and absorbing them.

The psychologists call this 'phantasy', and we shall have to distinguish between phantasy and imagination. The exploring of the mind at this level, directed by some inner need or urge and not tied down to realistic facts, i.e. pure day-dreaming, is phantasy. Imagination I see as the type of thought which relates the significant points of *that* world of day-dreams to *this* world of facts. That relation may be in various forms. It may be in the creation of a symbol which unites the two, as the day-dream stories of Cinderella and the Ugly Duckling do in fact represent something significant for us in the real world. It may be in the selection of an idea or thought occurring on that level which can become the inspiration of a theme to be worked out in the realm of controlled thought, as Mozart speaks of 'turning this morsel to account', or as a novelist gets the vague outline of a character to be given substance and built up into the backbone of a novel. Or it may be in seeing the relation between facts, the solution of a problem in fact, whether it is mathematical, social or personal. Or it may be the deliberate entering in imagination into another situation, allowing oneself to feel oneself into the part in a play or into the other person's shoes, by an imaginative projection followed by a period of quiet brooding. All these are examples of the interaction of the conscious mind and the level of autistic thought. But Ruth Griffiths [1] has shown how phantasy plays in fact a much more positive part in the development of the child. Phantasy can be looked on as an escape from reality, a compensation. Or it can be looked on as an exercise in preparation for real achievement—as the child plays at mothers and fathers and the adolescent plays at being in love—testing out certain feelings, advancing, retreating, selecting the appropriate response. Ruth Griffiths says: 'The child is not regarded as deliberately turning from reality in his phantasies or as being in any way hampered by his ego-centric attitude, but we consider that this attitude itself is necessary to his

[1] *Imagination in Early Childhood.*

development and can be shown to be ultimately of a social and not of an a-social nature.' Dr. Griffiths' research was carried out with two groups of young schoolchildren, one in London, one in Australia, who came to her every day over a considerable period. Each day she let them pour out their phantasies in many ways, through talking about what was interesting them, through free drawing, the interpretation of ink-blots, stories made up by them, telling their dreams of the previous night, and telling the images which they saw with their eyes covered up. She says: 'The careful study of children's day-dreams goes to show that during much of a normal child's time he is concerned with emotional problems. It appears, however, that the function of imagination in childhood involves more than a mere expression of emotion and may be shown indeed to be necessary to intellectual as well as emotional development.' Each of the children who came to her were pondering over at least one emotional problem, sometimes several at once. All their free play, their drawing (no subject was, of course, suggested), their day-dreaming, was concerned with that problem. For instance, Dick's problem—surely a very real one for all of us—of how to get possession of the goods he wanted. Dick's wants were symbolized by fruit, usually the apple—immemorial human symbol of the desired. He told a story about a little boy who wanted an apple and stole one off a street barrow. Next day, however, his mind was evidently running on the social consequences of such action because his story was concerned with a boy being punished for stealing. Then he tried another track. The next day the little boy in the story asked his mother for a penny to buy an apple, and then he went on to consider the ways in which a penny could be earned. His solution to his problem was coming into line with what was socially acceptable. There were then variations of the theme—the boy was given an apple as a gift. But Dick went on from there. Next time the little boy in his story was given an apple he kept the seeds and planted them and looked after the plantling till it grew big and then the tree bore apples and he could have all he wanted. Meanwhile this theme was recurring in all Dick's phantasy, painting, ink blots and dreams. When a solution was found in a way he felt would not lead him into conflict with his family and environment, his mind was able to go on, to ponder some other human problem which might occupy the wandering thoughts and dreams for several more weeks. The interesting thing is that a socially acceptable solution was largely found by Dick himself. It was not imposed on him from the outside. Having explored several possibilities, he arrived at this conclusion that desired things had to be worked for and earned in this world. This is only one of many fascinating stories in this delightful account of research into children's phantasy. Now, since Dr. Griffiths found that all or almost all the children (who were selected only in the sense that they covered a certain range of intelligence) had such problems and pondered them and worked them out in phantasy in this way, we are justified in presuming that the children we teach have the same sort of difficulties. But two points about her discoveries have a special significance for us as educationists. Firstly, the children could not indulge their gift for day-dreaming, until their attention was allowed to stray away from the objective world—even encouraged to do so. Their problems did not emerge so long as their attention was concentrated on their environment, either because it was strange and interesting, or because they were compelled to pay attention. But this is exactly what we are doing almost all the time in our schools. We are compelling the children's attention to something *other* than what is concerning them at the moment. We are destroying the conditions for phantasy. Even the 'activity method' schools, while starting from the children's interests, sometimes put too much stress on accomplishing something in actuality, and not enough on the solitary working through to a solution in the mind or the imagination. The second point is that while the teachers who knew those children well never discovered their imaginative power or suspected their problems, Dr. Griffiths got long stories, pictures, and recitals of dreams because she allowed a long time with each child. Some of the children quickly became accustomed to the procedure and settled down to draw or tell a story as soon as they came to her room. Others took much longer to settle down and would start several false hares before they came to work out the problem which was really worrying them. Dr. Griffiths never said 'tell me a story about a so and so', or suggested the subject for a picture. That would be to lead the mind away from its own problems, which can best be pursued in quietness and alone. She says, 'it is not by forcing the child to take part in group games that we can help him. To draw him from his problems is not to assist him in a solution.' So we arrive at the conditions in which the mind can work through to its own solution—lack of external distraction, quietness and mental solitariness (not necessary to be alone, but not to be impinged on by the group all the time), above all *time*, undisturbed time to ponder and day-dream.[1] When we face this fact, that these are conditions which most children in crowded homes seldom have before five and almost never after they go to school, we can hardly be surprised that their problems are not in fact solved satisfactorily, and that they grow into adults incapable of those acts of sympathetic imagination and creative thought to which we are all called. No one would suggest that the encouragement of day-dreaming would automatically solve all our problems and change the face of society, but it does appear that those are the *conditions* in which the imagination is fostered, just as freedom is

[1] Mozart, in the letter quoted, said 'provided I am not disturbed'.

the indispensable condition in which responsibility is fostered. Without these conditions we cannot begin to get anywhere. Nor am I suggesting that the whole school day should be given up to private and individual contemplation! The impact of the world, the response to the feelings and the claims of other people, are the other half of the picture. At present we are making it almost the whole. I do suggest that the years before five should be as free as possible, that the school years five to seven (if children must go to school at five) should definitely provide for and encourage a great deal of day-dreaming, and that from seven to twelve, when the child is naturally turning much more to the outside world and enlarging his environment all the time, we should still provide time and opportunity, and encourage for some part of each day, this more solitary phantasying. This is not to be done by saying to the children in effect 'Now stop doing anything and just dream'. If they do, in fact, do that often during lessons it may be an indication that concentrated thought over too long periods is being demanded of them. Such pondering may be passive in this sense, that it is all going on inside the children's heads, or it may be active in the sense of painting, modelling, story-telling, acting. But the conditions of phantasying will only be present in the lessons where we use these activities, provide a malleable material (one cannot express a phantasy with anything so intractable as beads, cane or matchboxes) and if we do not insist on the *subject* of the painting or the model of the story. In addition, the rates at which it is possible for humans to change one activity for another vary very greatly. We shall find, as Dr. Griffiths did, that some children can settle down to a new material or new subject quickly, some only slowly. Now this is simply a fact of human difference like colour of hair. It can be modified slightly but not eradicated. So it must be accepted. For the same temperamental reason the children who were slow to settle down may well be found to be absorbed when the time comes to do something else. So far as it is possible, any such activity should be carried on so long as the child is absorbed in it. But since this is not entirely possible in a class, it is a good idea to have a time set apart at the end of every school day when children can return to the things which have held their interest but not exhausted it during that day, a time set apart for them to return to those subjects which are still weighing on the mind so to speak.

The whole division of the junior school time-table into arbitrary periods has ignored the very important activity which goes on during this kind of pondering thought. We have agreed that the younger child cannot *concentrate* for any length of time, therefore periods which called for controlled thought must be short. But phantasying, which calls for much less energy, can be carried on for long periods. This is seen clearly in the normal children who for some reason or other are prevented from taking part in the usual school routine. Used to pursuing their own line of thought or phantasy for much longer periods, perhaps whole days or even day after day, they often find the division of the school day, if they are introduced to it between say seven and twelve, intensely irritating. Such children complain that they are swept from one subject to another, that they are never given time to finish anything. Their periods of controlled thought as well as of pursuing one phantasy appear to be much longer than the child who has been introduced to the school time-table at five and never been allowed to stay at anything for more than half an hour since. I suspect that we have been systematically destroying the capacity for sustained imaginative thought by our methods of early teaching. I have been struck by the fact that many of my own friends who had a developed power of sustained imaginative thought had almost all, through the circumstances of their childhood (either illness, or isolation in the country or abroad), been deprived of the first years of their school life. This led to my making a list of those writers who showed this imaginative capacity in a marked degree, and to a study of their early biographies. And it is surely suggestive that so many of these, including (to mention only near contemporaries) Osbert Sitwell, Virginia Wolff, Dylan Thomas, Neil Gunn, Herbert Read, James Joyce, Sean O'Casey, speak gratefully of the long hours spent wandering alone, pursuing phantasies during the years when the child in more normal circumstances would have been enslaved to the school bell. The childhood of our great imaginative writers would make a fruitful subject for research.

We have considered three of the four purposes of play Margaret Lowenfeld gives, those which in later life are related to work, to philosophy, to artistic self-expression. The fourth she calls 'relaxation'. It is heartening to find relaxation taken so seriously, and we cannot brush it aside as none of our concern as teachers but must regard it as a part of education. Autistic thought is the mental form of relaxation and must alternate with that tightening of the mind, that bending to a problem which is concentration. Complete relaxation of body and mind is the most desirable state of recuperation, but we seldom find this even in sleep. The physical training specialists are rightly giving care to the training in physical relaxation, and to those forms of rhythmical exercise which consist in relaxed movement. Certain preparatory stages in many crafts which provide just such rhythmical relaxed activity, such as preparing clay and teasing wool, and their relation to the rest of the process are discussed in Chapter V.

APPENDIX TWO

THE PLANNING AND EQUIPMENT OF A GENERAL CRAFT ROOM

In a Grammar or Secondary Modern School it is sensible to have two craft rooms or one and a Nissen hut. But with careful planning one room can be made adaptable for many crafts. By isolating clay equipment or carving, the messier part of the work can be kept to one end, or the room turned into a fabric printing or puppet studio. Two sinks are essential. To this suggested plan, a clay room is provided for messy work and storage, and the space just outside the door or french window can be utilized for drying troughs or kiln building for a school which takes its pottery seriously. A damp cupboard with fitted doors is essential if work is to be kept for a week and one in which one can stand to reach down work without disturbing other people is best. At the other end the corresponding space can be used for two or three stores according to the number of crafts envisaged. It is an inspiration to children to have some work of artist craftsmen in the room, where it is needed for discussion as well as room to display their own work.

Whereas in an art studio the type of light table which comes apart to form two easels and a large board serves well, in a craft room strong tables are needed. Ours are covered with Wareite, a strong plastic, but lino will serve well. They are easily wiped and can be converted for fabric printing by covering with felt and American cloth as suggested in the chapter on fabric printing. The fabrics (with aeroplane dryer) and clay equipments keep to different ends and work spreads from these.

Except for carving, it is not inconvenient to have the light coming from above, which leaves all the wall space for use. On the other hand it is delightful to have french windows to take the spinning or carving or modelling out on to a terrace in the summer.

For artificial lighting we have a combination devised on the spot, which is as close to daylight as I have seen. Phillips Blended bulbs are fitted in two-point sockets with a blue daylight bulb added to two out of every three. This proportion can be varied, as the depth of blue varies with the glass. Or the proportion of blue can be varied with 100 and 150 watt bulbs.

For ease of standing wooden floors are much the best, but concrete floors can be covered reasonably cheaply with semastic tiles (made of a kind of rubber composition), which can be washed and will stand up to most things except acid.

Padded topped stools which will fit under the tables or on top of the benches are convenient.

CRAFT ROOM ADAPTABLE FOR MANY CRAFTS

Planned here for Modelling, Pottery, Puppets, Carving, Fabric Printing, Dyeing, General Bookmaking. The emphasis can be changed by focusing on one end of the room or the other.

— Shelves at several levels.

— High cupboards.

— Working benches, wood or plastic tops—can have cupboards under, but stepped back.

— Working bench—slate or strong wood.

········· — Glass—windows or french windows.

— Wall in which are cupboards at height of about 4 or 4½ ft., which can be available from both sides, but also permit of outside being locked, when contents are available only from inside shelves through store.

— Walls with beaver board to hold illustrations, examples, etc.

A–A— Concrete pavement, possibly with roof over to provide working space outside french windows.

B–B— Corridor.

C— Store, with cupboards and shelves to hold fabric printing materials, etc. Aeroplane dryer overhead for printed fabrics.

D— Store, with cupboards and shelves, to hold puppets or books, etc.

E— Metal-topped bench with gas-rings, baths and dyeing equipment under; aeroplane dryer for wet things overhead. Cupboard for dyes here available from two sides.

F— Sink with draining-boards.

G— Tables—strong but movable.

H— Glass case for display. Seen also from corridor.

J— May be working bench with stepped-back cupboards under for keeping work and high shelves above. Or may be easily available cupboards for tools, with shelves for display of children's work all up the wall.

K— Press and card cutter, easily approached.

L–L— This part can be shut off by folding screen for pottery or carving, to isolate mess and, to some extent, noise. A mat well should be sunk here.

M–L— A partition (which might be glass) about 3½ or 4 ft. high to take the splashes of clay or chips from carving.

N, N, N— Room for three potter's wheels in good light, or continuation of long working bench N–O for carving, etc.

P–P— Wall with high cupboards available from both sides, which may be completed by two doors or simply by openings. Clay and stone could be stored under working benches.

Q— Outside door for delivering stores and for exit to kiln, etc.

R— Drain for hosing down floor.

S— Tea-chests for storing plaster, etc.

T— Bins for clay.

U— Damp cupboard—plenty of open strut shelves.

W— Working benches. One of these might have vices.

X— Bench outside.

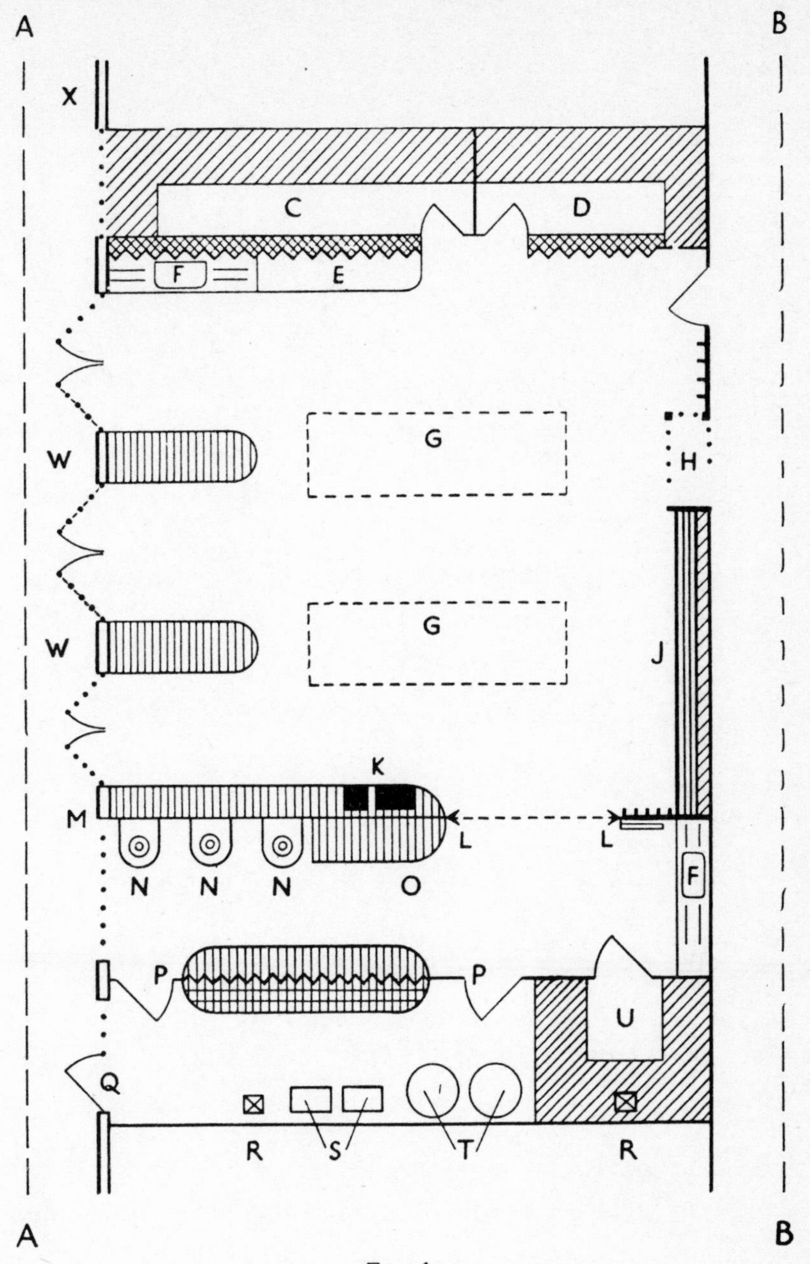

FIG. 64

INDEX

INDEX

INDEX